ZOMBIE APOCALYPSE

NOW!

WHY THE COLLAPSE OF CIVILIZATION IS NIGH

THORFINN SKULLSPLITTER

VOLUME 1

Zombie Apocalypse Now!
Thorfinn Skullsplitter
978-0-6484996-6-4

Thema Classification:
SZV (Survival Skills), VXQM3 (Zombies & Undead), RNR (Natural Disasters), JBFF (Social Impact of Disasters), RNPG (Climate Change)

MANTICORE PRESS
WWW.MANTICORE.PRESS

CONTENTS

Preface   *7*

CHAPTER 1

Why We Will Soon Star in Our Own Zombie Horror Movie   *15*

Discourse on the Metaphysics of the Zombie Apocalypse   30
The Coming Collapse of Civilization   38

CHAPTER 2

Lord of the Zombies   *47*

In Post Apocalyptica Will People Really Be De Facto Zombies?   61
But Won't We Be Able to Rebuild?   69
Conclusion: Kiss Liberalism (and Almost Everything Else) Goodbye   72

CHAPTER 3

Endgame – Our Journey to the End of the Night   *81*

Complexity, Chaos and Collapse   93
The Mechanisms of Collapse   98
Nothing to Sneeze at: Plagues, Pandemics and Social Breakdown   113
Ecological Collapse and Looming Resource Shortages   115
The Climate Cataclysm   130

CHAPTER 4

All You Need Is Lead(and a Few Other Things)   *149*

The Philosophy of Survivalism   157
Surviving the Zombie Apocalypse 101   162
Bug Out and Survival Retreats   165
Wilderness and Blackwood's Survival Philosophy   187
Disaster Preparedness, Philosophy   193
Self-Reliance and Self-Sufficiency Philosophy   203
Tools and the Craftsman   206
Zombie Apocalypse Preparation and Survival Philosophy   209

Conclusion Of Book 1   *215*

Brothers will fight
and kill each other,
sisters' children
will defile kinship.
It is harsh in the world,
whoredom rife
—an axe age, a sword age
—shields are riven—
a wind age, a wolf age—
before the world goes headlong.
No man will have
mercy on another.

Völuspá, The Poetic Edda (Stanza 45).

PREFACE

This Thing of Darkness...

ALTHOUGH ZOMBIES and the intrinsically related zombie apocalypse are cultural commodities worth billions in the global economy, cultural critics have argued that there is a serious message to be found in the mythos of the modern zombie, conceived as a *"relentlessly aggressive, reanimated human corpse driven by a biological infection."*[1] These "threshold creatures," standing in the apocalyptic wasteland between life and death, are "antisubjects," ultimate symbolic "Others" who "may be attacked and destroyed without violating increasingly rigid canons of politically correct behavior and utterance."[2] And, in their mindless apocalyptic fury they "signal the end of the world as we have known it."[3] Zombies are a power pack of English lit. *meat, albeit rotten.*

Zombie films, especially works of intellectual substance, such as George Romero's *Night of the Living Dead* (1968), function as contemporary morality plays, where existential anxieties about social disorder, death and civilizational decay can be safely explored without bringing an even colder and more brutal reality home to the viewer, and breaking now well-established thought and speech

---

[1] Matt Mogk, *Everything You Ever Wanted to Know about Zombies* (Gallery Books, New York, 2011), p. 6.

[2] Brian Anse Patrick, *Zombology: Zombies and the Decline of the West (and Guns)* (Arktos, London, 2014), p. 48.

[3] K. Paffenroth, *Gospel of the Living Dead: George Romero's Vision of Hell on Earth* (Baylor University Press, Waco, 2006), p. 13.

taboos. The zombie, as an "anthropomorphic plague," where "man has become the pathogenic agent of man," a consumer object of "our own devouring drive,"[4] represents our own dehumanization in an oppressive and mechanistic social order, where most of us have been reduced to the level of meat-machines, less than nothing.

Zombie outbreaks in film and literature are generally, but not always, associated with the victory of the rampaging hordes over civilization, so that a collapse of civilization occurs. Peter Dendle has said that this too is part of the mythos of the zombie as a "barometer of cultural anxiety":

> In twenty-first century America—where the bold wilderness frontier that informed American mythic consciousness for four centuries has given way to increasingly centralized government amidst a suburban landscape now quilted with mall strips and Walmarts—there is ample room to romanticize a fresh world purged of ornament and vanity, in which the strong survive, and in which society must be rebuilt anew. Post-apocalyptic zombie worlds are fantasies of liberation: the intrepid pioneers of a new world trek through the shattered remains of the old, trudging through shells of buildings and the husks of people.[5]

The zombie, in "inchoate, rampaging hordes," stands for "anything and everything that threatens to tear down 'civilized culture' and/or the established order."[6] Indeed, in this book it will be shown that this is an accurate description of how in the near future, people in this so-called "real" world, will face the same fate.

---

[4] Jorge Assef, "The Zombie Epidemic: A Hypermodern Version of the Apocalypse," *LCExpress*, vol. 2, no. 7, 2013, pp. 1-21, cited p. 6.

[5] Peter Dendle, "The Zombie as a Barometer of Cultural Anxiety," in N. Scott (ed.), *Monsters and the Monstrous: Myths and Metaphors of Enduring Evil* (Rodopi, New York, 2007), pp. 4-57, cited p. 54.

[6] Andre Austin, "Cyberpunk and the Living Dead," in S. Boluk and W. Lenz (eds), *Generation Zombie: Essays on the Living Dead in Modern Culture* (McFarland and Company, Jefferson, 2011), pp. 147-155, cited p. 147.

Given all of the above pearls of wisdom, in this book these observations will be taken to their logical conclusion, no doubt to the shock and horror of gentle academic souls. If "we are the walking dead" and "zombies are us," then perhaps humans really are as violent and destructive as zombies, and acting in social systems with an organized economy and military, perhaps even more so. Mankind stripped of the thin veneer of civilization, it will be shown in this book, is very zombie-like, and even more terrifying. Of course, in our world corpses do not literally reanimate, but as zombology expert Matt Mogk has said: "I would say from a practical point of view, if a raving maniac is trying to claw down my front door to get inside to attack me or eat me or turn me into one of them, I'm not really interested in having a philosophical conversation about: 'Is that really a zombie?'"[7] It will be "zombie" enough until the full zombie emerges from the lab of some bored genetic engineering PhD student with mental health issues.

One of the aims of this book is to set out the case, based upon an analysis of peer-reviewed scientific literature, that an environmental crisis encompassing a multitude on interconnected and compounding problems—global climate change, species/biodiversity decline, water shortages and the degradation of water quality, resource depletion, peak oil and "peak everything/doom"—is set, on the business-as-usual scenario of unrestrained global economic growth, to lead to a collapse of techno-industrial civilization as early as 2030, and maybe before. This proposition has been advanced by a minority of respected environmentalists, always with the caveat that a combination of technology and human goodness will be our *deux ex machina* (ἀπὸ μηχανῆς θεός *(apò mēkhanês theós)*), saving our unworthy hides, just in the nick of time. Now is the time to kick sand in the face of that illusion.

The collapse of civilization will occur first by a process of slow decay and disintegration, which, it is argued, is already well

---

7 Matt Mogk, cited from Bill Bradley, "How to Survive a Real 'Walking Dead' Zombie Apocalypse," November 1, 2014, at http://www.huffingtonpost.com.au/entry/walking-dead-zombie-apocalypse_n_6065332.html?section=australia.

underway, although the elites pretend that such decadence is actually progress. However, after some critical or catastrophe point, the social rot and entropy becomes sufficient to cause rapid breakdown, the same collapse that other civilizations experienced.[8] Both the Left and Right are usually optimistic about the prospects of long-term human survival, and hold that even if a collapse of civilization does occur, humans will have the ingenuity to rebuild. I put the case against this uncritical optimism, arguing for the "black pill," if not nihilistic thesis, that in the longish term, we are all dead. But, for the *short-term* … there are things that can be done.

Zombies and the zombie apocalypse then, may well be emanations from the collective unconscious, if there is such a thing, of the fear of the impending mega-death and destruction that the collapse of civilization will bring. If the world is presently ecologically unsustainable, as environmentalist tell us, and thus in a situation of ecological overshoot, future-eating environmental capital, then on a business-as-usual scenario of exponential economic growth, a crash is inevitable, and this will involve a vast die off of the bulk of the human race. This will be unpleasant, to say the least, and will mirror and even go beyond the events of apocalyptic fiction such as *The Walking Dead*, aborting a new world disorder of war and warlords, cannibalism and impalement, and savage rituals and human sacrifice as occurred in human pre-history. It happened once; it can happen again.

This book sets out the case that the zombie apocalypse is "real," or as real as anything in this possibly computer simulated "world," and has already begun. Whereas zombie fiction typically advances from the proposition that zombies → zombie apocalypse, this book reverses the arrow of causality: civilization collapse → "zombies" → zombie apocalypse. Chapters one and two give the brutal, grisly background to the social decay and exploding violence that is beginning to grip many cities in the West. With the "death of God," that is, secularization and the loss of the social significance of the

---

[8] Jared Diamond, *Collapse: How Societies Choose to Fail or Succeed* (Penguin, London, 2011).

transcendent in the life of the West, only consumer affluence and materialism function as social glues, holding the whole experiment of modernity together. As argued in chapter three, this structure is falling apart and a New Dark Age may replace it.

The response to this catastrophe, I argue in chapter four, should be, for those who want to survive (many will not and will accept oblivion; good for them), *survivalism*, a hyper-Darwinian philosophy of surviving whatever the cost and enduring whatever a cruel cosmos hurls at one, with metaphysical defiance. The chapter offers an overview of the main aspects of survivalism. However, the next book in this series, *The Barbarian Reborn: Weaponry and Survivalism in the Near-Term Post-Apocalyptic Wastelands*, goes further down the road of ruin, considering the physical culture and philosophical/ mental/spiritual changes needed to endure the coming of hell on Earth, a world without conventional gods and hope of salvation, only impending doom and destruction – *Ragnarök*! One must become a barbarian in a world that will be nothing short of barbaric, and the present author will be in character.

CHAPTER

Nature is a vast field of carnage. Between living creatures conflict takes place every second, every minute, without truth and without respite. It takes place first between separate individuals, then between collective organisms, tribe against tribe, state against state, nationality against nationality. No cessation is possible.

- J. Novicow (1886)[9]

Before the tribunal of nature a man has no more right to life than a rattlesnake, he has no more right to liberty than any wild beast; his right to the pursuit of happiness is nothing but a license to maintain the struggle for existence.

- William Sumner[10]

...and the life of man, solitary, poor, nasty, brutish, and short.

- Thomas Hobbes (1588-1679)[11]

[9]   Quoted by W. L. Langer, *The Diplomacy of Imperialism: 1890-1902* (Alfred Knopf, New York, 1965), p. 86.

[10]   William Sumner, *Earth-Hunger and Other Essays* (Yale University Press, New Haven, 1913), p. 234.

[11]   Thomas Hobbes, *Leviathan* (Penguin, Harmondsworth, 1968), I, 13, 9.

WHY WE WILL SOON STAR IN OUR OWN ZOMBIE HORROR MOVIE

Zombie Nation: Day of the Metaphysical Flesh Eaters

PROPOSITION 1: *Humans can be as savage, depraved, mindless and cannibalistic as any zombie/walker in* AMC's *The Walking Dead, and they will be exceptionally nasty in the extreme and violent circumstances posed by the coming collapse of civilization.*

SATURDAY, MAY 26 2012, was a seemingly normal day in Miami. As in most cities across the decaying West, rapists were raping, druggies were a-drugging and hookers, hooking. But, on the MacArthur Causeway, off-ramp to Biscayne Boulevard, a road ranger spotted two men, one naked and on top of the other. That in itself, in our enlightened day of sexual diversity would not normally raise an eyebrow. However, the actions were all-but-friendly from the man on top of the mount in the on-going ground 'n' pound. This man was literally gnawing at the face of bottom man. The road ranger, now Lone Ranger, shouted on his loud speaker for the naked attacker to back off, but this was no more effective than telling a hungry dog to stop gnawing on its bone. A woman riding her bicycle saw the attacker tearing off pieces of flesh from the face of his victim and devouring the meat. An observer at the scene told WSVN-Fox 7: "The guy just stood his head up like that, with a piece of flesh in his mouth, and he growled." He *growled*.

The officer at the scene told the attacker—later identified as Rudy Eugene, 31 years of age—to back off the victim, identified as Ronald Poppo, a homeless man who was living in the space under the causeway. Nevertheless, Eugene ignored the demand and continued his cannibalistic grazing. The officer fired his service handgun and delivered a torso hit. Eugene did not seem to notice being hit by the 9 mm round as it was dinner time for him and 9 mm lead was not going to keep him from his meal. The officer fired a number of times, scoring more ineffective torso hits. Then he tried something left-of-field and put one 9 mm slug into Eugene's head, killing him like… well, a zombie. The media and the blogosphere quickly called this case, the "Miami Zombie."

Zombie experts quickly took to the net telling us, we, the people, not to panic, as the long anticipated zombie apocalypse had not yet begun. There was no cause for alarm – *r-e-l-a-x!* But, what is a zombie? How would one tell if one was actually in a zombie apocalypse, rather than just in your garden variety of social collapse?

I will have more to say on the taxonomy or classification of zombies in due course. However, to simplify, the cause of zombieism may be biological (naturalistic) or supernatural, and a zombie itself (in a provisional definition), is a *"relentless aggressive reanimated human corpse driven by a biological infection"* and a "living zombie" is a "relentlessly aggressive human driven by a biological infection."[12] Apparently, real hard-core wizards and witches are short of the ground in Miami, so scratch the supernatural cause. Biological transmission via bites will follow the epidemiology of other infectious diseases.[13] That is, unless zombieism is some completely new phenomenon,

---

[12] Matt Mogk, *Everything You Ever Wanted to Know about Zombies* (Gallery Books, New York, 2011), p. 23.

[13] See P. Munz (et al.), "When Zombies Attack! Mathematical Modelling of an Outbreak of Zombie Infection," in J. M. Tchuenche and C. Chiyaka (eds), *Infectious Disease Modelling Research Progress* (Nova Science Publishers, New York, 2009), pp.133-150.

perhaps along the lines of an extra-terrestrial infection source, as hinted by George A. Romero in the classic zombie movie *Night of the Living Dead* (1968).

Eugene's cannibalistic and aggressive behavior and resistance to torso hits was first thought to be due to his consumption of "bath salts" or fake marijuana, synthetic cathinones that can cause violent psychotic behavior. Eugene "the zombie," eating 80 percent of the face of his victim, including his eyes, is an extreme case, but less dramatic cases of individuals going crazy, allegedly on "bath salts" had previously occurred in Miami. However, the toxicology report on Eugene revealed that he had not consumed "bath salts," only marijuana. Amusingly, when I described these events to an old lady friend of my dear deceased mother she said to me: "Dear, I will never put bath salts in my bath again!" Along similar lines in May 2015, an "ice" (meth) addict at John Hunter Hospital, Newcastle, Australia, gouged out his own eyeballs and ate them.

Following the next crazy media cycle was news that the "Canadian porno psycho" Luka Rocco Magnotta, 29, had been arrested outside an internet café in Berlin. Magnotta was charged with dismembering a Chinese student, Jun Lin, 33, and filming the killing. It included scenes of necrophilia and cannibalism. Magnotta, who considered himself a bisexual porn actor, then posted the gruesome spectacle online. He also remembered to mail severed limbs to Canadian political parties, with a human foot arriving via the post to the headquarters of Canada's Conservative Party. Magnotta obviously was not trying to lend them a hand.

Perhaps not to be outdone in the theater of horrors by the Americans, face eating has also occurred in China. A woman called "Du" was driving her car near a bus station in Wenzhou. A man ran into the street blocking her car. Meet "Dong." Dong jumped onto Du's car, pounding on the windshield, "Ding Dong" style, perhaps believing that he was a Chinese bell. Du was terrified by this lunatic and as in the movies, did the predictable thing and fled her car instead of using her car as a weapon. After all, from the safety of steel and glass she could have stayed in her car, accelerated, and then braked, dumping the lunatic. And, as in any H grade horror movie, Dong pursued the fleeing, screaming Du, and in a Chinese version of a zombie flick, caught up with her, jumped onto her and started eating her face. The police intervened. Dong, it seems was drunk on alcohol at the time. Who knows how he would have behaved if he had drunk a bathtub full of bath salts. The question now is: were his organs harvested?

In a place described by two of its past Prime Ministers as at the "arse (ass/anus) end of the world," Australia, the case of the "vampire" gigolo killer occurred. He claimed that he needed to drink human blood to survive. Nevertheless, there is a "zombie" theme in there as well: apart from slaying a male prostitute he savagely beat a woman and bit off her tongue.

Here is a cook's tour of a number of other gruesome killings or assaults involving cannibalism or threats of cannibalism that occurred in the West a few years ago.

In Sweden, a man believed that his younger wife was cheating on him, so he cut off her lips and ate them, thus chewing on her. In Texas, a mother was accused of eating her new-born son, including parts of his brain and biting off three of his toes. A Morgan State University student, killed, dismembered and ate his roommate, which involved eating his heart and parts of his brain. A New Jersey man stabbed himself and when police came, engaged in disembowelment and then threw part of his intestines at police, I suppose, in much the same way as fellow primates throw their excreta.

Lock up your dog as even the family Fido is not safe from human jaws. In Texas, a man smoked synthetic marijuana, assaulted friends and neighbors, and then ran around on all fours, growling and barking like a dog. Perhaps not wanting any canine competition, he then grabbed the family dog, choked it and began eating it. This takes America's passion for hot dogs to a completely new level.

Moreover, speaking of "hot dogs," Clear Food, a molecular food analysis group examined a sample of 345 individual hot dogs and sauces from 75 different brands sold at 10 food retailers. Human DNA was present in two percent of the samples and $\frac{2}{3}$ of these samples with human DNA were vegetarian products. The report did not identify where the human DNA came from, with most comments saying that it was probably a hygiene issue involving saliva, hair and bodily fluids such as sweat, as is common with restaurant foods, which sometimes also contains traces of human excreta from cooks with loose bowels who just don't care. Nevertheless, there is still the remote possibility that people are being thrown into the mincers or are ejaculating into the food, or both, ejaculating first of course.

In Georgia though, things did not get out of hand. A 21-year-old man ran out of the woods naked, a common enough thing to do. Police were called, who tasered and handcuffed him, also a common enough thing to do. But, as he was being dragged into the patrol car to be taken off for processing (criminal processing not pet food processing) he was heard to yell, "I'm a eat you," the joint he had smoked laced with bath salts obviously impacting upon his grammar. The kindly Georgian officers corrected him; the correct phrase for a naked wannabe cannibal is "I'm going to eat you" or "I'm a-goin' t' eat y'u." Suitably reprimanded, the man sat quietly, biting his lip and chewing things over in his drug-soaked head.

Crimes involving dismemberment and cannibalism are not recent, and as we have been told, "happen all the time." Thus, way, way back in the dim dark ages of 2010, a US cage fighter became convinced that his training partner was possessed by the devil. It happens. Usually it is all sorted out by the time his head hits the canvas, but cage-man this time had drunk a potent potion brewed by some evil chemical wizard, allegedly containing a powerful hallucinogen, wild mushroom tea. He then "ripped" open his partner's chest and tore out his still beating heart. At first, I was impressed and thought that he had done it with his bare hands as in the movie *Indiana Jones and the Temple of Doom* (1984). But, no, he used a knife. He cheated. It is not clear what his martial-arts trained victim was doing by way of self-defense at the time; apparently, nothing. However, heart now liberated, cage-man then cut off the victim's tongue and ripped off most of his face. The police found cage-man as happy as a pig in shit, standing naked over the dismembered body, drenched in blood, body parts such as eyeballs strewn untidily on the floor. Cage-man had taken the heart and other organs and cooked them to "stop the devil," which would only work if the devil was a tapeworm. Fortunately, this event did not give rise to a new species of reality TV show where losers of gladiatorial battles in martial arts cages found themselves, or their bodily parts, as the main event in a reality TV cooking show.

On September 7, 2012, in Hawley Borough, Wayne County Pennsylvania, a naked and profusely bleeding man, gnawed on a woman's head while "screaming like an animal." The 20-year-old man parked his car behind a house on Hudson Street and stripped to his underwear. He then unsuccessfully tried to break into a house and then succeeded in taking off his underwear, perhaps believing that his now liberated, freewheeling genitalia would improve his housebreaking skills. He then continued down Hudson Street and broke into an unoccupied house. Journeying up to that home's second storey, he jumped out of a window, severely injuring his arms and legs on impact. Literally oozing blood, he then approached two women walking down the street and attacked one woman, and as has been said, gnawed on her head and emitted an animalistic scream. Fortunately, the woman was able to escape and she called the police. The police tasered him. Even so, he was still able to punch an EMT in the face. When he was finally subdued, paramedics took him to the Geisinger Community Medical Center for treatment of his injuries. Police were uncertain of what cocktail of drugs, if any, he had wolfed down.

All of this is enough to make one lose one's head. In fact, in early 2016, to get the New Year to a raging start, just after the mass rapes in Europe by poor oppressed refugees suffering "sexual emergencies," a man from near Frankfurt, Germany, strangled and dismembered his wife. He then encased her head in concrete and used the concrete block as a weight as he drowned himself. Two suitcases containing the wife's other body parts were found near the shore of the lake Traunsee of the town of Gmunden, Upper Austria.

Here is one of my favorite stories and I hope that it will be yours too (apologies to *South Park*). Did you hear the one about the woman arrested for masturbating on the side of a Florida highway? The 35-year-old white woman was arrested after masturbating on the side of highway 484 Ocala, Florida. Traffic slowed down and many male drivers made illegal U-turns on the highway to get another eyeful. When a police officer (no doubt called by a woman) tried to pull up her pants, she tried to bite her! At the jail she "continued to resist the officers by spreading her legs, exposing her vagina and telling officers to kiss her "there" and refusing verbal commands to cooperate." Her connection to zombieism is tenuous, and this is added solely for amusement purposes. However, forced at tooth-point to give a straight answer, perhaps she simply wanted to be "eaten."

In Brazil, June 2019, a vibrating place at the best of times, a mum and her lesbian lover tore off her 9-year old son's penis, removed all of the skin from his face, and beheaded him, because, "he reminded her of her dad."[14] That ruled out necrophilia I suppose.

While not exactly causing people to eat others, krokodil (dihydrodesoxymorphine), cheap Russian heroin, has been called a "zombie drug" that rots the skin from the inside out. This synthetic opiate in a pure form was patented in the 1930's under the brand name *Permonid*. A highly impure version, popular in Russia, is made from codeine, iodine and red phosphorus, with highly toxic impurities from gasoline, paint thinner and industrial cleaning oil. "Krokodil" is a Russian word for "crocodile;" it is estimated that up to one in a million users end up with a scale-like appearance to their skin. Bodily damage comes from gangrene, among other pleasantries, giving the life expectancy of addicts of about two years. The flesh literally rots of the bones of addicts, making them almost "the walking dead." The drug has spread to the US, naturally enough, because almost every insane thing spreads to the US, or comes from the US, the universal salad dressing. If such drug users were also exposed to "Devil's Breath" or scopolamine, then we would move even closer to chemically creating a zombie. This Colombian drug, delivered by blowing it in someone's face, eliminates free will and

---

[14] https://www.thesun.co.uk/news/9300395/mum-son-lesbian-lover-murder-killed-brazil/.

blocks memories. People under its influence, have emptied bank accounts and even given up organs.

There were reports of a flesh-eating disease in the Philippines in 2013 in the province of Pangasinan, of an unknown origin. Another flesh-eating disease, Leishmanisis disease, in 2015 and 2017, was spreading in ISIS-controlled areas of Syria, arising from parasites feasting on rotting human corpses lying in the streets. A mysterious "nodding disease," thought to be caused by a parasitic worm, has been debilitating children in northern Uganda, causing epilepsy-like seizures and producing strange symptoms such as starting fires. Presumably, if these diseases could get together and make sweet genetic love, we also would be moving towards zombieism. As well, if the infected person was unfortunate enough to simultaneously acquire Cotard's syndrome, or "walking corpse illusion," where the person actually believes that one he/she is dead and putrefying, this would be like being in *The Walking Dead*, only with half the fun. "God" certainly has blessed us with a diversity of diseases, biologically enriching the planet.

My own personal encounter with a proto-zombie occurred in June 2012. As in any good story, it was a bitterly cold winter's night. I had returned to the city after clearing feral trees on a property in the West Texas hills. I was about to enter a small independent supermarket when I saw, at a nearby crossing, a small guy wearing only a pair of briefs. He began jumping in front of cars, clearly intending to be hit by drivers; the drivers braked, but impacts still occurred. Mr. Underpants was tossed up onto the bonnets of the cars, slid down and then tried to punch the drivers. Everybody sped off and soon people were not stopping at the lights, running reds to escape this lunatic. Only a few pedestrians were on the street and he ran at them, screaming wildly. By this time, his body was cut and bleeding but he was oblivious to his injuries. I watched in amazement. So did a Chinese fellow who decided to say: "You must stop doing that; it is very bad." Crazy man heard that and said: "So, we have a hero here do we? And who is the hero?" He looked at me on the sidewalk, (the Chinese man had wisely fled) and pointed at me and said: "You're the hero!" He then ran at me, threatening to tear out my heart, among other things. However, he stopped when he got within striking range. This time he did not face a soft urban man, but instead an ageing powerlifter and martial artist of over 50 years of experience, and still a lean 303 pounds. Also, someone who appreciated that the human race is essentially degenerate filth, present company excluded. Not wanting to find out what diseases he had in his blood, I military pressed, a wheeled shopping cart and spat this line at him: "Try to touch me, you fucking lunatic, and you can wear this." He stopped in his tracks, shocked, and then turned and ran. Perhaps the resistance was too much for him. I immediately left the area as he may have run off to get his handgun. As I walked off I noticed how the trail of blood that he had left on the pavement was being was being washed away from the falling rain. Good on you, rain. Perhaps some SJW (Social Justice Warrior) will write a song about this one day; the answer is flowin' in the rain.

All of these examples involve *individuals* losing their heads. What about larger social groups? Consider Papua New Guinea, where after the "zombie apocalypse" events just listed occurred, various acts of savagery happened suggesting the "mutant zombie biker" (MZB) theme. The MZB, perhaps first mentioned by David Crawford in *Lights Out*[15] and depicted in the *Mad Max/Road Warrior* movies and *The Road* (2009)[16] is a metaphor for those who reject the values of civilization and stand ready to revert to savagery. "Normal" humans are capable of greater brutality than any zombie in *The Walking Dead*, which is the thesis of this chapter.

For example, the first episode of AMC's spinoff *Fear the Walking Dead* (2015), takes us to the time when the zombie apocalypse was just beginning, but the level of social decay, violence and drug-addicted

---

[15] David Crawford, *Lights Out* (Halffast Publishing, San Antonio, 2010), Chapter 20, "Mutant Zombie Bikers." The attackers in this case were not literally "bikers" but a motorized gang of scum.

[16] Matt Mogk in *Everything You Ever Wanted to Know About Zombies*, as above, says that the movie *The Road*, with its roaming bands of cannibalistic killers, gives a "more realistic picture of an undead planet" (i.e. a zombie planet) than much of the recent zombie literature and film. (p. 113)

dysfunction is quite consistent with a comparable apocalypse. It is essentially our world a little further down the track. Who needs the flesh-eating zombies to be terrified? They are just the rotting icing on a decaying cake. It is the humans who are truly terrifying, which is the core theme of the zombie genre.

Consider the following. An elderly woman was abducted in Lopel Village PNG on April 2, 2013, by a crazed mob of villagers. They believed that the old woman was a witch who had used sorcery on a former schoolteacher who had died. Relatives of the deceased teacher, constituting said crazy mob, held her captive and tortured her for three days with knives and axes. Police attended the village but were hopelessly outnumbered by the mob. (There was no mention of the use of firearms.) The mob then beheaded her in front of the police. A few days before this, in the Southern Highlands of PNG, six women were accused of sorcery and tortured with hot irons.

In March 2013, in the town of Mount Hagen, in the western Highlands of PNG, a 20-year-old mother was abducted by a mob consisting of relatives of a young boy who had died. She was accused of killing the boy using sorcery. The mob stripped her naked and tortured her with a branding iron, then covered her in gasoline and burnt her alive on a pile of trash, topped off with car tyres.[17] Police, again were outnumbered by the mob and did not use weapons to prevent the burning, and apparently did not even pass around donuts in a desperate bid to use saturated fats and sugars to calm the savage mob.

Another 20-year-old PNG woman was found dead in her family's food garden with her arm hacked off. Former teacher, Helen Rumbali, was beheaded; her sister, Nikono, was kidnapped and tortured by villagers.

Rape in PNG is at epidemic levels, with 70 percent of PNG women expected to be raped or physically/sexually assaulted in their

---

[17] Meredith Bennett-Smith, "Accused 'Witch' Kepari Leniata Burnt Alive by Mob in Papua New Guinea," *Huffington Post*, February 7, 2013, at http://www.huffingtonpost. com/2013/02/07/kepari-leniata-young-mother-burned-alive-mob-sorcery-papua-new-guinea_n_2638431.html.

lifetime. A US academic was pack raped near Madang, a 14-year-old girl was raped and murdered in Lae, and an Australian man was killed and his Filipino friend raped in Hagen.

Less media coverage has been given to racially based attacks. There have been in recent times a number of killings of Asians. For example, in June 2013 in Port Moresby, four Chinese people were hacked to death in their store and bakery, and one was beheaded. A group wearing masks, who did not harm any Papua New Guineans present at the time, attacked them. The Chinese embassy in PNG then warned Chinese residents to stay in their homes and workplaces "for the time being."

A PNG cult leader known as the "Black Jesus," convicted rapist Steven Tari, escaped from Beon prison in Madang in March 2013, along with 48 other prisoners. Villagers killed him on August 29, 2013, at the remote Gal village about 20 kilometers outside of Madang. He and one of his followers were attacking a young woman at the time. They were hacked to death and the Black Jesus was castrated and dragged by means of a cane around his neck to a shallow pit where his body was dumped to rot. Tari had raped girls in his sect, claiming that they were married to him because God said so, or at least did in his imagination. As well, the cult was a true zombie cult and practiced cannibalism. Young girls had been sacrificed in blood rituals and then eaten.

Tari is not the only one in PNG to do this in the last few years: in 2011, PNG police arrested dozens of people involved in a cannibalism cult, accused of killing at least seven people, eating their raw brains and making soup from their penises. It is unknown how much soup they were able to make.

Voodoo killings are making a comeback, worldwide. For example, as a cholera epidemic raged in Haiti in 2010, voodoo murders soared. Forty-five people were killed, being accused of using black magic to spread cholera. Most of the murders were in the coastal town of Jérémie. These people had been lynched, set on fire or hacked to death with machetes. About half of Haiti's population practice voodoo.

Voodoo, along with human sacrifice has come to the West with African and Caribbean immigrants. The "Thames torso boy" gave a dramatic illustration of this. An African child's torso, without arms, legs or a head (and drained of blood) was found in the Thames on September 21, 2001, near London's Globe Theatre, something "Willy-the-Shake" (Shakespeare) would have found dramatically inspiring. The boy, named by the police "Adam," had a substance in his stomach identified as a black magic potion used in West Africa, made from calabar beans, a highly toxic plant. Small clay pellets with tiny particles of gold were also found, indicating a Muti ritual killing, widespread in sub-Saharan Africa. Forensic scientists at Scotland Yard, using an isotope/bone analysis, traced "Adam" to Nigeria. The boy was likely to have been purchased for a sacrificial killing and smuggled into Britain. Once there, a voodoo priest administered the poison which acted as a paralyzing agent (but not anesthetic). In agony, Adam had his throat cut, his head and limbs removed and the body drained of blood. Finally, after the voodoo ritual, his torso was tossed into the Thames.

Children are often used in Muti ritual killings because their body parts are believed to be sacred. The body parts are plopped into potions to bring good luck, but not obviously to those dismembered. Modern human sacrifice is not restricted to black children; in Belgium, the mutilated torso of a white child was found. However, black Africans are the main victims. The United Nations Children's Emergency Fund (UNICEF) estimates that 200,000 children are trafficked out of central and western Africa annually to be exploited as slave laborers and/or sex slaves. Along with this, there are around 100 Muti killings in South Africa alone each year. With the coming collapse of civilization expect to see a rise in human sacrifice, since historically sacrifice has served the ruling elites as a method of terror to maintain power in hierarchical societies.[18]

Apart from human sacrifice, there is an illegal bush meat trade from West Africa to Britain involving exotic meats such as bush rat,

---

[18]   J. Watts (et al.), "Ritual Human Sacrifice Promoted and Sustained the Evolution of Stratified Societies," *Nature*, vol. 532, 2016, pp. 228-231.

chimpanzee and—human flesh! Human flesh "on sale in London"—
"roll up ladies and gentleman, don't miss out on the bargains! All
parts must go!" Heathrow airport's meat transport director (in 2002)
has been cited in the media as saying that he believes that the trade in
human meat is linked to criminal gangs smuggling drugs and people.
The trade in bush meat continues in not-Great Britain, with in 2019,
reports of bushmeat from poor animals such as chimpanzees, more
intelligent beings than most of the eaters, openly on sale in UK
markets.[19] It is one thing for dumb humans to butcher each other,
but quite another for life forms superior to most humans, namely
primates, to be destroyed.

Cannibalism, witchcraft, human sacrifice, human trafficking
and slavery – these horrors were thought by our enlightened liberal
intelligentsia to be dark stains of the past, banished by the light of
reason and learning. Not so – these monsters are rising again,
albeit at present of limited virulence. However, if all this can occur
within civilized order, a collapse of civilization will almost certainly
project these practices far beyond immigrant groups. There is
nothing "special" about Europeans and Asians, for we all partake
in the unspeakable depravity of the human condition as the great
philosophical pessimists across the ages have clearly shown,[20] and as
will be argued for in the next chapter in this book.

In times of starvation, humans are not averse to a bit of human
meat. For example, evidence has recently emerged of cannibalism
among the first English colony at Jamestown, Virginia, during the
"starving time," the winter of 1609-1610.[21] The first colony faced the
worst drought in 800 years and endured food shortages between 1607
and 1625. Corpses were dug up from graves and eaten. A 14-year-old
girl's remains were discovered in 2012 in an old cellar that was filled
with the bones of horses and other animals eaten in desperation. Her

---

[19]   https://www.thesun.co.uk/news/9265043/chimpanzee-meat-smuggled-sold-britain/.

[20]   Arthur Schopenhauer, *The World as Will and Representation*, translated by E. F. J. Payne
(Dover Publications, New York, 1966).

[21]   "Evidence of Cannibalism Found at Jamestown, 1st English Colony in America," May 1,
2013, at http://www.ctvnews.ca/sci-tech/evidence-of-cannibalism-found-at-jamestown-1st-
english-colony-in-america-1.1261918.

skull was smashed. There were crude chop marks to the head and body, indicating that her brain was removed as well as her body being butchered. She was probably dead before all this happened.

Captain John Smith also documented the case of a man "salting" and eating his pregnant wife. It did not do him much good as he was later executed. According to Smith:

> One amongst the rest did kill his wife, powdered her, and had eaten part of her before it was known, for which he was executed as well he deserved. Now whether she was better roasted, boiled or carbonado'd [barbequed], I know not, but such a dish as powdered wife I never heard of.[22]

Europeans in the late medieval period to the end of the 18th century, and in some places well into the 19th century, used corpse parts regularly in the medical practice of the day, "corpse medicine" and "corpse pharmacology."[23] While the ancient Romans drank the blood of slaughtered gladiators as a remedy for epilepsy, Europeans made use of blood, fat, bones and even the moss growing on human skulls to treat a wide range of ailments, no doubt trading on a placebo effect rather than any intrinsic healing power of the body parts. Europeans believed, at a time when the church kept society ignorant about the working of the human body by the suppression of the physiological/anatomical research,[24] that bodies contained a "life force" or "vital energy" that could be consumed.[25] The drinking of human blood of a recently beheaded person, as well as the "pickling" of their flesh for

---

[22] D. Zabarenko, "Starving Virginia Settlers Turned to Cannibalism in 1609: Study," May 1, 2013, at http://www.reuters.com/article/2013/05/01/us-cannibalism-jamestown-idUSBRE9400UY20130501.

[23] Louise Noble, *Medicinal Cannibalism in Early Modern English Literature and Culture* (Palgrave, Macmillan, New York, 2011).

[24] Paul Barber, *Vampires, Burial and Death: Reality and Folklore* (Yale University Press, New Haven and London 1988).

[25] P. Bethge, "Europe's 'Medicinal Cannibalism': The Healing Power of Death," *Spiegel Online*, January 30, 2009, at http://www.spiegel.de/international/zeitgeist/europe-s-medicinal-cannibalism-the-healing-power-of-death-a-604548.html.

consumption, was a common practice right through Europe.[26] The blood of Charles I from his execution was mopped up and consumed by on-lookers, it being thought to have special healing powers.[27] At the same time as Europe practiced "corpse medicine," there was widespread horror at the reports of cannibalism practiced in the Americas.

Gough's Cave in Somerset, discovered in the 1880s, revealed a deposit of human bones intermingled with the bones of large butchered mammal remains. The bones were radiocarbon dated to be about 14,700 years old. There was evidence of the human bones being cracked so that the marrow could be obtained, as well as defleshing, with human teeth marks on the bones. During the Magdalenian period (15-12,000 years BCE), most human burial sites have cut-marked and broken human bones, as also seen in the Dordogne area in France and the Rhine Valley in Germany. Most individual remains are highly fragmented and around 40 percent exhibited evidence of defleshing.[28]

The "zombie" has been an integral part of Western civilization. We are, already, but a few steps away from being "the walking dead."

Conclusion: If all this carnage happened once, there is no reason why it cannot happen again, especially when confronted by the ecological terror of the collapse that awaits us, poor, bare, forked animals. Humans are as dangerous, if not more so than Hollywood zombies.

As "The Collapse" comes closer, watch out for an increase in beheadings and severed heads being placed on sticks, classic barbarian stuff. For example, throughout 2014 and 2015 Islamic State fighters beheaded many Western journalists. Boko Haram gunman

---

[26] F. Macrae, "British Royalty Dined on Human Flesh (but Don't Worry it was 300 years Ago)," *Daily Mail*, May 21, 2011, at http://www.dailymail.co.uk/news/article-1389142/British-royalty-dined-human-flesh-dont-worry-300-years-ago.html.

[27] M. Dolan, "The Gruesome History of Eating Corpses as Medicine," May 6, 2012, at http://www.smithsonianmag.com/history/the-gruesome-history-of-eating-corpses-as-medicine-82360284/

[28] S. M. Bello (et al.), "Upper Palaeolithic Ritualistic Cannibalism at Gough's Cave (Somerset, UK): The Human Remains from Head to Toe," *Journal of Human Evolution*, vol. 30, 2015, pp. 1-20.

beheaded 23 people and set their homes on fire in Buratai, northwest Nigeria on the eve of the March 2015 general elections. The aim was, apparently to disrupt the polls, preventing voting. The trend towards beheadings, even by gunman, symbolically represents a return to barbarian values of blood and steel; nothing gets the animal spirits stirring, as much as dispatching one's enemies by a blade.

Next, expect severed heads to be shrunk (techno-barbarian) *Predator*-style and carried around the warrior's neck. ISIS has already performed executions by dissolving prisoners to death with nitric acid, and hacking them in half with a chainsaw. Although popular "debunking" sites claim that this did not happen, the *New York Post* cites testimony from eye witnesses that victims of the French Bataclan Theatre massacre, November 14, 2015, had eyes gouged out, genitals sliced, castration and disembowelment. [29]

Discourse on the Metaphysics of the Zombie Apocalypse

PROPOSITION 2: *The zombie apocalypse is a metaphor for impending civilization collapse. Almost all zombie movies and literature feature an out-of-control zombie plague bringing down the world as we know it. The aspect of civilization breakdown is more important than the actual zombies.*

The above scene-setting events are of course not evidence of a zombie apocalypse as *conventionally* defined. Of course not. How could it be? For a start, the main players are not the reanimated dead – not by a long shot. Brain-dead, perhaps, but not the living dead. Their victims who survived a munching have not yet become zombies.

---

[29] I. Vincent and L. Italiano, "Horrifying Details of the Bataclan Theater Massacre Revealed," *New York Post*, July 15, 2016, at www.nypost.com/2016/07/15/horrifying-details-of-the-bataclan-theatre-massacre-revealed/.

And further, the US Centers for Disease Control declared that there was no zombie apocalypse as the "CDC does not know of a virus or condition that could reanimate the dead, or one that could present zombie-like symptoms."[30] Indeed, we all know from season 1, episode 5 ("Wildfire") of AMC's *The Walking Dead*, which featured the last CDC survivor Dr Edwin Jenner, that this must be correct because, one, the government is the fountain of truth and wisdom and two, the government never lies. Just ask B. Hussein Obama, Hillary Clinton, and President Donald Duck.

The theme of "zombies 'r' us" has become prevalent in American culture and across the world.[31] It was suggested in the various zombie walks in many cities across the world and was a theme of the Occupy Wall Street protests, which used zombie dress-up to illustrate their protest.[32] Apparently, there are plans to turn downtown Detroit, a crime infested city, devastated by the US car industry collapse, into a zombie theme park, where one can actually pay to be terrified, compared to the present, where one does not need to pay to be terrified.[33]

The "Health Ranger," Make Adams, who on his popular website champions alternative medicine, nutrition, "superfoods" and a critical attitude towards orthodox medicine and "Big Pharma," when he is not banned, sees the cultural interest in zombies as an implicit awareness of civilization collapse, for like the present author, he too believes that our present techno-industrial civilization is doomed.[34] Adams believes that the "average American consumer"

---

[30] "CDC Declares 'There is No Zombie Apocalypse' After Spake of Cannibal Killings," June 4, 2012, at http://www.news.com.au/technology/science/cdc-declares-there-is-no-zombie-apocalypse-after-spate-of-cannibal-killings/story-fn5fsgyc-1226382746704.

[31] Kelly J. Baker, *The Zombies are Coming! The Realities of the Zombie Apocalypse in American Culture* (Bondfire Books, Kindle Edition, 2013).

[32] Christopher M. Moreman and James Rushton Cory (eds), *Zombies are Us: Essays on the Humanity of the Walking Dead* (McFarland and Company, Jefferson, 2011).

[33] Jill Stark, "Playing Dead: Zombies March into the Mainstream," February 2, 2014, at http://www.smh.com.au/entertainment/playing-dead-zombies-march-into-the-mainstream-20140201-31u5e.html.

[34] Mike Adams, "Zombie Apocalypse Becomes Reality in Miami as Police Shoot Naked, Mindless Man Literally Eating Face Off Another Man," NaturalNews.com, May 27, 2012, at http://www.naturalnews.com/035990_zombie_apocalypse_Miami_police.html.

is "half-zombie now, because of mechanized, ritualistic lifestyles, meaningless work practices and unhealthy, if not toxic, diets."[35] He has said that reason is "an alien concept to most people."[36] Surely, he is being too generous.

Dylan Charles, also writing from a holistic health perspective, highly critical of modern mass society, sees people becoming "hypnotized automatons," with their individuality eliminated as they embrace "the hypnotic indulgences of a poisoned, consumer driven, media controlled way of life," a life that has become so mundane, "dead" and mechanical, that for all effective purposes, people are zombies.[37] Thus, the zombie apocalypse can be taken as the prevailing metaphor of our times. It is now a situation of "every cannibal for himself." Millions of Americans are preparing for social collapse and the end of the world as we know it (TEOTWAWKI) and are concerned with individual rather than community defense, for the zombified masses care not what happens to their fellow man.

Mike Adams goes further and the following is an accurate summary of the position taken in this book: "I predict that the human race will destroy itself and collapse back to a tiny population of ragged survivors." There is no such solution to the environmental crisis because,

> we're such an infantile race of stupid creatures just barely more intelligent than apes, we are going to ride this crazy train of idiocy right into the ground. We are going to burn out this planet, kill the ecosystem, poison the waters and taint the skies. And most of the population is going to giggle all of the way to their own graves

---

[35] Mike Adams, "CDC Warms Americans to Prepare for Zombie Apocalypse (Really)," NaturalNews.com, May 19, 2011, at http://www.naturalnews.com/032454_zombie_apocalypse_CDC.html.

[36] Mike Adams, "The Zombie Apocalypse is Already Here: Mindless Masses Do Whatever They're Told, Then Invent Empty Logic to Justify It," May 18, 2015, at www.naturalnews.com/049754_zombie_apocalypse_mindless_voters_irrational_thinking.html#.

[37] Dylan Charles, "5 Reasons the Zombie Apocalypse is the Prevailing Metaphor of Our Times", *Waking Times*, May 3, 2012 at http://www.wakingtimes.com/2012/05/03/5-reasons-the-zombie-apocalypse-.

as they perish from the very same systems of self-destruction they voted for at the polling booths.[38]

That is just on a good day.

Before Adams, Erich Fromm, a Frankfurt school theorist said:

In the nineteenth century, the problem was that God [is] dead; in the twentieth century the problem is man is dead. In the nineteenth century inhumanity meant cruelty; in the twentieth century it means schizoid self-alienation. The danger of the past was that men became slaves. The danger of the future is that men became robots. True enough, robots do not rebel. But given man's nature, robots cannot live and remain sane, they became 'Golems,' they will destroy their world and themselves because they cannot stand any longer the boredom of a meaningless life.[39]

Colin Mason in *The 2030 Spike: Countdown to Global Catastrophe*, also says about proposed solutions to the environmental crisis: "if proposed solutions don't take the lowest common denominator of human nature realistically into account, they will not work."[40]

The pessimistic sentiment about the "lowest common denominator of human nature" is defensible and a pessimistic tradition of philosophical thought, antagonistic to progressive liberalism and humanism, and even nationalism, supports this.[41] For example, the Spanish philosopher Jóse Ortega Y Gasset (1883-1955) in *The Revolt of the Masses* (1930),[42] saw the early 20th century

---

[38]   Mike Adams, "The Overpopulation Myth MYTH," NaturalNews.com, March 15, 2013, at http://www.naturalnews.com/039490_overpopulation_myth_ecological_footprint_population_collapse.html.

[39]   Erich Fromm, *The Sane Society* (Cowl Books/Henry Holt, New York), 1955, pp. 359-360.

[40]   Colin Mason, *The 2030 Spike: Countdown to Global Catastrophe* (Earthscan, London, 2003), p. 8.

[41]   On the pessimistic view of human nature and life see James Sully, *Pessimism: A History and Criticism* (Henry S. King and Co., London, 1887); R. Scrutton, *The Uses of Pessimism: And the Danger of False Hope* (Oxford University Press, Oxford, 2010).

[42]   Jóse Ortega. Y Gasset, *The Revolt of the Masses* (George Allen and Unwin, London, 1961, published in Spanish in 1930).

as a "levelling period" where the mass-man, our friend the "sheeple," "feels himself lord of his own existence" and "crushes beneath [him] everything that is excellent, individual, qualified and select." A dumbing down and collapse of culture is hence inevitable: "[t]he characteristics of the hour is that the commonplace mind, knowing itself to be commonplace, has the assurance to proclaim the rights of the commonplace and impose them wherever it will."[43] All of that, decades before the "cultural wars."

The zombie apocalypse has as a philosophical subtext, as a very insightful Wikipedia article has put it, that "civilization is inherently fragile in the face of truly unpredictable threats and that most individuals cannot be relied upon to support the greater good if the personal cost becomes too high."[44] Frank Darabont, creator of early AMC's *The Walking Dead*, also sees the zombie apocalypse as an allegory of civilizational collapse: "I think we're coming to grips with the fact that we've created something here that is unsustainable as a civilization. The sheer numbers and resources we're consuming, there's a real sense of great potential death about to befall us."[45]

The zombie apocalypse phenomenon "represents a profound disturbance in the Western collective unconscious caused by anxieties over the decline of Western civilization," Brian Anse Patrick observes in *Zombology*.[46] Zombies are a sign "for disorder, chaos, overpopulation, civil breakdown and more."[47] Zombies, Delfino and Taylor say, "are a projection of some of our worst fears… [and] the idea of a "zombie apocalypse"… calls to mind a kind of Judgement Day – "the wrath of god."[48] "The zombie apocalypse is an illustration

---

[43] As above.

[44] "Zombie Apocalypse," https://en.wikipedia.org/wiki/Zombie#Zombie_apocalypse.

[45] Frank Darabont, quoted in Graeme Blundell, "Heroes or Villains," *The Weekend Australian (Review)*, October 12-13, 2013, p. 26.

[46] Brian Anse Patrick, *Zombology: Zombies and the Decline of the West (and Guns)* (Arktos, London, 2014), p.25.

[47] As above, p.168.

[48] Robert A. Delfino and Kyle Taylor, "Walking Contradictions," in Wayne Yuen (ed.) *The Walking Dead and Philosophy: Zombie Apocalypse Now* (Open Court, Chicago, 2012), pp.39-51, cited p.51.

of the "fatally soft" and weakness of modern humanity, a state produced by our own technology."[49] Zack Snyder, director of the zombie apocalypse movie *Dawn of the Dead* (2004) sums up this matter as follows: " I have a feeling that our whole way of life is like an eggshell that we think is so impervious, but once you put a crack in it everything comes apart pretty quick."[50] Our "unthinkable world" of planetary horrors, Eugene Thacker has observed, produces "an absolute limit to our ability to adequately understand the world at all."[51]

Tauriq Moosa asks how our world differs from Thomas Hobbes' state of nature and the zombiescape.[52] The difference is one of degree as there are daily doses of misery facing the majority of humankind, not so much in the developed world, but certainly in the developing world, with disease; lack of resources (e.g. clean, safe drinking water); armed militants killing, raping and looting; natural disasters; violence and atrocities. For example, across much of sub-Saharan Africa, violence—including murder, cannibalism, torture and rape —is a way of solving social problems in a world where police forces are totally corrupt and powerless against gangs and warlords. Over in India, visitors to the Ganges River can usually see corpses floating downstream, often to lodge at the banks of the river, to be eaten by feral dogs. (No cultural/racial criticism or imperialism etc. implied by the way. These places are just in "advance" of the times. Our turn is just around the corner.) That is close to *The Walking Dead* in terms of shock value (at least when first one sees it, the corpse-eating dogs, that is).

---

[49] Jonathan Maberry, "Take Me to Your Leader: Guiding the Masses Through the Apocalypse with a Cracked Moral Compass," in J. Lowder (ed.), *Triumph of the Walking Dead: Robert Kirkman's Zombie Epic on Page and Screen* (Smart Pop, Dallas, 2011), pp. 15-34, cited pp. 18-19.

[50] Zack Snyder, quoted from Matt Mogk, *Everything You Ever Wanted to Know About Zombies*, p. 99.

[51] Eugene Thacker, *In the Dust of this Planet [Horror of Philosophy Vol. 1]* (Zero Books, Winchester, 2010, cited p. 1.

[52] Tauriq Moosa, "Babies in Zombie Land," in Wayne Yeun (ed.) *The Walking Dead and Philosophy: Zombie Apocalypse Now* (Open Court, Chicago, 2012), pp. 231-242.

Moosa says that our world may be *worse* than even the zombie apocalypse and for many people "a zombie apocalypse would be an improvement" for "[z]ombie attacks are like animal attacks, they're unfortunate when they happen, but they're not the horror of thugs raping you or your family, killing your neighbors, and burning your village to the ground. It's obvious that the thugs are worse and, what makes it more so is that the thugs exist right now."[53] Many examples of such terrors can be cited: the 2014 Islamic State beheadings of Lebanese soldiers, Kurds, British aid workers, American journalists and French nationals who had their heads hacked off with knifes; the brutal murder of British soldier Lee Rigby in Southeast London, stabbed and hacked to death by British-born, Nigerian-descent jihadists; the multitude of stabbings, hit-and-run car attacks, shootings and explosions, committed in Jerusalem and Tel Aviv against ordinary Israelis by Palestinian extremists, and the Paris shootings of November 13, 2015, where three Islamic terrorists killed 130 people. Much more on this later in this book.

Few in the comfortable West shed a tear for hate crimes committed against homosexual people in Africa, involving machete and hammer attacks, vigilante groups brutally beating gays and the "corrective rape" of lesbian women by gangs. One horrific crime involved a 23-year old gay man who was decapitated and had his genitals severed and inserted into his mouth. Another ghoulish crime occurred in 2011, where a lesbian was murdered by being stabbed to death with glass shards, mutilated, her genitalia cut out and a bottle inserted into the wound. Her body was then dumped in a ditch and rocks and used condoms tossed on her face.

Neo-masculinity writer Jack Donovan has given another take on the zombie apocalypse.[54] He notes that not everyone is rattled by guilt and fear about growing social inequality. In the wilds of 'merica news about the face-chewing incident gave some tough guy a hard-on as he lovingly stroked his AR-15 and perhaps other weapons featured in

---

[53] Moosa, as above, p. 236.

[54] Jack Donovan, "Zompocalypse Now: America's Training Wheel Tribalism," July 8, 2012, at http://www.jack-donovan.com/axis.

Guns & Ammos' Zombie Nation.[55] His guns may be loaded with special ammunition produced by Hornady for the zombie apocalypse, the "Zombie Max Ammo"[56] and on his belt may be one or more of Ka-Bar's range of zombie apocalypse blades (Ka-Bar ZK (zombie killer) series), handles in ghoulish apocalyptic green.[57] The zombie apocalypse gives men the prospect of returning to a life on the edge, where being alive means fighting for survival, not tap dancing on computer keys. Donovan quotes the tagline form *The Walking Dead* graphic novel: "[i]n a world ruled by the dead, we are forced to finally start living." This represents a return to a way of life lived by men for most of history, where one's right to life was fought for and defended. Zombie apocalypse preparation is a way for modern detribalized men, "to dip their toes into a kiddie pool of tribalism and get used to the feel, texture and temperature of blood."[58] To continue this line of thought, the zombie apocalypse is a metaphor for the coming collapse of civilization and the rise of the neo-barbarian.[59] That is the argument of this book, and the next one.

CONCLUSION: *The zombie apocalypse is a metaphor for the collapse of civilization, with zombies being a "death's head." The symbolization of death and destruction is culturally more important than considerations of these literally being the "living dead." The (brain) dead living are more frightening because we dwell amongst them.*

---

[55] *Zombie Nation, Guns & Ammo*, July 5, 2012, at http://www.gunsandammo.com/blogs/zombie-nation/.

[56] On the Hornady "Zombie Max Ammo," see http://www.hornady.com/ammunition/zombiemax and also http://www.youtube.com/watch?v=bQWb-5nblx4.

[57] See www.kabar.com/.

[58] Donovan, as above.

[59] Venkat, "The Return of the Barbarian," March 10, 2011, at_http://www.ribbonfarm.com/2011/03/10/the-return-of-the-barbarian.

The Coming Collapse of Civilization

PROPOSITION 3: *The zombie apocalypse, representing a coming collapse of civilization, is no more fiction. There is a substantial body of research, particularly from environmentalists, indicating that techno-industrial civilization is doomed, with a breakdown occurring as early as 2030, and perhaps sooner.*

It has been argued by those who have examined the evidence of the array of converging and compounding crises,[60] that due to the interplay of a multitude of interacting and compounding factors and forces—such as natural human aggressiveness and violence; the lack of survival adaptability of modern humanity to life without advanced technology and infrastructure (which has made people into domestic human battery hens) and the immense destructive impact of the contemporary world upon ecological services and resources—that there will be no soft landing or green, tree-hugging transition to "sustainability." Instead, there will be a "rapid descent" into a Dark Age of barbarism and savagery. Civilization—represented by life in concentrated nucleated settlements, cities—is a product of the abundance of resources, especially energy resources, and an impending collision with the mountain of ecological scarcity will lead to civilization's destruction.[61] Civilization involves "political consolidation, economic specialization, social stratification, some sort of monumental architecture, and a flowering of artistic and intellectual endeavour."[62] Logically, a collapse of civilization involves a breakdown of these factors, and a Dark Age.[63]

A Dark Age, as Widdowson defines it, is a "time without government, without trade, and without any sense of community. It

---

[60] See for example, J. M. Greer, *Dark Age America: Climate Change, Cultural Collapse, and the Hard Future Ahead* (New Society Publishers, Gabriola Island, 2016).

[61] David Price, "Energy and Human Evolution," *Population and Environment*, vol.16, 1995, pp.301-319.

[62] As above, p. 315. See further V. Gordon Childe, *Social Evolution* (Watts, London, 1951).

[63] Roberto Vacca, *The Coming Dark Age* (Doubleday, New York, 1973), p. 174.

is a time of everyone for himself or herself. During the Dark Age, mere survival is the only concern. No one has the leisure for a higher activity, including keeping records. That is why a Dark Age is dark. Its principal feature is that we know little of what took place in it. The collapse that precipitates the Dark Age is abrupt and unexpected."[64] Shorter and sweeter (depending on your point of view) is James Ballou's definition in his *Long-Term Survival in the Coming Dark Age*, of a period of time "marked by frequent warfare and a virtual disappearance of urban life," as civilization, involving organized political power, the rule of law and some form of sociocultural and economical structure and organization, collapses.[65] Thus, it will be *Mad Max/Road Warrior*, sans the hot cars (fuel depletion), sans the leather-clad homoeroticism, and after a time, no ammunition. Moreover, given *Fury Road* (2015), it will also be sans feminism. The vision depicted in the movie and book *The Road* (2009),[66] with some qualifications, is essentially correct.

The collapse of civilization or the zombie apocalypse needs to be distinguished from, I argue in chapter three of this book, the extinction of the human species itself from existential threats such as comet strikes, black hole collisions, runaway high energy experiments or even if the human race has a use-by-date because of a species-genetic biological clock.[67] The human race seems to have survived a climate-change induced drought that almost extinguished our species 70,000 years ago, reducing human numbers to as little as 2,000, but here we are, for the time being.[68] Civilization though, is not as resilient and inevitably crashes.

The thesis of collapse is widely accepted by environmentalists, but most see a silver lining to a very dark cloud. Thus W. H. Kötke

---

[64] Mark Widdowson, *The Phoenix Principle and the Coming Dark Age: Social Catastrophes – Human Progress 3000 BC to AD 3000* (Amarna LTD, Bedford, UK, 2001), p. xi.

[65] James Ballou, *Long-Term Survival in the Coming Dark Age: Preparing to Live After Society Crumbles* (Paladin Press, Boulder, Colorado, 2007), p. 1.

[66] Alan Weisman, *The World Without Us* (Picador, New York, 2008).

[67] D. M. Raup, *Extinction: Bad Genes or Bad Luck?* (W. W. Norton, New York, 1991).

[68] D. M. Behar (et al.), "The Dawn of Human Matrilineal Diversity," *American Journal of Human Genetics*, vol. 82, 2008, pp. 1130-1140.

in *The Final Empire: The Collapse of Civilization and the Seed of the Future*,[69] believes that the collapse of civilization is inevitable because economic growth has reached ecological limits and there are no more frontiers on Earth. Thus, our generation "is on the verge of the most profound catastrophe the human species has ever faced." Our present world is a "culture of suicide" and the only hope for humanity is "to regain balance with the earth" by creating "a utopian paradise, a new Garden of Eden." Dream on; based on the initial assumptions, we are doomed, doomed, doomed, and maybe doomed a wee bit more.[70]

Carolyn Baker, in *Sacred Demise: Walking the Spiritual Path of Industrial Civilization's Collapse* (2009),[71] expresses collapse optimism, a "sacred demise." For Baker, collapse is "more stable" than a "zombie apocalypse" and involves "subtle patterns of abandonment and decay that unfold over long periods of time."[72] Even so, the breakdown of techno-industrial civilization "is likely to be the most devastating holocaust in the recorded history, and will be the end of the world as any of us has known it." There will be "unprecedented escalations of violence."[73]

Not as sweet, the "Health Ranger" Mike Adams sees the collapse of techno-industrial society occurring relatively soon.[74] There will be "untold human suffering and death," but a rebirth of human civilization will occur along with "human spiritual awakening." He says "[i]t is my belief that the majority of today's living population

---

[69] W. H. Kötke, *The Final Empire: The Collapse of Civilization and the Seed of the Future* (Arrow Point Press, Portland, OR, 1993).

[70] Craig Dilworth, *Too Smart for Our Own Good: The Ecological Predicament of Humanity* (Cambridge University Press, Cambridge, 2010), pp. 453-454.

[71] Carolyn Baker, *Sacred Demise: Walking the Spiritual Path of Industrial Civilization's Collapse* (iUniverse; http://www.iuniverse.com, 2009).

[72] Carolyn Baker, "What if Collapse Happened and Nobody Noticed?" May 3, 2012 at http://carolynbaker.net/2012/05/03/what-if-collapse-happened-.

[73] Carolyn Baker, *Collapsing Consciously: Transformative Truths for Turbulent Times* (North Atlantic Books, Berkeley, 2013), p. 45.

[74] Mike Adams, "How to Prepare Yourself for the Collapse of the Age of Human Delusion (and the Arrival of Human Spiritual Awakening)," NaturalNews.com, July 14, 2014 at http://www.naturalnews.com/045991_age_of_delusion_spiritual_awakening_mental_practice.html.

will not survive the inevitable sequence." Nevertheless, after about a century a rebirth will occur. That is nonsense in my opinion, for once the great spiral down has happened it will be virtually impossible for humanity to rise out of the primeval mud. However, Adams wisely recommends that people strive to achieve physical, mental and spiritual toughness and the cultivation of all-round survival skills.

Clive Hamilton in *Requiem for a Species*,[75] focusing on climate change and humanity's inability to deal with the climate crisis, sees the end of modern civilization, if not the human species: "[t]he prospect of runaway climate change challenges our technological hubris, our Enlightenment faith in reason and the whole modernist project."[76] The evidence of global climate change shows that, "the world is now on a path to a very unpleasant future and it is too late to stop it."[77]

More controversially, Guy R. McPherson in *Going Dark*[78] argues that the Earth may no longer be a habitat for humans beyond the 2030's and that near-term human extinction will occur because of self-reinforcing feedback loops in the global climate system. Collapse will include the catastrophic meltdown of around 440 nuclear power plants destroying most organisms, as shutting down nuclear power plants requires 1-2 decades of "careful planning."

McPherson is an "extreme" example of an eco-collapse theorist, but he has made a plausible cause for human extinction, as I argue in chapter 3. However, many other scientists and theorists have expressed alarm that the "compounding crises,"[79] "shock of history,"[80]

---

[75] Clive Hamilton, *Requiem for a Species: Why We Resist the Truth about Climate Change* (Allen and Unwin, Crow's Nest, New South Wales, 2010).

[76] As above, p. 31.

[77] As above p. viii.

[78] Guy R. McPherson, *Going Dark* (Publish America, Baltimore, 2013).

[79] Will Steffen and David Griggs, "Compounding Crises: Climate Change in a Complex World," in P. Christoff (ed.) *Four Degrees of Global Warming: Australia in a How World* (Routledge, London and New York, 2014), pp. 121-138; A. J. McMichael, "Health Impacts in Australia in a Four Degree World," as above, pp. 155-171.

[80] Dominique Venner, *The Shock of History* (Arktos, London, 2015).

and "converging catastrophes"[81] including the climate change crisis, energy scarcity, food and water insecurity, biodiversity destruction, economic insecurity, international terrorism and militarization, threaten us with civilization collapse, if present trends continue.

GENERAL CONCLUSION: *In chapter 3, I argue that a civilization collapse because of the environment is inevitable. This will lead to a great die-off of the bulk of humanity in waves of hyper-violence, as environmentalists implicitly acknowledge. Rather than fruitlessly hoping that this tsunami of blood does not occur, those who want to survive need to fight fire with fire and embrace the way of the neo-barbarian. Our salvation will be via weaponry and the cultivation of individual toughness. These books are the self-help books for a journey to hell.*

There are some other excellent books taking a similar type of personal transformative approach to the zombie apocalypse, the impending collapse of civilization. Forrest Griffin former light heavyweight champion of the UFC (Ultimate Fighting Championship) has *Be Ready When Shit Goes Down: A Survival Guide to the Apocalypse,*[82] which is a big-balled approach to survivalism, stacked full of jokes; which is not to say that I agree with the twisted sentiment in all of these jokes, just with the freedom to make them. Who would have thought that TEOTWAWKI could be so much fun?

On the other hand, *The Disaster Diaries* by Sam Sheridan[83] traces this mixed martial artist's attempt to master a wide-range of survival skills, from knife fighting to wilderness skills, to deal with various doomsday threats. The final chapter of the book though says that the evidence is against *The Walking Dead* world of dog-eat-dog. Hurricane Katrina's reports of human savagery were false; the extent of violence and social breakdown in the aftermath of

---

[81]   Guillaume Faye, *Convergence of Catastrophes* (Arktos, London, 2012).

[82]   Forest Griffin and Erich Krauss, *Be Ready When the Shit Goes Down: A Survival Guide to the Apocalypse* (itbooks, HarperCollins, New York, 2011).

[83]   Sam Sheridan, *The Disaster Diaries: One Man's Quest to Learn Everything Necessary to Survive the Apocalypse* (Penguin Books, New York, 2013).

Haiti's earthquake, were exaggerated. Contrary to Sheridan, this book defends the social Darwinist, dog-eat-dog view of humanity, and maintains that humans are even more degenerate than conventionally thought.[84] However, Sheridan does say that "man is wolf to man", "when the resources run low, when people are starving, they start eating each other." Nevertheless, even though "long-term, grid down TEOTWAWKI is different to a normal disaster," it is unlikely he believes. After all, predictions of the apocalypse or even "collapse" are as old as recorded history, and haven't all such predictions been wrong? Well, no, they haven't – all past civilizations did collapse. Shit really does happen and does not merely hit the proverbial fan, but often buries it. The question to be investigated in chapter 3 is: why should techno-industrial civilization be any different?

---

[84] Martha Stout, *The Sociopath Next Door* (Three Rivers Press, New York, 2006).

CHAPTER

2

Listen up, maggots! You are not special. You are not a beautiful or unique snowflake. You're the same decaying organic matter as everything else.

-Tyler Durden, *Fight Club* (1999)

There exists no man who is not an enemy.

-Kanti I, King of Egypt, (C 2500 BC), *Teachings*.[85]

Most men are bad.

-Bias of Priene, (C 600 BC, *Maxims*) [86]

Civilization is a thin varnish, built up painfully over centuries; when it is removed, you discover egotistical, violent, and cruel human beings. Take a normal person and put him out in the cold, the rain, amid hunger and thirst, take away his comfort and habits, his television, beer, booze, cigarettes, and other drugs, and you will soon see the savage within. [...]And if you think fraternity and social bond are still there after decades of consumerist, hedonist, narcissist, egocentric culture, you are in for a big surprise. A society that encourages immediate satisfaction of our basest desires and whims can only, in a crisis situation, transform itself into a horde of violent psychopaths.

-Piero San Giorgio[87]

The human race will be the cancer of the planet.

-Julian Huxley (1887-1975)[88]

How many people there are could be described as mere channels for food, producers of excrement, fillers of latrines, for they have no purpose in this world; they practice no virtue whatsoever; all that remains after them is a full latrine.

-Leonardo Da Vinci (1452-1519) (attributed to)[89]

---

[85] Quoted from A.R. Pratt, *The Darkside: Thoughts on the Futility of Life from the Ancient Greeks to the Present* (Citadel Press Books/Carol Publishing Group, New York, 1994), p. 4.

[86] As above p. 7.

[87] Piero San Giorgio, *Survive the Economic Collapse: A Practical Guide* (Radix/Washington Summit Publishers, Whitefish, 2013), p. 171.

[88] Quoted from Pratt, as above, p. 230.

[89] K. Krull, *Leonardo da Vinci* (Puffin Books, New York, 2005), p. 39.

LORD OF THE ZOMBIES

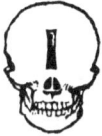

I T WAS the ancient Greek philosopher Heraclitus (c. 535-c. 475 BC), who held that "fire" (energy?) was the primordial substance of the universe and that all things were in perpetual flux, who also said: "Those unmindful when they hear, for all they make of their intelligence, may be regarded as the walking dead."[90] The idea here is that the "unmindful," those who live their lives as unenlightened sleepwalkers, might just as well be the "walking dead," what we today would call "zombies."

Contemporary zombie popular culture has also drawn a direct connection between "us" and zombies.[91] George Romero's film *Dawn of the Dead* (2004), set in a shopping mall, has a scene where Peter says to Stephen regarding the zombies outside: "They're us. That's all." Robert Kirkman in his graphic novel *The Walking Dead # 24* expresses the same sentiment: "WE ARE THE WALKING DEAD." AMC's *The Walking Dead* extends the theme running through Romero's films and many other zombie flicks, that humans are their worst enemies and that human hubris and selfishness will lead to our ultimate destruction.[92]

---

[90] Heraclitus, Fragment 3, cited from Dale Jacquette, "Zombie Gladiators," in Richard Greene and K. Silem Mohammed (eds), *Zombies, Vampires, and Philosophy: New Life for the Undead* (Open Court, Chicago and La Salle, 2010), pp.105-118, cited p. 105.

[91] Roger Luckhurst, *Zombies: A Cultural History* (University of Chicago Press, Chicago, 2015).

[92] C. D. Evans, *"They're Us": Infectious Trauma and the Zombie Apocalypse* (PhD Thesis, University of Arkansas, May 2009).

Hollywood zombies, born in George Romero's film *Night of the Living Dead* (1968) are reanimated bodies, "a living body that has died and come back to life," due to various causes, typically naturalistic.[93] Matt Mogk in *Everything You Ever Wanted to Know about Zombies*,[94] says that a zombie is a "scientific monster," "*a relentlessly aggressive, reanimated human corpse driven by a biological infection.*" That definition rules out a supernatural/magic cause for zombieism. In the Afro-Caribbean voodoo concept of zombieism, the zombie was usually a living person, controlled by the "magic" of a sorcerer. Early "zombie" movies including *White Zombie* (1932), *Revolt of the Zombies* (1936), *King of the Zombies* (1941), and *I Walked with a Zombie* (1943), did not have zombies as cannibals, eating human flesh and brains, but were people under a spell, who usually were able to break the spell in the end. Thus, the Mogk definition, whilst working perfectly fine for most of modern culture, needs fine-tuning; the biological agent could have a supernatural/magic origin (indirect cause) or supernatural/demonic forces may directly cause the zombieism. In the TV series *Supernatural*, Dean and Sam Winchester face "zombies" of two types; those raised from the dead by necromancy, magicians or by demons, and humans infected by the Croatoan zombie virus, demonically created. Hence, zombies can have a supernatural cause, and at least in the world of fiction, and supernaturally caused zombies get over the problem of how the dead reanimate.

In *Dead Snow* (2009), zombies are reanimated by pure evil. Sam Raimi's *The Evil Dead* (1981), *Evil Dead 2* (1987) and now concluded TV version, *Ash vs Evil Dead* (2015-2018), starring Bruce Campbell (of *Burn Notice* fame), featured necromantic reanimation by demonic possession, produced by an ancient reborn evil. The possessed have many zombie-like elements (although zombologist purists will not classify these ghouls as "zombies") and they are not destroyed by

---

[93] David Wang, "5 Scientific Reasons a Zombie Apocalypse Could Actually Happen," October 29, 2007, at http://www.cracked.com/article_15643_5-scientific-reasons-zombie-apocalypse-could-actually-happen.html.

[94] Matt Mogk, *Everything You Ever Wanted to Know About Zombies* (Gallery Books, New York, 2011).

head shots. Well, maybe they are. In the 2015-2018 TV series, *Ash vs. Evil Dead*, head shots, which completely blow the head away, stop these ghouls, although only blowing away say half a head, will not. Ash's trusty chain saw arm weapon though, beheads and minces these demon spawn and stops their evil. At least, we hope so.

In HBO's now concluded *Game of Thrones*, there were White Walkers in the TV show and "Others" in George R.R Martin's books, which are an ancient, mystical race, hostile to humans. In the distant past, in a bitterly cold winter lasting a generation, known as the "Long Night," White Walkers invaded the southern regions of men and cut down all in their path. The human and animal dead were reanimated as *Wights*. Wights, either human or animal, are the near-mindless minions of White Walkers, the dead magically reanimated. Unlike conventional zombies, decapitated corpses still attack, and limbs, which are slashed off, can still move. Fire is the principal weapon used to destroy Wights, while dragonglass weapons—obsidian—a form of volcanic glass, is the only weapon able to kill White Walkers, which in the hasty ending of the series in season 8, the Battle of Winterfell (2019), occurred too easily. When White Walkers are stabbed or slashed by dragonglass weapons they freeze up and fall apart. Wights can use basic weapons, unlike most zombies. Once again, zombologist professors would not see Wights as zombies, and perhaps not even quasi-zombies, but both creatures share common attributes, and have their fan base.

The zombie idea has been in human culture in various forms for thousands of years. For example, in *The Epic of Gilgamesh* (c. 2100 BCE), Ishtar was in a rage from perceived insults from Gilgamesh, whom she wanted as her husband. Gilgamesh rejected her, reciting a long list of her previous lovers and all the harm and horrors that she brought on them. Ishtar, pissed off with this rejection, returned to the heavens and requested of her father Anu, who possessed the "Bull of Heaven," to kill Gilgamesh or she would carry out this threat:

I will knock down the Gates of the Netherworld,

I will smash the doorposts, and leave the doors flat down,

And will let the dead go up to eat the living!
And the dead will outnumber the living![95]

To cut to the chase, she gets the Bull of Heaven to attempt to destroy the Earth, but Gilgamesh and the wild man Enkidu, kill the Bull of Heaven. Which goes to show that people have been speaking bull for thousands of years.

The Old Testament has one quasi-zombie passage: Zechariah 14: 12-13: "This is the plague with which the Lord will strike all the nations that fought against Jerusalem: Their flesh will rot while they are standing on their feet, their eyes will rot in their sockets, and their tongues will rot in their mouths. On that day people will be stricken by the Lord with great panic. They will seize each other by the hand and attack one another." The flesh rotting, while people attack, is zombie-like, although there is no mention that the dudes "that fought against Jerusalem" are the walking dead, but no doubt when all that mayhem goes down, they may have wished that they were. At least in the hard fairy tale world of religion.

In the New Testament, Revelation 9:6 states: "During those days people will seek death but will not find it; they will long to die, but death will elude them." This is some distance from even quasi-zombiedom, but is still an interesting deviation: those unable to die may still deteriorate, perhaps becoming as decayed as zombies. This is much like, I suppose, the traitorous new class who now fill our universities, and seem never to disintegrate, but become increasingly putrid over time, feasting and festering on the public purse.

In European folklore and superstition, the idea of the dead returning to haunt, hunt and prey upon the living was common, although ghosts, demons and vampires had pride of place in the pantheon of terror. For example, archeologists in Bulgaria have uncovered two skeletons dated from the Middle Ages, which were found pierced through the chest with iron rods, presumably to keep

---

[95] *The Epic of Gilgamesh*, Tablet VI, cited at http://www.ancienttexts.org/library/mesopotamian/gilgamesh/tab6.htm.

them from turning into vampires.[96] The skeletons were discovered in an archeological dig in the Bulgarian Black Sea town of Sozopol. According to Bulgaria's national museum chief, Bozhidar Dimitrov, this was a common practice in some Bulgarian villages up until the first decade of the 20th century. It was considered that people regarded as bad during their lifetime might return after death as vampires to suck the blood of the living in the night, unless stabbed in the chest with an iron rod or wooden stake, to pin them in their graves. About 100 such "vampire" corpses have been discovered in Bulgaria, and there are many other similar finds in central and Western Europe. This practice may be revived in the ruins of the West, in the near future, to pin down forever our brood of blood suckers of the new class.

Ancient Greeks believed that the dead could rise from their graves as "revenants," being in a state of neither living nor dead, arising to harm the living. In a cemetery known as "Passo Marinaro," near the Greek coastal town of Kamarina in south-eastern Sicily, used for graves from the fifth to the third centuries BCE, one individual's head and feet were completely covered by large amphora fragments (a large two-handled ceramic vessel), used to pin the individual in the grave. A second individual was a child buried with five large stones on the top of its body.[97]

The Norse *draugr* or "again-walker" is a reanimated corpse with superhuman strength, who may guard treasure buried with it, or seek revenge over those who wronged them in life.[98] They slay victims through various means, including flesh eating. The draugr can drive the sane, insane, and was thought to have magical powers such as shape-changing, increasing their size and being able to see into the future.[99] Unlike the modern zombie, the draugr can, shades of Freddie

---

[96] R. Nuwer, "Vampire Grave" in Bulgaria Holds a Skeleton with a Stake through its Heart," October 13, 2014, at https://www.smithsonianmag.com/smart-news/vampire-grave-bulgaria-holds-skeleton-stake-through-its-heart-180953004/.

[97] C. L. S. Weaver, "Walking Dead and Vengeful Spirits," *Popular Archaeology*, vol. 19, Summer, 2015.

[98] Hilda Ellis-Davidson, *The Road to Hel* (Cambridge University Press, Cambridge, 1943).

[99] Ellis-Davidson, as above, p. 163.

Krueger, enter the dreams of the living. Anticipating zombies, in the Norse *Eyrbyggja Saga*, a shepherd killed by a draugr arises from the dead the next night as a draugr.[100] Unlike the modern zombie, the draugr is generally immune to weapons wielded by ordinary men, but in the *Grettir's Saga* and *Eyrbyggja Saga*, a hero can fight the draugr back to the grave.[101]

The Germanic *nachzehrer* eats already dead bodies, but a living person is not transformed into a nachzehrer by being bitten by one. The nachzehrer arises after death, typically the death of a suicide. It is destroyed by placing a coin in its mouth (good luck with that one) and then beheading it.[102] Both of these European creatures of terror can be contrasted with the *jiangshi*, a reanimated corpse in Chinese folklore. It moves with outstretched arms seeking the life force of the living. The corpse is stiff and moves by hopping.[103] No doubt the present vampire and zombie cults stir up deep racial memories of fear and dark forces from our past that the thin walls of civilization have only precariously held at bay.

In contemporary culture, the zombie apocalypse is viewed through the conceptual framework of science, rather than traditional folklore and superstition. Max Brooks in his best-selling book *The Zombie Survival Guide*[104] is one leading source of information about Hollywood zombies. Zombieism arises from a virus, simply named *solanum*. The origin of solanum is a mystery; perhaps it arose as a genetic engineering experiment gone wrong (compare to the T-virus in the *Resident Evil* series). Nevertheless, solanum uses cells from the human frontal lobe for replication, destroying the cells in the process.

---

[100] Kathryn Hume, "From Saga to Romance: The Use of Monsters in Old Norse Literature," *Studies in Philology*, vol. 77, 1980, pp. 1-25.

[101] As above. Skuld ("by evil Norns, ill created") in *The Saga of King Hrolf Kraki* (Penguin Books, London, 1998), in a battle, raises dead Viking warriors as quasi-zombie minions: "Skuld," Badass of the Week, at http://www.badassoftheweek.com/skuld.html.

[102] N. K. Chadwick, "Norse Ghosts (A Study of the *Draugr* and the *Haugbúi*," *Folklore*, vol.57, 1946, pp. 50-65.

[103] "Jiangshi," at http://en.wikipedia.org/wiki/Jiangshi.

[104] Max Brooks, *The Zombie Survival Guide: Complete Protection from the Living Dead* (Three Rivers Press, New York, 2003).

Bodily functions cease, the person "dies," but the brain is dormant as the virus causes cells to mutate to create a new brain, which acts independently of oxygen. The body is then reanimated, with some bodily functions remaining, but others shutting down. Usually this process is complete in under 24 hours. For humans the virus is 100 percent communicable and 100 percent fatal, which is thematically convenient.

It is not waterborne or airborne (contrasting with *I am Legend* (2007), where there is an airborne virus as well as one transmittable through bites). Infection comes from direct fluid transfer by a bite or splatter. The solanum virus is similar to rabies insofar as both diseases are transmitted by infected bites, and in the case of both diseases, the infected have a propensity to attack and bite. Solanum differs from rabies, as there is no cross-species active infection (rabies being transmitted to humans from bites from infected animals such as dogs, wolves, and bats), because solanum is fatal to all animals, but presumably not plants. Reanimation only occurs in humans (contrasted to the infected dogs in the *Resident Evil* series and *I am Legend*, if this is taken to be a zombie film rather than a vampire or hybrid vampiric-zombie film).

Brooks-zombies do not have superhuman abilities; they have visual and sound detection, a keen sense of smell to detect human prey, no sense of touch, no powers of regeneration, and a lifespan on average of 3-5 years depending on environmental conditions, with zombies in cold climates generally lasting longer than zombies in hot climates. The solanum virus apparently slows down normal decomposition. Nevertheless, zombies ultimately decompose, if for no other reason than that their bodies do not regenerate and they wear away. Zombies may raise their rude finger to existing physiological knowledge, but they are still bound by the laws of physics (e.g. the second law of thermodynamics, of increasing entropy).

Unlike your unfriendly neighborhood cannibal, human flesh is not food for Brooks-zombies, whose digestive system is decomposing; presumably, they eat out of primal savagery. Such zombies have no circulatory system, just tubes of congealed blood, which makes transmission of the virus by blood splatter used by melee impact weapons, difficult, but not impossible. They have the same strength as the living (unlike vampires), but do not fatigue.

Brooks-zombies have ultra-low intelligence, and little capacity to learn or use weapons. They are dispatched by destroying the brain's cerebellum (which controls motor skills and co-ordination) and the brain stem by piercing through the brain's dura matter into the white matter. The standard Romeo/ Brooks zombie is "slow," but there are also "fast" zombies ("the infected"), as in *28 Days Later* (2002), *28 Weeks Later* (2007) and *World War Z* (2013). In this case a mere drop of infected blood into one's eye can transform one into a zombie in as little as 12 seconds *without* actual death (as in *World War Z* (2013)), whereas in *The Walking Dead*, the transformation involves some hours, *with* death and reanimation. Hence *World War Z*-style zombies are not the "living dead," but brain-destroyed, crazed and savage humans, who primarily do not eat flesh, but could tear flesh with their teeth as part of their "rage" (e.g. *28 Days Later, 28 Weeks Later*). Matt Mogk in *Everything You Ever Wanted to Know about Zombies*, argues that the creatures of *28 Days* and *28 Weeks* are technically not zombies, with the ghouls dehydrating/starving in 28 days, whereas conventional zombies do not. While that argument about the title of "28 days" seems plausible, it does not hold for the film *28 Weeks*, which surely refers to the time of the zombie apocalypse. In any case, the ghouls on *Zombieland* (2009) are not the "living dead" and Mogk says, "almost anyone will tell you that *Zombieland* is a zombie movie."[105] Thus, "zombies" may not be the "living dead," "reanimated human corpses," and need not be flesh-eaters and such, although they are typically human flesh *destroyers*. Further, the living ghouls traditionally classified as the mere "infected," are in the light of film developments, such as Brad Pitt's *World War Z* (2013), justifiably classified as zombies. The term "zombie" is as spongey and open-textured as the entities it denotes.

---

[105] Matt Mogk, *Everything You Ever Wanted to Know About Zombies*, p. 22.

George Romero's *Night of the Living Dead* (1968) was inspired by Richard Matheson's novel *I am Legend* (1954).[106] The novel, which has vampires instead of zombies, has been made into three films: *The Last Man on Earth* (1964) (starring Vincent Price), *The Omega Man* (1971) (starring Carlton Heston) and *I am Legend* (2007) (starring Will Smith). *I am Legend* (2007) involves a genetically engineered viral-based vaccine for cancer being administered to the entire human race (extremely unlikely). The virus (probably in a live attenuated vaccine (LAV)) mutates, killing off 90 percent of humanity. The rest become vampiric-zombie creatures. Like vampires, they are vulnerable to light, fast moving with almost Spider-Man-like climbing abilities, and agility and strength far beyond normal humans. Perhaps such beings are just a type of vampire or genre-benders, mixing vampires and zombies. Such creatures do not appear to be decaying.

One of the major conceptual problems about zombies is inconsistency of their nature. Most zombie movies have the "living dead" as devoid of higher cognitive functions. Zombie reanimation restarts the brain stem, although the neocortex is dead. The problem is that "walkers" do things inconsistent with being literally "the walking dead"—sounds like gunfire attract them and they see lights and detect smells—implying that major organ systems and the parts of the brain supporting them must still be intact. The movement of limbs requires functioning nerves and muscles, making *The Walking Dead*-style zombies, "walking contradictions."[107] If only the brain stem was reanimated, zombies could not walk and sense. To be able to attack and eat prey requires a functioning motor cortex, parietal lobe, part of the neocortex (for seeing and hearing) and also the temporal and occipital lobes. Romero/Brooks/*The Walking Dead* zombies are physiologically impossible beings if the cause of zombieism is viral. However, if the cause is supernatural, or maybe even alien nanobot technology (as part of a nanobot attack to exterminate us (as in *Plan 9 From Outer Space* (1959) and *Slither* (2006), where the alien organism

---

[106]   Richard Matheson, *I am Legend* (Gollancz, London, 2006; first published 1954).

[107]   Robert A. Delfino and Kyle Taylor, "Walking Contradictions," in Wayne Yuen (ed.) *The Walking Dead and Philosophy: Zombie Apocalypse Now* (Open Court, Chicago and La Salle, 2012), pp. 39-51.

causing the zombie apocalypse crashes to earth in a meteor), such zombies may be physically possible if their causal agents exist.

The neurology and psychology of zombies remain something of a philosophical problem for the genre as Matt Mogk notes in one of his "Romero rules," zombies are capable of communication, using weapons, retaining memories and "eventually even out-smart humans."[108] Thus, the zombies in Romero's *Day of The Dead* (1985) are capable of learning new skills and using weapons. In *The Walking Dead* season 1, episode 2, ("Guts"), inconsistently, a zombie in a crowd in one scene uses a rock to break through the glass doors of an Atlanta department store.

In *The Crazies* (2009), starring *Justified* series star Timothy Olyphant, a US military bioweapons program gone wrong, contaminates the water of a small US town, turning most of the population into ultra-violent quasi-zombies (meaning that this, for zombie purist, may not be a zombie movie), who while not appearing to desire to eat flesh, certainly seek to destroy it, using fire and weapons such as pitch forks to impale people. In the film *Dog House* (2009) "zom-birds" who prey exclusively on men, use a variety of weapons of murder, including scissors, an axe, a metal cleaver and even a broadsword. In the Japanese zombie movie *Chanbara Beauty* (2008) (directed by Yohei Fukuda), as a result of experiments by mad scientist Sugita, smarter zombies capable of using weapons roam the Earth. However, Aya (Eri Otoguro), clad in a fluffy bikini, and wielding big tits and a katana, proves more than a match for them (and probably most guys).

The trend of zombies having intelligence and some quasi-moral sense, which would entail the survival of a fair part of the neocortex, began with Romero's *Land of the Dead* (2005) (i.e. use of a softball bat by Number 9, a softball player turned zombie), and is taken to its logical or illogical conclusion in *In the Flesh* (2013) and *Warm Bodies* (2013). In *Warm Bodies*, the zombie "R" develops a love interest in a warm bodied female, taking modern liberalism's universal cosmopolitan love philosophy to its *reductio ad absurdum*. However,

---

[108]   Matt Mogk, *Everything You Ever Wanted to Know about Zombies*, as above, p.51.

it was only a matter of time before it happened. The question is: given the lack of blood circulation in zombies, will R have erection problems or is he already stiff?

Harvard psychiatrist Steven Schlozman, author of *The Zombie Autopsies*[109] has moved some distance from the Romero/*The Walking Dead* "living dead" zombie to suggest a scientifically more credible zombie. A virus, as yet undiscovered, causes Ataxic Neurodegenerative Satiety Deficiency Syndrome (ANSD). It destroys key parts of the brain except the amygdala, that part of the limbic system responsible for the fight or flight response. The brain stem also survives. The destruction of the ventromedial hypothalamus results in an insatiable appetite as there is no neural mechanism regulating eating. That would explain the bug eating in *Night of the Living Dead*, the attack on Rick's horse on season 1, episode 1 and 2 in AMC's *The Walking Dead*, and the zombie munching on the family dog in season 1, episode 3 ("The Dog") of *Fear the Walking Dead*.

Neurologists Timothy Verstynen and Bradley Voytek, authors of *Do Zombies Dream of Undead Sheep?*[110] believe that a more "realistic" conception of zombies entails seeing them not as the walking dead, but as blood-thirsty, stimulus-driven humans suffering from CDHD – Consciousness Deficit Hypoactivity Disorder. This is characterized by a "loss of rational, voluntary and conscious behavior replaced by a delusional/impulsive-reactive aggression, stimulus-driven attention, and the inability to coordinate motor or linguistic behaviours." The impulsive-reactive aggression disorder arises from the loss of orbitofrontal control signals to the amygdala. Ataxic movements occur because of cerebellum loss. Other brain damage in the zombie brain includes loss of the arcuate language circuit; bilateral hippocampal damage (lack of memory consolidation); damage to the secondary somatosensory cortex, resulting in lack of pain response; bilateral damage to the posterior parietal cortices

[109]   Steven Schlozman, *The Zombie Autopsies: Secret Notebooks from the Apocalypse* (Grand Central Publishing, New York, 2011).

[110]   Timothy Verstynen and Bradley Voytek, *Do Zombies Dream of Undead Sheep? A Neuroscientific View of the Zombie Brain* (Princeton University Press, Princeton, 2014).

(co-ordination difficulties); ablation of the claustrum (lack of "meta-consciousness") and finally, the dysfunctioning of ventral striatal reward pathways, leading to an addiction to flesh-eating. For the non-neurophysiologist, the zombie is just a special type of brain-damaged human. Verstynen and Voytek distinguish between the "slow" zombies of *The Walking Dead* (suffering from CDHD-1) and the "fast" zombies of *World War Z, 28 Days Later* and *28 Weeks Later* (suffering from CDHD-2), by the degree of brain damage suffered. Neither type of zombie is literally the "walking dead."

In conclusion, working through zombie fiction returns us to the real horrors of our world. Max Brooks in his zombie works was not presenting a parody of a horror genre, but was attempting to capture a contemporary fear that "the systems are breaking down," as seen in "neighbors knifing each other for food, women being raped, the cops not showing up, children dying of starvation."[111] This fear of civilizational collapse is represented in zombies and is well-captured in season 1 of *Fear the Walking Dead* (2015), where the stench of socio-economic collapse precedes the zombie apocalypse. Mel Brooks, Max Brook's father and comedy legend has said:

> the zombies aren't comedy. It has to do with life-and-death survival, the *modus operandi* for the need to survive.

In this context emergency authorities in the United States and Canada have also used the metaphor of the zombie apocalypse as a study guide to help people prepare for more probable threats such as severe storms, tornadoes, floods, hazardous material spills, earthquakes, tsunamis, landslides, nuclear disasters and other fun things. In the US state of Montana, hackers broadcasted a zombie apocalypse warning in February 2013, claiming (falsely of course), that the bodies of the dead were rising from the grave. This illustrates

---

[111] Taffy Brodesser-Akner, "Max Brooks is Not Kidding about the Zombie Apocalypse," *The New York Times*, June 21, 2013, at http://www.nytimes.com/2013/06/23/magazine/max-brooks-is-not-kidding-about-the-zombie-apocalypse.html.

what I believe is something of a collective unconscious awareness, if not perverse desire and fetish, for death, destruction and doomsday.[112] If one is ready for the zombie apocalypse, then presumably one is ready for anything, including death.[113]

Ali S. Khan's "Preparedness 101: Zombie Apocalypse," published online at the US Centers for Disease Control and Prevention website on May 16, 2011, attracted considerable attention.[114] An online comic, *Preparedness 101: Zombie Pandemic*, was also available.[115] The basic CDC strategy is for people to get together an emergency kit (also known as a bug out kit, discussed in chapter 4. This bag should contain water, food, medication, first aid supplies, sanitation and hygiene goods, tools and supplies, clothing and bedding and important documents (e.g. passport, driver's license). Then one needs an emergency plan, where to go so that the authorities can help ("Never fear – CDC is ready"). That is fine assuming that the CDC has not been zombiefied or otherwise destroyed, as illustrated in season 1, episode 6 ("TS-19") of *The Walking Dead*. No mention is made of self-defense weapons and the comments section of the CDC blog rams this point home, sharply and firmly up to the large intestine.[116]

By contrast, the Missouri Department of Conservation website has an article "Invasive Species Alert: Zombies," where it is stated: "Chainsaws, axes and machetes are excellent weapons for quickly

---

[112] "Hackers Broadcast Zombie Apocalypse Alert," February 13, 2013, at http://www.telegraph.co.uk/news/worldnews/northamerica/usa/9864063/Hackers-broadcast-zombie-warning-on-US-TV.html.

[113] "Zombie Preparedness Week: Are You Ready?" At https://www.emergencyinfobc.gov.bc.ca/zombie-preparedness-week-are-you-ready/.

[114] Ali Khan, "Preparedness 101: Zombie Apocalypse," US Centers for Disease Control and Prevention, May 26 2011, at http://blogs.cdc.gov/publichealthmatters/2011/05/preparedness-101-zombie-Apocalypse/.

[115] US Centres for Disease Control and Prevention, *Preparedness 101: Zombie Apocalypse*, at http://www.cdc.gov/phpr/zombies.htm.

[116] See "Zombie Apocalypse," at http://www.cdc.gov/phpr/zombies.htm; (zombie blog), http://blogs.cdc.gov/publichealthmatters/2011/05/preparedness-101-zombie-apocalypse/, (social media), http://www.bt.cdc.gov/socialmedia/zombies.asp.

'dispatching' zombies."[117] Whether these are "excellent weapons" for zombie dispatching or not, will be discussed in book 2.

The Pentagon also has a plan stop a zombie apocalypse.[118] The document "CONOP 8888" is a zombie apocalypse survival plan that recognizes that zombies are fictional, but sees merit in using them as a training exercise. CONOP 8888, also known as "Counter-Zombie Dominance" (April 20, 2011), uses zombies to avoid the public mistake of a "real plan" with a real world enemy. The document covers familiar ground of the causes of the zombie apocalypse (e.g. radiation, evil magic extra-terrestrial origin, weaponized (genetically engineered, nanotech), symbiont-induced, plant-only eating zombies (e.g. the game *Plants vs. Zombies* and many sequels and spinoffs), with the danger from consumption of food resources)). The CONPLAN phases to deal with a zombie apocalypse are:

1. Shape – zombie awareness in formation.
2. Deter – large-scale training.
3. Seize initiative – personnel to duty stations, fortification.
4. Dominance – lock down for 30 days.
5. Stabilization – recon teams deployed after 30 days.
6. Restore civil authority – aid surviving civil authorities and restore basic services.

Interestingly enough, the lockdown of all USSTATCOM operating locations for 30 days, without an energetic attempt to curb the growth in zombie numbers, will according to mathematical models of the zombie apocalypse,[119] lead ineluctably to societal collapse. Thus, USSTATCOM, after their lock down may be surprised to find little

---

[117] Missouri Department of Conservation, "Invasive Species Alert: Zombies," at http://mdc.mo.gov/zombies.

[118] G. Lubold, "The Pentagon's Plan to Stop the Zombie Apocalypse," May 18, 2014, at http://www.stripes.com/news/us/the-pentagon-s-plan-to-stop-the-zombie-apocalypse-1.283263.

[119] P. Munz. (et al.), "When Zombies Attack! Mathematical Modelling of an Outbreak of Zombie Infection," in K. M. Tchuenche and C. Chiyaka (eds), *Infectious Disease Modelling Research Progress* (Nova Science Publishers, New York, 2009), pp. 131-150.

remaining of humanity and hence no civil authorities to restore basic services. In fact, the report essentially goes on to admit as much. USSTRATCOM forces do not have adequate contingency stores of food and water for 30 days of barricaded counter-zombie operations. The zombie hordes are likely to overrun almost all protected military facilities in the first few days of an outbreak and Airborne Command Centers may not be viable after the first week as support bases are overrun by zombies. There will also be a degradation of military readiness due to political, social and economic instability. In other words, the world depicted in AMC's *The Walking Dead* is not too far from the truth.

In Post Apocalyptica Will People Really Be De Facto Zombies?

They are already. Consider: Lara Logan, then, CBS foreign correspondent, was subjected to a horrific mass rape by a crazed mob of about 200 Egyptian men during the short-lived euphoria of "Arab Spring," February 11, 2011. The mob torn her clothes to shreds, took pictures of her nude body with their cell phones and began beating her with flagpoles and sticks. Then she was raped vaginally and anally (presumably, digitally) "over and over and over again." The victim told the media in a CBS *60 Minutes* interview on May 1, 2011: "[t]hey were tearing my body in every direction... and they were trying to tear off chucks of my scalp." "They really enjoyed my pain and suffering. It incited them to more violence." Fortunately, a group of Arab women saved Logan before she was torn apart. These women closed ranks around her and apparently, the men were not willing to treat their own women the way they just treated an American. Logan was treated for severe bruising, joint injuries and vaginal and anal tears and has been hospitalized a number of times since the vicious attacks. None of the rapists have been brought to justice.[120] If the

---

[120] Scott Pelley, "Lara Logan Breaks Silence on Cairo Assault," May 1, 2011, at http://www.

crazed mob had succeeded in tearing off her flesh, they would be only one-step (the eating step), away from becoming *28 Days*-style zombies. Perhaps their sexual aggression makes them even more frightening: Hollywood zombies do not rape. A lengthy discussion of the migrant rape culture of Europe, especially the rape of British children by migrant grooming gangs, made in numerous daily online sources, with one horror story trumping the next, need not be made to make the same point.[121]

If people can act like that in the "spring time" then how do they fare during times of disaster? Sociologists generally dispute that widespread looting and violence occur after *natural* disasters, seeing, in general, that people band together to help each other.[122] For example, in the case of Hurricane Katrina, the media came to retract earlier-made reports about widespread violence, looting and raping, such as claims that babies were raped. Sociologists claim that during natural disasters people exhibit prosocial helping behaviours. Looting is said to be common in civil disturbances, but rare in the aftermath of natural disasters. Thus, earlier media reports, such as that a seven-year-old child in the Superdome had her throat cut, of 30-40 bodies being stored in a freezer in the Superdome and of 300 bodies piled high at Marion Abramson High School in Eastern New Orleans, were *false*. The claims were soon retracted by the media, to be replaced by the other extreme, that there was not one official report of rape or sexual assault, and that likewise, looting was minimal.

Against this, there are many sources, while accepting that the savage, zombie-like murders and rampaging did not occur, do affirm from personal observations and reliable witnesses and photographs, that widespread violence, looting and raping did occur. Brian Thevenot says that wide spread looting was "definitely not a myth, I

cbsnews.com/news/lara-logan-breaks-silence-on-cairo-assault/.

[121]   P. McLoughlin, *Easy Meat: Inside Britain's Grooming Gang Scandal* (New English Review Press, London, 2016).

[122]   E. L. Quarantelli, "The Myth of the Realties: Keeping the Looting 'Myth' in Perspective," *Natural Hazards Observer*, March, 2007, at http://www.colorado.edu/hazards/o/archives/2007/mar07/mar07.pdf; L. G. Sun, "Disaster Mythology and the Law," *Cornell Law Review*, vol. 96, 2011, pp. 1131-1208.

can confirm as an eyewitness."[123] Photographs of looters stealing not just food and essential items, but expensive electronic goods, can be viewed at various websites.[124] In fact, after Hurricane Katrina hit, the police arrested so many people for robbery that the New Orleans jails were soon full and temporary jails were set up. In early September 2005, 8,000 prisoners were moved out of New Orleans jails and transported to state prisons.[125]

Rape is an under-reported crime; the US Department of Justice estimates that in the US over 300,000 women are raped every year, but less than one in three women report the rape to the police.[126] A number of sources have claimed that the incidence of rape was greater in the aftermath of Hurricane Katrina than the "normal" incidence of rape and that most rape victims did not report it.[127]

A study of Hurricane Katrina crimes, as a Master of Public Administration thesis by Kevin Bailey,[128] concluded that some types of crime increased after the disaster, but others decreased. In New Orleans, *most* crime rates increased significantly in January 2006, but returned to pre-Hurricane Katrina levels by December 2007. The annual murder rate increased in the years 2006 and 2007.

It has been claimed that there was no crime wave among Hurricane Katrina evacuees.[129] Others dispute this; one report states:

---

[123] Brian Thevenot, "Myth-Making in New Orleans," *American Journalism Review*, December/January 2006, at http://www.ajr.org/article.asp?id=3998.

[124] See for example: http://web.archive.org/web/20140704005914/http://jtf.org/america/america.hurricane.katrina.htm.

[125] "At the Train Station, New Orleans' Newest Jail is Open for Business," September 6, 2005, at http://www.komonews.com/news/archive/4163081.html.

[126] K. Bishop, "Preparing for THE Worst," at http://www.preparednesspro.com/preparing-for-the-worst.

[127] See, "40 Rapes Reported in Hurricane Katrina, Rita Aftermath," http://www.wdsu.com/news/5627087/detail.html. http://www.frfrogspad.com/disastr.htm.

[128] Kevin Bailey, *An Evaluation of the Impact of Hurricane Katrina on Crime in New Orleans, Louisiana* (Master of Public Administration Thesis, Department of Political Science, Texas State University, San Marcos, 2009).

[129] S. Vergano, "Report: No Crime Wave among Hurricane Katrina Evacuees," February 15, 2010, at http://usatoday30.usatoday.com/tech/science/columnist/vergano/2010-02-12-hurricane-katrina-crime_n.htm.

[w]hen New Orleans residents streamed into Houston six months ago to escape the floodwaters caused by Hurricane Katrina, they brought in gangs and the violence that goes with them. The city had 170 homicides from September through February 22, 28 percent more than in the same period a year earlier, according to the Police Department. In 29 cases, displaced Louisianans were the victims, the suspects or both.[130]

At the time, police said that once gangs had moved in and drug and prostitution rings were re-established, old scores were settled. To combat this the police formed the Gang Murder Squad to help prevent a further increase in the murder rate.

L.G. Sun has said that prior research on looting in disaster situations may be skewed, being based on "small western populations experiencing more limited disasters in scale and scope."[131] Most research on the alleged absence of looting after disasters has been in developed countries, and in fact, "studies have occasionally observed large-scale looting after natural disasters in the developing world." For example, in the wake of Super Typhoon Haiyan in November 2013 in the Philippines, soldiers and police were deployed to halt large-scale looting; even a Red Cross convoy was attacked. Survivors were suffering from a lack of food, water and shelter in a landscape littered with rotting corpses. However, the prevalence of *illegal* guns carried by insurgents and criminal gangs, challenged security.

One alleged counter-example to this claim of increased crime in the wake of disasters is Superstorm Sandy during October/November 2012 in the US. Crime dropped by a third during the storm – e.g. murder dropped by 86 percent, rape by 44 percent, assault by 31 percent, but burglaries rose by 3 percent. Although this seems to support, *prima facie*, the position of Rebecca Solnit in *A Paradise Built in Hell*,[132] that people tend to work together in disasters, there

---

[130]   J. Kennett, "Louisiana Gangs That Fled Katrina Heighten Houston Murder Rate," March 3, 2006 at http://www.bloomberg.com/apps/news?pid=newsarchive&sid=az6n8C6gsqfo.

[131]   Sun, as above, p. 1139.

[132]   Rebecca Solnit, *A Paradise Built in Hell: The Extraordinary Communities That Arise in*

is contrary evidence. First, crime was down because the goblins and ghouls were off the street; they did not want to be injured. Second, there was some nasty, collapse-style forms of looting, such as people pretending to be Con Ed workers, holding people up and looting. There were also tweets from Twitter accounts by twits intending to loot when the storm hit, mainly to secure electronic goods. This is hardly an example of the milk of human kindness. Reflecting on the issue of violence and disaster, environmentalist/peak oil theorist Richard Heinberg has concluded that for "every heart-warming anecdote about the convergence of rescuers and caregivers on a disaster site, there is a grim historic tale of resource completion turning normal people into monsters."[133]

So much then for disasters unleashing the "inner monster," what then about your garden vanity social breakdown? Consider flash mob crime involving "polar bear hunting," where people, using social media for organization, converge to a certain spot, destroy private property, riot, commit acts of violence and then disperse – quickly. This may be a hit-and-run *group* crime against a *group* of people of another particular group. It may also involve a *group* or an *individual* targeting another small *group* or *individual*, who are the "polar bears," and knocking them down i.e. bashing them into unconsciousness or death – hence its name, "the knockout game." The distinguished black scholar Thomas Sowell sees this as "early skirmishes in a race war,"[134] and who am I to disagree?

Fernando "Ferfal" Aguirre, a collapse-survivalist whose work I will consider in a later chapter, believes that life after economic collapse will be much the same as it is now – but worse. That is, it will not be a zombie apocalypse.[135] Aguirre lived through the economic

Disaster (Penguin, New York, 2010).

[133] Richard Heinberg, "Conflict and Change in an Era of Economic Decline, Part 2: War and Peace in a Shrinking Economy," December 12, 2012 at http://www.carolynbaker.net/2012/12/12/conflict-and-change-in-the-era-of-economic-decline-part-2-war-and-peace-in-a-shrinking-economy-by-richard-heinberg/.

[134] Thomas Sowell, "Early Skirmishers in a Race War," October 24, 2013, at http://www.nationalreview.com/article/362030/early-skirmishes-race-war-thomas-sowell.

[135] Fernando "Ferfal" Aguirre, "Life after an Economic Collapse: The Same… Only Worse,

collapse of Argentina in (1998-2002) and reports on lessons learnt from that experience. As we will see in chapter 3, even though Ferfal rejects the idea that *economic* collapse will lead to a type of world like *The Walking Dead*, the world of *economic* collapse, even with a limited and dysfunctional government, will be a violent and dangerous place.

Likewise, Dmitry Orlov, author of *The Five Stages of Collapse*,[136] who lived through the collapse of the Soviet Union (USSR), predicts the coming crash of the United States, and ultimately of techno-industrial civilization. This will be through resource shortages, passing through five stages of collapse (financial, commercial/economic, political, social and cultural), leading to a more primitive Hobbesian existence where life is "nasty, brutish, and short." This is more to my taste.

British philosopher John Gray in *Straw Dogs* observes that even with the present growth of knowledge "[t]he human animal will remain the same: a highly inventive species that is one of the most predatory and destructive."[137] Harold Bloom in *The Lucifer Principle* argued that "evil" is a part of nature and moves the human world "to greater heights of organization, intricacy, and power."[138] The explanatory assumption of "inborn evil" makes sense of the blood bath of human history. Bloom's "barbarian principle" is also relevant to this book. Civilized societies ultimately become over-civilised and weak and are overcome by barbarians: the ancient Egyptians conquered by the Hyksos; the Babylonian Empire conquered by the Persians; the Persians conquered by the Greeks, even defeating Emperor Xerxes army of 1,700,000 men (according to Herodotus), with Alexander the Great later conquering the entire Persian empire.

Part I," November 6, 2014 at http://ferfal.blogspot.com.au/2014/11/life-after-economic-collapse-same-only.html.

[136]   Dmitry Orlov, *The Five Stages of Collapse: Survivor's Toolkit* (New Society Publishers, Gabriola Island, 2013).

[137]   John Grey, *Straw Dogs: Thoughts on Humans and Other Animals* (Granta books, London, 2002), p. 4.

[138]   Harold Bloom, *The Lucifer Principle: A Scientific Expedition into the Forces of History* (Atlantic Monthly Press, New York, 1995), p. 2.

Today, they are all but an historical memory and we of the West will be lucky to be even that.[139]

Supporting empirical material for this pessimistic view of human nature is given by Le Blanc and Register in *Constant Battles*,[140] who show that the idea of the peaceful noble "savage" is a myth and that warfare and violence, primarily for resources, including females, has been present throughout human history and in our evolutionary past. Lawrence Keeley in *War before Civilization* says that primitive warfare was much more deadly than that conducted between civilized states because of the greater frequency of combat and the more merciless way it was conducted. "Primitive war was very efficient at inflicting damage through the destruction of property, especially the means of production and shelter, and inflicting terror by frequently visiting sudden death and mutilating its victims."[141] Prisoners, for example, were generally not taken, and if not killed on the spot, were stored, to be tortured and/or fattened and eaten.[142] Primitive societies were constantly at war and if modern societies had the same casualty rate in the 20th century, wars would have yielded two billion deaths. On average, tribal societies lost 0.5 percent per annum of their populations due to war.[143] Sixty five percent of primitive societies were at war continuously and 87 percent fought more than one war annually.[144] According to Wade:

Warfare between pre-state societies was incessant, merciless, and conducted with the general purpose, often achieved, of annihilating the opponent. As far as human nature is concerned,

---

[139] Patrick J. Buchanan, *The Death of the West* (St. Martin's Griffin, New York, 2002).

[140] S. Le Blanc and K. E. Register, *Constant Battles: Why We Fight* (St Martin's Press, New York, 2004); Lawrence Keeley, *War before Civilization: The Myth of the Peaceful Savage* (Oxford University Press, Oxford, 1996).

[141] Keeley, as above, p.174.

[142] Nicolas Wade, *Before the Dawn: Recovering the Lost History of our Ancestors* (Duckworth, London, 2007), p. 151.

[143] As above, p. 152.

[144] Keeley, as above, p. 33.

people of early societies seem to have been considerably more war-like than people today.[145]

That includes the Australian Aborigines:

The Australian Aboriginal tribes seemed to have lived in a state of constant warfare, with defended territories and neutral zones marked for trading. Their tool kit, designed for easy transport over long distances, included weapons like heavy war clubs, a special hooked boomerang, and spear-throwers.[146]

It is a myth to suppose that humans have lived in a harmonious ecological balance with their natural environment; rather, technological limits have limited human destructiveness.[147] Pre-civilization was no peaceful Garden of Eden. The violence of pre-civilization is well illustrated by the discovery of Neolithic mass graves in Europe of 6,000 to 7,000 years old, containing human skeletons and hacked off body parts.[148] One circular pit, uncovered in Bergheim, France, had seven human skeletons as well as an infant skull section laying on the remains of seven human left arms that had been hacked off, probably by axes, perhaps done for war trophies. Other mass graves in Europe have incomplete skeletons, indicating mutilation, and maybe cannibalism and the shinbones of victims are frequently broken, so it is likely torture occurred.[149]

Steven Pinker in his study of human violence, *The Better Angels of our Nature*,[150] concludes that the growth of cites, states, technology,

---

[145]   Wade, as above, p. 151.

[146]   As above, p. 84.

[147]   T. Flannery, *The Future Eaters: An Ecological History of the Australasian Lands and People* (Reed books, Port Melbourne, 1994).

[148]   F. Chenel (et al.), "A Farewell to Arms: A Deposit of Human Limbs and Bodies at Bergheim, France, c. 4,000 BC," *Antiquity*, vol. 89, December, 2015, p. 1313.

[149]   C. Meyer (et al.), "The Massacre Mass Grave of Schöneck-Kilianstädten Reveals New Insights into Collective Violence in Early Neolithic Central Europe," *Proceedings of the National Academy of Sciences*, vol. 112, 2015, pp. 11217-11222.

[150]   Steven Pinker, *The Better Angels of our Nature: The Decline of Violence in History and its*

commerce and cosmopolitan morality and culture—in short, modern civilization—has dulled to a significant degree the edge of the normally sharp sword of human violence. He accepts that humans, like chimpanzees have a genetic trait for violence (i.e. are hardwired for violence), but modern civilization has constrained violence and kept it on a tight leash. Given the extent of violence in the past, Pinker, I believe, has made a strong case for his thesis. Nevertheless, if this is so, consider the logical consequence of Pinker's position: if modern civilization collapses then the restraints holding back the pit bull of human aggressiveness and violence will be removed, and Hobbesian humans in a war of all against all (or tribe against tribe) will stalk the earth once more. Given the principle "the bigger they are (or higher they fly), the harder they fall," the collapse could very well lead to levels of violence not yet experienced as "collapse shock" leads to many losing their "heads."[151]

In Post Apocalyptica, people really will be *de facto* zombies, and if all of the nuclear power plants on earth meltdown before, during or after the collapse, spreading ionizing radiation across the planet, stricken with radiation poisoning, they will be for all effective purposes, "zombies," complete with radioactive rotting flesh, as seen in *Fear the Walking Dead* season 5 (2019).

But Won't We Be Able to Rebuild?

Annalee Newitz in *Scatter, Adapt, and Remember*,[152] accepts that humanity is heading towards disaster: "whether the disaster is caused by humans or by nature, it is inevitable."[153] Humanity has experienced population crashes in the past, but bounced back over thousands of years. The fundamental survival strategies are to scatter/bug

---

Causes (Penguin, New York, 2011).

[151] See Nicholas Monsarrat, *The Tribe that Lost its Head* (House of Stratus, Looe, 2000).

[152] Annalee Newitz, *Scatter, Adapt, and Remember: How Humans Will Survive a Mass Extinction* (Anchor Books, New York, 2014).

[153] As above, p. 1.

out, adapt to the new environment, and seek to preserve as much accumulated knowledge as possible.

Lewis Dartnell in *The Knowledge: How to Rebuild our World from Scratch*,[154] goes further and shows how, using the basic scientific method—empirical observation, experimentation and testing, instrument construction and theorization—civilization can allegedly be rebuilt after The Great Collapse.

Dartnell argues that preservation of the scientific method would enable many basic technologies to be rediscovered if lost from an apocalyptic disaster. The core scientific beliefs include the fundamental ideas of physics and chemistry, such as the atomic hypothesis (i.e. matter is composed of particles such as atoms), and the postulate of methodological materialism (explaining the physical world using physical rather than spiritual entities). On this basis, for example, the germ theory of disease would be preferred over say, the evil spirit theory. Sound principles of public health would be adopted, such as don't empty your bowels within 100 meters of your water source, and cover your poo-poo with dirt to prevent flies spreading your dung around when they feed on it and then land on your ham and cheese sandwich, and so on.

Dartnell also accepts another fundamental assumption of this book: that modern humans are weak, especially those in the developed societies. In former times "everyone was a survivalist, with a far more intimate connection to the land and the methods of production," but today people in the developed world "are astoundingly ignorant of even the basics of the production of food, shelter, clothes, medicine, materials or vital substances. Our survival skills have atrophied to the point that much of humanity would be incapable of sustaining itself if the life-support system of modern civilization failed, if food no longer magically appeared on the shop shelves, or clothes on hangers." Core skills need to be relearnt if post-apocalyptic survivors are to continue living.

---

[154]   Lewis Dartnell, *The Knowledge: How to Rebuild Our World from Scratch* (Bodley Head, London, 2014).

Even a humble pencil, because of the sourcing of raw materials and dispersion of production methods, could not be made from scratch. Dartnell's proposal for rebuilding civilization is based on the proposition that there would be vast quantities of resources left for survivors after certain global disasters, thus giving a safety margin for the reboot of civilization.

Most knowledge, especially that on the internet would be lost, and many textbooks would only be accessible to specialists. Most books contain no relevant practical knowledge at all. Dartnell also accepts another core proposition of this book, that after The Collapse, violence and looting will be a way of life and even once law-abiding citizens will now do what is necessary to survive. This will require having a gun (or many), as well as gangs/tribes of people uniting into a protective force to protect perimeters.

Darnell's proposal is based on a "sudden and extreme depopulation that leaves the material infrastructure of our technological civilization untouched."[155] The "best" way for the world to end, on this scenario, would be a nuclear holocaust or massive coronal mass ejection, although Dartnell strangely does not consider the health impacts of ionizing radiation produced from the meltdown of nuclear power plants. He says that if there is a collapse without immediate depopulation: "[t]his wastes the grace period, and society promptly descends into *Mad Max*-style barbarism and subsequent mass depopulation, with little hope of rapidly bouncing back."[156] As Fred Hoyle put it:

It has been often said that, if human species fails to make a go of it here on Earth, some other species will take over the running. In the sense of developing intelligence this is not correct. We have, or soon will have, exhausted the necessary physical prerequisites so far as this planet is concerned. With coal gone, oil gone, high-grade metallic ore gone, no species however competent can make the long climb from primitive conditions to high-level

---

[155] As above, p. 22.
[156] Dartnell, as above, p. 24.

71

technology. This is a one-shot affair. If we fail, this planetary system fails so far as intelligence is concerned. The same will be true of other planetary systems. On each of them there will be one chance, and one chance only.[157]

Apart from this problem, Dartnell says in an internet post that survivors will face a problem of learning practical skills, such as metalwork from guide books, as to obtain such skill takes years of an apprenticeship under a master.[158] There is also the problem of maintaining basic intellectual skills such as reading and mathematical knowledge and passing it on to the next generation. I believe that it should be possible to pass on basic reading and writing skills, even in a small group of survivors. Elementary mathematics—arithmetic, geometry, trigonometry and basic algebra at a high school level— should also be possible in survival group having a mathematically educated person. However, there may not be the time and resources to preserve much of higher mathematics (symbolic logic, metamathematics, transfinite set theory, projective and differential geometry etc.). The joy of solving complex mathematical problems, such as nonlinear partial differential equations—perhaps a higher pleasure than an orgasm—will be sadly lost to humankind. Well, this is the apocalypse and sacrifices will have be made.

Conclusion: Kiss Liberalism (and Almost Everything Else) Goodbye

This chapter has discussed in more detail the meaning of the zombie apocalypse in contemporary culture, especially film. The position taken in this book is that the zombie apocalypse is a metaphor for the death of civilization. It is the aspect of collapse that is of central importance in almost all zombie apocalypse fiction. Organized

---

[157]   Fred Hoyle, *Of Men and Galaxies* (University of Washington Press, Seattle, 1964), p. 64.

[158]   Lewis Dartnell, "Tacit Knowledge and Loss of Reading," at http://the-knowledge.org/en-gb/tacit-knowledge-loss-reading/.

society with functioning technology could easily deal with bunches of mean biting "humans," effortlessly mincing them with any number of instruments of death. But when organized society no longer exists, and the biters are seeking your flesh – then it gets interesting. The collapse of civilization can lead to people acting in a zombie-like fashion (as depicted in the movie *The Road* (2009)) and as we have seen, there are plenty of real-world examples of humans behaving in frightening violent ways. The forces of civilization breakdown, such as climate change,[159] will generate a hyper-violent world once The Collapse occurs. Further, it has been argued, humans are unlikely to be able to claw their way back to a civilized state once "The Fall" has occurred.

The coming "zombie apocalypse" may be of interest to those who are opposed to liberal globalist society and its ideologies. There is, of course, a lively conventional academic attack upon liberalism,[160] but there is also a critique coming from the Dissent Right[161] and "Dark Enlightenment" rejecting universalism, egalitarianism, the "Cathedral" (the power elites and new class) and embracing ethnocentric religion and ancestral folkways.[162] The Dark Enlightenment is a diverse array of positions including paleo-conservatism, tribalism and nihilism, opposed to the existing globalist/cosmopolitan/progressive regime and its constitutive ideologies of democracy, egalitarianism, socialism, modernity (but also "post-modernity"), and instead emphasizing the importance of organic community, the value of tradition and culture.

For example, conservatives may be interested in the remarks by Ashley Barkman, in her paper "Women in a Zombie Apocalypse."[163]

---

[159]   J. Barnett and W. Neil Adger, "Climate Change, Human Security and Violent Conflict," *Political Geography*, vol. 26, no.6, 2007, pp. 639-655.

[160]   Alasdair MacIntyre, *After Virtue: A Study in Moral Philosophy* (Duckworth, London, 1981).

[161]   R. Houch, *Liberalism Unmasked* (Arktos, London, 2018).

[162]   Alfred W. Clark, "What are the Characteristics of the Dark Enlightenment?" April 27, 2013, at https://occamsrazormag.wordpress.com/2013/04/27/what-are-characteristics-of-the-dark-enlightenment.

[163]   Ashley Barkman, "Women in a Zombie Apocalypse," in Wayne Yuen (ed.), *The Walking*

She said: "[i]n a zombie apocalypse feminism is pretty much dead in the water" and Barkman rejects the trendy feminist idea that sex and gender are social constructions: "men and women are not just biologically different (male and female), but also spiritually different: differences between masculine and feminine exist at conception." This proposition is known to be true "naturally," as a matter of empirical observation. Men are, in general, naturally stronger and more aggressive than women due to higher testosterone levels, and women of a childbearing age (if fertile) are vulnerable to pregnancy. Here is the kicker: "masculinity has qualities that lend itself to leadership, whereas femininity leads itself to being led." Hence, in a zombie apocalypse, feminism "which argues that gender is a social construct and thus woman should be given the same roles and duties as men is not only unrealistic, but also ineffective and inefficient." They can quietly argue about that one after class in the Womyn's Room, or the "safe space."

The scenario depicted in *Mad Max: Fury Road* (2015), which has a feminist warrior, Imperator Furiosa (played by Chalize Theron), who can out-shoot and out-fight a hardened warrior like Max, is possible, but improbable. It remains a fantasy, much like *Kill Bill* (volume 1, 2003; volume 2, 2004). The situation is more likely to be as Barkman has depicted. This observation follows from a lifetime of street awareness, being in and witnessing fights, as well as from the theoretical considerations that Barkman references.

Another, more likely scenario for women has been given by Megan Hurwitt, an intelligent, attractive, young lady featured in an episode of season one of *Doomsday Preppers* (2012). When the crash comes she sees people killing each other for food. Moreover, for women who do not prep she said: "you don't want to have to resort to whoring yourself out; that's what a lot of women would face." Tragically, a large number of men are likely to become, as seen in war zones across history, sexual predators, making rape both a sport and political weapon. It is already happening.

Dead and Philosophy: Zombie Apocalypse Now (Open Court, Chicago and La Salle, 2012), pp. 97-106.

A contemporary example of this return to savagery is supplied by the capture of Yazidi women by Islamic State fighters beginning in 2014. The Yazidi is, or was, a Kurdish community with many woman having blond hair and blue or green eyes. Isis stated that it wanted to "smash this "blond bloodline" by impregnating thousands of kidnapped Yazidi women, and has done so, while the West did little specifically about this.

The Islamic State issued a document by its research and fatwa department, which "justified" using captured woman as *sabaya* (sex slaves) and permitted the raping of pre-pubescent girls who are "fit." According to the October 2014 edition of the Islamic state's digital Magazine *Dabiq*, the revival of slavery is part of their belief that the end of the world was coming.[164] The "rape manual" states that woman can also be beaten. Thousands of captured Yazidis woman have been sold as sex slaves in slave markets, with blue-and green-eyed young girls bringing "top price." Some Yazidi were dragged into sexual slavery by their hair.[165] Price tags were apparently placed on the women.[166] Teenage girls abducted by Islamic State fighters were sold in slave markets for as little as the price of a packet of cigarettes. Girl's that did not convert to Islam were tortured, raped and murdered. Many raped Yazidi girls committed suicide, and in June 2016, ISIS burnt 19 Yazidi girls to death in iron cages after refusing to have sex with jihadists.[167] In "brothels" run by British female jihadis,[168] women were raped at a rate of up to 30 times in just a few hours; as

---

[164] Nour Malas, "Ancient Prophecies Motive Islamic State Militants: Battlefield Strategies Driven by 1,400-Year-Old Apocalyptic Ideas" *The Wall Street Journal*, November 18, 2014, at http://www.wsj.com/articles/ancient-prophecies-motivate-islamic-state-militants-1416357441.

[165] A. Lloyd, "Yazidi Girls Dragged into Sex Slavery by Their Hair," *The Australian*, December 23, 2014, pp. 1, 4.

[166] Ivan Watson, "'Treated Like Cattle': Yazidi Women Sold, Raped, Enslaved by ISIS," November 7, 2014, at http://edition.cnn.com/2014/10/30/world/meast/isis-female-slaves/.

[167] J. Newton, "ISIS Burn 19 Yazidi girls to Death in Iron Cages After they Refused to have Sex with Jihadists," June 6, 2016, at http://www.dailymail.co.uk/news/article-3627063/ISIS-burn-19-Yazidi-girls-death-iron-cages-refused-sex-jihadists.html.

[168] "British Female Jihadis Running ISIS "Brothels" Allowing Killers to Rape Kidnapped Yazidi Women," http://www.mirror.co.uk/news/uk-news/british-female-jihadis-running-isis-4198165.

one headline put it: "I've been raped 30 times and it's not even lunch time."[169]

While the rape and genocide of the Yazidis was proceeding, on December 16 2014 the Al-Qaeda affiliated terrorist group Tekreek-e-Taliban Pakistan, conducted a school slaughter of unmitigated depravity. Seven jihadists, who wore suicide bomb vests, attacked the Army Public School in the Pakistani city of Peshawar ("City of Flowers"). The massacre of 132 teenage children and nine teachers (121 children and three staff were wounded), involved shooting them at point blank range, throat slitting, head severing and burning them alive. The jihadists, cornered by Pakistan's Special Service Group, detonated their suicide bomb vests, all seven dying.

In general, these attacks have been seen as a product of Islamic extremism, shaped by their medieval outlook and philosophy. While this is undoubtably true, these acts of brutality arise from those who have put themselves beyond the pale of civilization and who see the end as nigh, and we would expect similar, if not more extreme acts of savagery during the collapse of civilization, the zombie apocalypse and in Post Apocalyptica. So, the phenomenon is not just a product of radical Islam. All of this and more will be coming to your street, if you survive and remain in the cities.

The coming zombie apocalypse will differ from *The Walking Dead*, which maintained, at least in the first few seasons, a conventional moral universe, with Rick decked out in police uniform, with the now-discontinued, anachronistic, Colt Python .357 Magnum at his side, a John Wayne-symbol of order, and right vs wrong. Rather, the world will be more like *Dead Set* (2008), a zombie apocalypse five-part series created by Charlie Brooker, set in the UK Big *Brother House*. As in the reality TV show, people essentially destroy each other, self-destruct, and no one is "saved."

---

[169] John Hall, "'I've Been Raped 30 Times and It's Not Even Lunch Time': Desperate Plight of Yazidi Women who Begged West to Bomb her Brothel after ISIS Militants Sold her into Sex Slavery," *Daily Mail Australia*, October 21, 2014, at http://www.dailymail.co.uk/news/article-2801353/i-ve-raped-30-times-s-not-lunchtime-desperate-plight-yazidi-woman-begged-west-bomb-brothel-isis-militants-sold-sex-slavery.html.

The considerations so far in this book suggest an answer to the question posed by physicist Enrico Fermi (1901-1954) (the Fermi paradox), "where is everybody?" This is the *prima facie* contradiction between the alleged high probability of intelligent life in the universe (even our galaxy) and the lack of human contact. Who, with even half a brain, let alone two heads, would want to visit a planet containing killer animals, a miserable bunch of fuckers, such as the human race? To a higher intelligence, would not the entire human race, and that includes all races etc., appear to be little more than a bunch of brainless … zombies?

There is another answer as well to the Fermi paradox, and that is that intelligent life may have existed on other worlds, but is there no more having gone extinct, just as we are about to.[170] That is the subject of the next chapter.

---

[170]   A. Frank (et al.), "The Anthropocene Generalized: Evolution of Exo-Civilizations and Their Planetary Feedback," *Astrobiology*, vol. 187, 2018, pp. 507-518; B. Specktor, "Climate Change Killed the Aliens, and it Will Probably Kill Us Too, New Simulation Suggests," June 6, 2018, at https://www.livescience.com/62750-climate-change-killed-aliens-easter-island. html.

We are in for a period of sustained chaos whose magnitude we are unable to foresee.

-Dennis Meadows[171]

[T]he coming years will prove increasingly cynical and cruel. People will definitely not slip into oblivion while hugging each other. The final stages in the life of humanity will be marked by the monstrous war of all against all: the amount of suffering will be maximal.

-Pentti Linkola[172]

The world oil production peak represents an unprecedented economic crisis that will wreak havoc on national economics, topple governments, alter national boundaries, provoke military strife, and challenge the continuation of civilized life. At peak, the human race will have generated a population that cannot survive on less than the amount of oil generated at peak – and after peak, the supply of oil will decline remorselessly. As that occurs, complex social and market systems will be stressed to the breaking point, obviating the possibility of a smooth ride down from the peak phenomenon.

-James Howard Kunstler[173]

After four decades of developing an interpretation of history out of my theories of size, I come to the same conclusion as Charles de Gaulle, who confided to André Malraux shortly before his death that in all his years of highly successful leadership he knew of not a single problem that had ever been solved – or ever would be. And the same applies to the problem of excessive size. Not that is could not be solved. Of course, it could. But it never will. "Men," as Hesiod wrote twenty-eight centuries ago, "will go on destroying the towns of other men"; and looking around me 2,800 years later gives me little reason for hope that it will ever be otherwise.

-Leopold Kohr[174]

---

[171]   Dennis Meadows, quoted from M. Mukerjee, "Apocalypse Soon: Has Civilization Passed the Environmental Point of No Return?" *Scientific American*, May 23, 2012, at http://www.scientificamerican.com/article/apocalypse-soon-has-civilization-passed-the-environmental-point-of-no-return.

[172]   Pentti Linkola, *Can Life Prevail? A Radical Approach to the Environmental Crisis* (Integral Tradition Publishing, 2009), p. 157.

[173]   James Howard Kunstler, *The Long Emergency: Surviving the Converging Catastrophes of the Twenty-First Century* (Atlantic Books, London, 2005), pp. 24-25.

[174]   Leopold Kohr, *The Breakdown of Nations* (E. P. Dutton, New York, 1978), pp. 223-224.

CHAPTER

ENDGAME – OUR JOURNEY TO THE END OF THE NIGHT:
WHY THE COLLAPSE OF CIVILIZATION IS INEVITABLE

Collapseology: Is Earth Already "Fucked"?

LEADING BRITISH scientist Sir Martin Rees, in his book *Our Final Century?* (2003),[175] states that "humanity is more at risk than at any earlier phase in its history" and he believes that "the odds are no better than fifty-fifty that our present civilization on Earth will survive to the end of the present century." There is considerable literature, too immense to summarize fully here, which indicates that Rees is too optimistic in his Bayesian probability (personal probability estimate) and that the probability of the destruction of modern civilization, if not the human species and perhaps life on Earth itself, is greater than fifty-fifty.[176] The late Stephen Hawking (1942-2018), physicist, believed that the fate of humans on Earth is sealed already by the socio-political and environmental problems which we face, and that the probability of survival will be increased by abandoning Earth and seeking other planets and space colonies.[177]

---

[175]   Martin Rees, *Our Final Century? Will the Human Race Survive the Twenty-First Century?* (William Heinemann, London, 2003).

[176]   Donald A. Collins, "Heading for a World Apocalypse? *Journal of Social, Political, and Economic Studies*, vol. 35, no.1, Summer, 2010, pp. 242-254.

[177]   "Stephen Hawking's Warning: Abandon Earth – or Face Extinction," at http://bigthink.com/dangerous-ideas/5-stephen-hawkings-warning-abandon-earth-or-face-extinction.

Brad Werner in his paper "Is Earth Fucked?" (his actual title), delivered to the American Geophysical Union in 2012, used a numerical computer model of human-environment interactions, and concluded: "the dynamics of the global coupled human-environmental system within the dominant culture precludes management for stable, sustainable pathways and promotes instability."

Along similar lines Motesharrei (et al.) used a mathematical model (Human and Nature Dynamic Model, (HANDY), based on predator-prey models, to model the human population as a "predator" and nature as "prey."[178] With economic stratification, collapse "within decades" was difficult to avoid because the elites/the rich consume resources until collapse occurred. Similar conclusions have been reached by a limits to growth study by Graham Turner, who concludes from a survey of the scientific literature on resource depletion that on a business as usual scenario the world is already on the cusp of collapse with the first stage of collapse already beginning, and with death rates rising from 2020 onwards.[179]

What is "collapse"? Jared Diamond has defined collapse as "a local drastic decrease in human population numbers and/or in political, economic, or social complexity."[180] Butzer and Endfield give a "broader, integrative" definition of "social collapse" as representing a "transformation at a large social or spatial scale, with long-term impact on combinations of independent variables: (i) environmental change and resilience; (ii) demography or settlement; (iii) socio-economic patterns; (iv) political or social structures; and (v) ideology or cultural memory."[181] Collapse, really is the end of the

---

[178]   S. Motesharrei (et al.), "Human and Nature Dynamics (HANDY): Modeling Inequality and Use of Resources in the Collapse or Sustainability of Societies," *Ecological Economics*, vol. 101, 2014, pp. 90-102.

[179]   G. Turner, "On the Cusp of Global Collapse? Updated Comparison of *The Limits to Growth* with Historical Data," *Gaia*, vol. 21, no. 2, 2012.

[180]   Jared Diamond, "Ecological Collapses of Past Civilizations," *Proceedings of the American Philosophical Society*, vol. 138, 1994, pp. 363-370, cited p. 363.

[181]   Karl W. Butzer and Georgina H. Endfield, "Critical Perspectives on Historical Collapse," *Proceedings of the National Academy of Sciences*, vol. 109, no.10, 2012, pp. 3628-3631, cited p. 3628.

world as we know it. However, we won't "feel fine," contrary to the band R.E.M.[182]

Media commentators and journalists ridicule those who propose that there are ecological limits to economic growth and that the world may be rapidly approaching such limits with respect to environmental sustainability[183] from water,[184] soil,[185] food resources[186] and other variables such as biodiversity[187] and human population growth. In June 2019, the UN Population Division had a further revision of its demographic statistics: UN Department of Economic and Social Affairs, *2019 Revision of World Population Prospects*. The populations of some African countries were thought to be certain to at least more than double, with Africa's population of an estimated 1.3 billion in 2020, exploding to 4.3 billion in 2100.[188]

However, Anglia Ruskin University's Global Sustainability Institute, using computer modelling, predicted a collapse of society on a business-as-usual scenario.[189] A catastrophic collapse of the global food supply would occur due to human population expansion and ecological destruction. Commenters on this study took comfort that its predictions were based on "things" continuing as they are, but they chirped, people will change their behavior. It is argued in this book that they will not and in fact people will consume more, not

---

[182]   https://www.youtube.com/watch?v=OA_CndlBuog.

[183]   M. Wackernagel (et al.), "Tracking the Ecological Overshoot of the Human Economy," *Proceedings of the National Academy of Sciences*, vol. 99, no. 1, 2002, pp. 266-271.

[184]   S. Postel, *Pillar of Sand* (W. W. Norton, New York, 1999).

[185]   D. R. Montgomery, *Dirt: The Erosion of Civilizations* (University of California Press, Berkeley, 2007).

[186]   L. R. Brown, "Could Food Shortages Bring Down Civilization?" *Scientific American Magazine*, April 22, 2009, at http://www.scientificamerican.com/article.cfm?id=civilization-food-shortages.

[187]   S. Pimm (et al.), "The Biodiversity of Species and their Rates of Extinction, Distribution, and Protection," *Science*, vol. 344, 2014, pp. 1246752-1 – 1246752-10.

[188]   UN Department of Economic and Social Affairs, *2019 Revision of World Population Prospects*, (United Nations, New York, 2017), https://population.un.org/wpp/.

[189]   Global Resource Observation, *Climate Change, Resource Scarcity and Conflict*, (Anglia Ruskin University, Cambridge, September, 2014), at http://www2.anglia.ac.uk/ruskin/en/home/microsites/global-sustainability-institute.html.

less and economic globalization will accelerate resource depletion, producing increasing environmental degradation and catastrophic shifts in the planet's ecosystems.[190]

Further, Lloyd's Emerging Risk Report, *Food System Shock* (2015), points out that global agricultural production needs to more than double by 2050 to meet food demands by expanding populations and rising affluence, but this makes food systems vulnerable to food shocks such as water stress, climate change, globalization and political instability. Climate change and related impacts could lead, they say, to wide-spread economic chaos, food riots, civil unrest and terrorist-style attacks.[191]

Intellectuals from the optimist camp also attack the very idea of such pessimism which calls into question the fundamental basis of our present techno-industrial society: there are no limits to growth, technology and economics will ultimately solve all problems and humans are "special," not just another vicious animal species. Thus, French philosopher Pascal Bruckner sees the Western world as flirting with the trendy idea of apocalyptic angst which is chic and "cool" for the chattering class.[192] According to Bruckner, non-European people,

> are likely to receive our professionals of environmental faith with polite indifference. Billions of people look at economic growth, with all the pollution that accompanies it, to improve their condition. Who are we to refuse it to them?

---

[190] J. Zalasiewicz (et al.), "Colonization of the Americas, 'Little Ice Age' Climate, and Bomb-Produced Carbon: Their Role in Defining the Anthropocene," *The Anthropocene Review*, vol. 2, no. 2, 2015, pp. 1-11.

[191] Lloyd's Emerging Risk Report, *Food System Shock: The Insurance Impacts of Acute Disruption to Global Food Supply* (2015), at https://www.lloyds.com/~/media/files/news%20 and%20insight/risk%20insight/2015/food%20system%20shock/food%20system%20shock_ june%202015.pdf.

[192] Pascal Bruckner, "Apocalyptic Angst of the Western World," *The Weekend Australian*, April 21-22, 2012, p. 20.

According to other intellectuals, the West would not in the future be able to stop the Asian dragons, even if it wished to, for societies such as China are set to eclipse the declining West and consume like there is no tomorrow – because there will not be.

Environmental angst may well be a potent symbol of the alleged decline, decay and fall of the West – or alternatively, a reflection of the decadence of Western intellectuals and universities, not naming anyone in particular. However, such angst, whatever its social cause, does not merely by its alleged existence demonstrate that there is no rational, scientific basis for believing that modern techno-industrial civilization is immune to collapse. Indeed, pursuing this idea to its logical conclusion, we should conclude that the cultural decadence of the West premise presents a piece of evidence for the collapse thesis explored in this book. I explain further.

Mark Steyn in *American Alone* (2006)[193] said that "much of what we loosely call the Western world will not survive the twenty-first century and much of it will effectively disappear within our lifetimes, including many if not most European countries." America stands alone to preserve civilization (and neo-liberal capitalism of course), and if America fails then "much of the map is reprimitivized" and a New "Dark Age" will occur. But, in Steyn's later book, *After America: Get Ready for Armageddon*,[194] he is pessimistic about America's future, seeing America as facing the same fate as Europe unless a radical 11th hour movement away from Big Government and the oppressive ideologies of centralist control occur. This form of cultural pessimism arises essentially from seeing neo-liberal market forces being frustrated by centralist control, and the pessimism about civilizational collapse is contingent on that assumption. As ecological limits are approached, financial collapse becomes likely without cheap fossil fuels to maintain the system. Rising energy costs and availability ultimately leads to financial collapse. Tim

---

[193] Mark Steyn, *America Alone: The End of the World as We Know It* (Regnery Publishing, Washington DC, 2006).

[194] Mark Steyn, *After America: Get Ready for Armageddon* (Regnery Publishing, Washington DC, 2011).

Morgan in a Tullett Prebon Strategy Insights publication, sees the coming economic crisis as due to a "perfect storm" of economic mismanagement, resource depletion and rising costs.[195] Thus, matters are much worse than even in Mark Steyn's worst neoliberal nightmare.

Apart from economic liberty considerations, Steyn's pessimism about Europe's survival is based on development of Samuel Huntington's "clash of civilizations" thesis,[196] which sees fundamental incompatibilities and tensions between Western liberalism and Islamic fundamentalism. Steyn and others[197] predict a transformation of Europe into "Eurabia" due to massive Islamic immigration (e.g. Germany's 2015-2019, Syrian "refugee" intake), high Islamic migrant birth rates and Europeans having below replacement level fertility rates.

The grooming rapes of British children in Rotherham, right through the UK and Northern Europe, the sexual assaults, rapes and bashings (*taharrush gamea* and *taharrush el-ginsy*: collective harassment and sexual assault) on New Year's Eve 2016 at Cologne, Hamburg, Stuttgart, Dusseldorf, Frankfurt, Bielefeld, Vienna, Salzburg, and also in Sweden and Finland, and many other assaults, rapes, murders and tortures, could be seen as an indication of how well immigration is performing. Some see this as a "colonization of Europe," if not the end, or collapse of Europe, by demographic swamping.[198]

US President Donald Trump predicted that the influx of migrants could lead to the "end of Europe," a prediction also made for Germany

---

[195] Tim Morgan, *Perfect Storm: Energy, Finance and the End of Growth*, Tullett Prebon, Strategy Insights, Issue 9, 2013 at http://ftalphaville.ft.com/files/2013/01/Perfect-Storm-LR.pdf.

[196] Samuel Huntington, *The Clash of Civilizations and the Remaking of World Order* (Simon and Schuster, New York, 1996).

[197] Mark Steyn, *Lights Out: Islam, Free Speech and the Twilight of the West* (Stockade Books, 2009).

[198] Frank Salter, "Germany's Jeopardy: Could the Immigration Influx "End European Civilization"?" January 15, 2016, at http://www.eurocanadian.ca.

by Thilo Sarrazin, *Deutschland schafft sich ab* (*Germany Abolishes Itself*), (Deutsche Verlags-Anstalt, 2010). Contrary to Obama, two-thirds of all migrants are male and young. Due to the age, the influx in Germany could cause a cultural transition within one generation.[199]

Along similar cultural conservative lines are the works of Lee Harris,[200] Patrick J Buchanan,[201] John Derbyshire,[202] Thomas W. Chittum[203] and Morris Berman.[204] Berman sees a Dark Age, a time of cultural and moral decay, "cultural disintegration" and "spiritual death" occurring. He believes that collapse is inevitable, being built into "the process of civilization itself."

Collapse is especially evident in America, Berman argues, because of: (1) accelerating social and economic inequality; (2) declining marginal returns with respect to the investment of effort in organized solutions to socioeconomic problems; (3) declining levels of literacy and general intellectual awareness in the population and (4) spiritual death i.e. the dumbing down of culture. Thus, in America the top one percent of the nation owns more than the bottom 90 percent, 11 percent of young adults cannot locate the United States on a world map, 45 percent of the US population believe that space aliens visited the Earth,[205] 69 percent of under 30 years olds do not know basic facts of US history—such as America declaring its independence in 1776—and

---

[199] Adorján F. Kovács, "Wahrheiten zur Flüchtlingskrise," ("Truths about the Refugee Crisis"), *The European Magazine*, December 28, 2015, at http://www.theeuropean.de/adorjan-f-kovacs/10622-einwanderung-oder-zuflucht.

[200] Lee Harris, *Civilization and Its Enemies* (Free Press, New York, 2004), *The Suicide of Reason* (Basic Books, New York, 2008).

[201] Patrick Buchanan, *Suicide of a Superpower: Will America Survive to 2025?* (Thomas Dunne Books/ St. Martin's Press, New York, 2011).

[202] John Derbyshire, *We Are Doomed: Reclaiming Conservative Pessimism* (Crown Forum, New York, 2009).

[203] Thomas W. Chittum, *Civil War Two: The Coming Breakup of America* (Lexington and Concord Partners, Ancon, Panama City, distributed in the USA by American Eagle Publications, Inc. 1996).

[204] Morris Berman, *The Twilight of American Culture* (W. W. Norton, New York, 2001), *Dark Ages America: The Final Phase of Empire* (W. W. Norton, New York, 2007), *Why American Failed: The Roots of Imperial Decline* (John Wiley, New York, 2011).

[205] Berman, *Dark Ages America*, as above, p. 6.

almost 30 percent of the US population believes that the sun revolves around the Earth or is unsure of which revolves around which.

Berman's specific critique of the United States is that the "American dream" is based on a hustling paradigm that is not about working hard and playing fair, so that one can have a better lifestyle than one's parents in a wholesome community, but rather about hustling, cheating, swindling, conning and manipulating the system. One aims to get more than one's fair slice of the "pie" and to hell with ethics, compassion and the community. Self-interest and greed have replaced the idea of the common good because there is little "common" now which is good. Consequently, Berman sees America as doomed because the social capital necessary to sustain society has been eroded. By implication, other nations, including much of the West, based upon the same values of economic selfishness and crude utilitarianism, also face implosion or rot and decay.

Journalist Robert D. Kaplan in his "coming anarchy" thesis, gave a perhaps bleaker vision of humanity's future.[206] Here the interplay of environmental disintegration and social unrest could lead to a breakdown of societies as has occurred in West Africa in failed states such as Somalia. Kaplan says that the United States may not survive the 21st century in its present form and states that although "the distant future will probably see the emergence of a racially hybrid globalized man, the coming decades will see us more aware of our differences than of our similarities."[207] He does not explain how "globoperson" will arise, especially as conflict, polarization and segregation may increase if economic decline and ultimate economic collapse occurs.

Robert Harvey,[208] for example, sees the possibility of "doomsday-global anarchy" occurring unless America and the West prevent it.

---

[206] Robert D. Kaplan, "The Coming Anarchy: How Scarcity, Crime, Overpopulation, Tribalism and Disaster are Rapidly Destroying the Social Fabric of Our Planet," *The Atlantic Monthly*, February, 1994, pp. 44-76, *The Coming Anarchy: Shattering the Dreams of the Post Cold War* (Vintage Books, New York, 2000), "Why So Much Anarchy?" February 5, 2014, at https://www.stratfor.com/weekly/why-so-much-anarchy.

[207] Kaplan, *The Coming Anarchy*, as above, pp. 49-50.

[208] R. Harvey, *The Return of the Strong: The Drift to Global Disorder* (Macmillan, London, 1995); R. Harvey, *Global Disorder*, (Constable, London, 2003).

However, if the conservative pessimists such as John Derbyshire, Thomas Chittum, Morris Berman and Mark Steyn are correct about the decline and fall of America, and by a domino effect, the rest of the West, Harvey's "doomsday-global anarchy" is essentially "in the bag."

Niall Ferguson in *The Great Degeneration*,[209] argues that Western institutions are already exhibiting evidence of decay. French New Right intellectual Alain de Benoist in his article "La fin du monde a bien en lieu,"[210] puts the case that the world has already "ended"—that is, a Traditional world based on communities of meaning—to be replaced by a culturally fluid world where the only fixed meaning is the religion of self-gratification and consumption in the global supermarket and where profit and greed trumps all values. Such a world, which seems overwhelming and invincible to Traditionalist Right thinkers, will I argue, itself be smashed by the stronger forces of ecological scarcity.

In his book *Immoderate Greatness Why Civilizations Fail*,[211] William Ophuls puts the case that civilizations inevitably breakdown and collapse because of human hubris or what Edward Gibbon (1737-1794) in his *The History of the Decline and Fall of the Roman Empire* described as follows:

[t]he decline of Rome was the natural and inevitable effect of immoderate greatness. Prosperity ripened the principle of decay; the causes of destruction multiplied with the extent of conquest; as soon as time or accident had removed the artificial supports, the stupendous fabric yielded to the pressure of its own weight.[212]

---

[209] Niall Ferguson, *The Great Degeneration: How Institutions Decay and Economics Die* (Allen Lane, London, 2012).

[210] Alain De Benoist, "La fin du monde a bien eu lieu," *Eléments*, no.146, January-March, 2013.

[211] William Ophuls, *Immoderate Greatness: Why Civilizations Fail* (CreateSpace, North Charleston, 2012). The discussion to follow is greatly in debt to this superb book, especially for some references.

[212] Edward Gibbon, *The History of the Decline and Fall of the Roman Empire*, edited and abridged by David P. Womersley (Penguin, New York, 2001), p.435.

Collapse was thus inevitable after a certain point of decay; instead of asking *why* Rome fell, Gibbon wrote, "we should rather be surprised that it had subsisted so long."[213] Civilizational destruction is thus often a form of suicide; as Will Durant has put it: "A great civilization is not conquered from without until it has destroyed itself from within."[214]

Ophuls gives a general theoretical argument for civilizational breakdown that I expand and develop in this chapter. First, there is the problem of ecological resource exhaustion and the limits to growth. Prosperity may be a short-term wonder, but in the long-term, it results in the destruction of a civilization's basis for its own sustainability, because economic systems mask environmental decline: the economy can grow and bloom while the ecology dies. Conventional economists, in particular, have an inability to understand exponential growth and how collapse can sneak up on a society. The human mind is still essentially Paleolithic, hardwired for a hunter-gatherer lifestyle and is not well adapted to understand the concept of *entropy*, a trend towards increasing disorder and breakdown as available energy over time is transformed into less useful forms.[215] The "thermodynamic vicious circle" of civilization is that high civilization means high production and consumption and the larger the entropy increase the greater the "depletion, decay, degradation, and disorder" in the system. At some point "a civilization exhausts its thermodynamic "credit" and begins to implode."

Second, civilizations are complex ("complexity" referring to both the quantitative size of the number of interrelationships as well as the qualitative dimension), and no past civilization is as complex as ours is. The growth in complexity leads to a compounding of problems, and even though more people does mean more problem-solvers, it also means more problem-creators, a situation of problem overload and an "ingenuity gap," a lack of ability to solve problems. Problems that were

---

[213]   As above, p. 435.

[214]   Will Durant, *Caesar and Christ: The Story of Civilization*, vol.3, (Simon and Schuster, New York, 1994), p.665, cited from Ophuls, as above, p. 4.

[215]   N. Georgescu-Roegen, *The Entropy Law and the Economic Process* (Harvard University Press, Cambridge, MA, 1971).

once seemingly separate "begin to coalesce into a "problematique," a nexus of problems that mutually aggravate each other."

Complex socio-ecological systems are also non-linear and exhibit "chaotic" behaviour, making accurate prediction impossible. Such systems become unstable after a certain critical threshold is reached and are subject to catastrophic collapse. Ophuls gives a general theoretical argument is his book *Immoderate Greatness* in support of this proposition, but evidence is presented in this chapter, which indicates that the Earth's ecosystems are fast approaching such critical thresholds.

Another human factor leading to the collapse of civilizations is that humans are not supremely rational problem-solvers, but typically "muddle through," making suboptimal decisions. The ruling elites of the society may know that the system is decaying and dying, but may not act because they do not want to endanger their share of the loot. They will have comfortable lives, for a time, while the great unwashed slowly suffer. Ultimately, the heads of the elites' rest on the chopper. Moreover, beyond this, most people, especially "intellectuals," are blindly and unthinkably committed to the ruling ideologies of the day and move to punish free and critical thinkers. Chris Hedges in an article "The Treason of the Intellectuals," powerfully sums up this point:

> [t]hose who doggedly challenge the orthodoxy of belief, who question the reigning political passions, who refuse to sacrifice their integrity to serve the cult of power, are pushed to the margins. They are denounced by the very people who, years later, will often claim these moral battles as their own. It is only the outcasts and the rebels who keep truth and intellectual inquiry alive. They alone name the crimes of the state. They alone give a voice to the victims of oppression. They alone ask the difficult questions. Most important, they expose the powerful, along with their liberal apologists, for what they are.[216]

---

[216] Chris Hedges, "The Treason of the Intellectuals," March 31, 2013, at http://www.uruknet. info/?p=96437.

Civilizations, as Oswald Spengler and Ophuls have proposed, are like organisms, going from birth, to adolescence, to the prime of their lives, and finally to twilight and ultimate death. Put alternatively, civilizations go through a rise and fall from an age of pioneers and/ or conquest, to an age of commerce, affluence and intellect, before suffering moral decay and disintegrating in an age of decadence. In the beginning a people believes in itself and the virtues of sacrifice, courage and determination, which eventually leads to success, riches and luxury. But when the love of money replaces the love of honor, courage and the in-group, greed and selfishness begin to kill off society as the exuberant growth of weeds might strangle a once ordered vegetable garden. The society begins to wither and decay from within. With a loss of identity, mass immigration is undertaken, with the influx of eager foreigners cashing in on the existing affluence. The result, as Ophuls puts it "is an increasingly polyglot population that no longer shares the same values. This diversity overload alone poses a substantial challenge to social sustainability."[217]

Combine biophysical entropy and moral decay and one has, Ophuls concludes, *over-determination*, more than enough factors for collapse. As our techno-industrial civilizations is now global, collapse will be global, with a vast die off of the human race. The loss of life will be so high because human hubris being what it is, most people even if they believed that a collapse of civilization was inevitable, and soon, would not prepare.

Ophuls is not the only one who has said this; writing about the zombie apocalypse, Jonathan Maberry says that humanity is ill-prepared for a global catastrophe of this magnitude. The odds are against most of us surviving:

We have become fatally soft, weakened by the technology that has allowed us to conquer the rest of the planet. The weaknesses come from being continually resource-rich in our daily lives. We have clothing, multiple forms of transportation, medicine, readily available food sources, deliveries of foods, affordable repairs or

---

[217]   Ophuls, as above, p. 86.

replaceable parts, and access to virtually endless information via cell phones and internet. ... The fact that we are surrounded by structure encourages us to believe in its effectiveness and permanence.[218]

When systems fail, people no longer know how to adapt because "the average person in a post-industrial society is not skilled in repairs, combat, farming, emergency medicine, outdoor survival, general mechanics, or other useful trades."

Ophuls in an earlier book, *Plato's Revenge*, expressed hope that an ecological politics of consciousness will develop, ushering the world into a "smaller, simpler, humbler vessel"[219] from the doom-bound *Titanic* which humanity is presently on. He wants America to return to a Jeffersonian, limited republican government, basically what is was like in the beginning. America, as I stated earlier in this chapter is more likely to spiral into "Civil War II," and ultimate destruction.

Complexity, Chaos and Collapse

One of the themes running through the collapseology literature is that complex systems are vulnerable to collapse because complexity itself means that there are more components that can break down.

Roberto Vacca in his *The Coming of the Dark Age* thought (so far, wrongly) that a collapse of modern civilization would occur in the early 21st century because technological systems are becoming so complicated that they are reaching "critical dimensions of instability"[220] and becoming uncontrollable. Thus, a "chance concomitance of

---

[218] Jonathon Maberry, "Take Me to Your Leader: Guiding the Masses through the Apocalypse with a Cracked Moral Compass," in James Lowder (ed.), *Triumph of the Walking Dead: Robert Kirkman's Zombie Epic on Page and Screen* (Smart Pop/Ben Bella Books, Dallas, 2011), pp. 15-34, cited pp. 18-19.

[219] William Ophuls, *Plato's Revenge: Politics in the Age of Ecology* (MIT Press, Cambridge MA, 2011), p.208.

[220] Roberto Vacca, *The Coming Dark Age* (Doubleday, New York, 1973).

stoppages in the same area could start a catastrophic process that could paralyse most developed societies and lead to the deaths of millions of people." The deaths of substantial numbers of the scientific and technological elite would contribute to this paralysis, and spiral down, and if enough of the elite died, the end of science would occur: "[a]lmost no one will be free from immediate burdens and able to think with detachment about abstract and general issues." This great die off will leave plenty of houses "once the corpses have been removed," but ultimately the world as we know it will crumble away due to lack of maintenance.

In this context, both the United States and India's infrastructure, to cite but two examples, are "on the brink" of collapse. In July 2012, the electricity grid supplying electricity to half of India collapsed in a cascading failure. The failure was due to the inadequate response of the government to have enough power capacity to meet India's demands from its rapid industrialization. India's power grid, like its road and railway infrastructure, is poorly constructed and constantly tottering on breakdown.[221] The United States' infrastructure received a "D" grade from the American Society of Civil Engineers, its drinking water infrastructure a "D-" aviation a "D," energy a "D+" and roads a "D-." Bridges have collapsed and the power infrastructure failed during the July 1-3, 2012 heatwave. Beneath the streets of most cities in the West, water and sewerage pipes continue to age, many being over a century or more.[222]

Ancient Rome's concrete structures lasted over 2,000 years but ours will be crumbling in under a century. High strength (Portland) concrete structures are falling apart twice as fast as pre-1930s concrete structures. The concrete cracks and erodes, leading to air, moisture and chemicals oxidizing the rebar, which then expands in diameter, wrecking the rest of the concrete. Infrastructure across the world is crumbling, including highway bridges, sewer pipes,

---

[221] Mike Adams, "Grid Down Catastrophe Strikes India; Half the Population Stranded with No Electricity," NaturalNews.com, July 31, 2012 at http://www.naturalnews.com/036640_India_power_grid_failure.html.

[222] American Society of Civil Engineers, http://www.asce.org/reportcard/.

plumbing stations and so on.[223] The West really is in an advanced state of decay.

Infrastructure deficiencies in the US already cost US $129 billion a year from decaying roads, railways, bridges, and transit systems and an investment of US $1.7 trillion is needed to stop costs growing exponentially. This infrastructure is unlikely to be repaired in the crisis times ahead, so watch America literally fall apart.[224]

Vacca, while seeing the cities as we know them ultimately crumbling away, predicted in the short term that dwellings would become fortified citadels, manned by armed inhibitors and security guards. Cities such as Johannesburg today confirm this prediction. Sieges, he also thought, will become common. There will be a return of man the warrior:

[t]hough modern firearms will be available, physical strength will also be important. It will be necessary in man-to-man combat, in trifling day-to-day emergencies once dealt with by machines, and also in handling obstacles caused by nature or the enemy.[225]

A number of scientists and thinkers have defended the idea that the complexity of modern civilisation is a vulnerability that can lead to collapse. The cover story edition of *New Scientist*, April 5, 2008 "The Collapse of Civilization: It's More Precarious than We Realized," featured an article by Debora MacKenzie, "Are We Doomed?"[226] summarizing the ideas of theorists who can see breakdown and collapse as inherent in societies once a certain point of complexity is reached. The work of Professor Joseph Tainter, an archaeologist

---

[223]   Alice Friedemann, "A Century from Now Concrete will be Nothing but Rubble," January 19, 2014, at http://energyskeptic.com/2014/enough-energy-left-to-rebuild-concrete-infrastructure.

[224]   "ASCE: Infrastructure Delay Costs Billions Each Year," July 28, 2011, at http://www.think-harder.org/think-concrete-blog/11-07-28/ASCE_Infrastructure_Decay_Costs_Billions_Each_Year.aspx.

[225]   Vacca, as above, p. 191.

[226]   Debora Mackenzie, "Are We Doomed?" *New Scientist*, vol. 197, no. 2650, April 5, 2008, pp. 32-35.

at the University of Utah and author of *The Collapse of Complex Societies*,[227] is highly relevant. Tainter believes that complex societies can collapse because of the diminishing returns of increased complexity. His position is that: (1) human societies are problem-solving organizations; (2) socio-political systems require energy for their sustainability; (3) increased complexity results in increased costs per capita; (4) investment in social complexity as a problem-solving response to problems yields declining marginal return.[228] The cost of increased complexity results in societies becoming less capable of dealing with challenges and threats over time leaving societies vulnerable to social collapse.

The complexity of modern technological systems also has an inherent vulnerability as Robin Hanson has observed:

[The] intricate coordination that makes a society more productive also makes it more vulnerable to disruptions. For example, productivity in our society requires continued inputs from a large number of specialized systems, such as electricity, water, food, heat, transportation, communication, medicine, defense, training, and sewage. Failure of any one of these systems for an extended period can destroy the entire system.[229]

Mike Adams has put it thus: "[t]he more complex a society becomes, the more the loss of efficiency in just one small area of service or manufacturing ripples across the entire economy, magnifying its negative effect."[230] Thus, the long-term disruption of the supply of even one resource, such as rubber, would grind modern transportation systems to a halt. Any number of events may cause

---

[227]   Joseph Tainter, *The Collapse of Complex Societies* (Cambridge University Press, Cambridge, 1988).

[228]   As above, pp. 118-120.

[229]   Robin Hanson, "Catastrophe: Social Collapse, and Human Extinction," in N. Bostrom and M. M. Ćirković (eds.), *Global Catastrophic Risks* (Oxford University Press, Oxford, 2008), pp. 363-377, cited p. 366.

[230]   Mike Adams, "Is the Fabric of Industrialized Society Starting to Unravel? Highly Complex Civilizations are More Vulnerable to Collapse," Natural News.com, December 29, 2011 at http://www.naturalnews.com/034517_complex_societies_collapse_2012.html.

supply-line disruptions, but they may also occur by what Sidney Dekker calls the "drift to failure."[231] The "drift into failure" occurs when an organization, by a "slow incremental process," "gradually borrows more and more from the margins that once buffered it from assumed boundaries of failure," so that over time, under conditions of competition and scarcity, the very pursuit of the organization's mandate "creates the conditions for its eventual collapse." Complex systems often have a sensitivity to small influences (chaos), so that system instabilities may arise once some "critical state" is reached, making systems catastrophically unstable.[232]

Self-organized criticality applies to the Earth's biosphere as well.[233] Barnosky (et. al) have argued that local ecological systems have been known to shift abruptly and irreversibly across critical thresholds once "tipping points" are reached, and that global ecosystems also exhibit state shift changes when human influence causes the planet to reach critical transition points: "[c]ritical transitions lead to state shifts, which abruptly, override trends and produce unanticipated biotic effects."[234] Global scale forcing mechanisms operating today— including human population growth, habitat transformation, energy production and consumption and climate change—exceed both the rate and magnitude of the last global-scale state shift. That was the last glacial-interglacial transition, 14,300-11,000 years ago. It involved a rapid warm-cold-warm fluctuation, caused by Earth's orbital changes, that affected solar insolation, leading to the extinction of around half of the species of large mammals and several species of large birds and reptiles. Present global-scale shifts may have already been initiated, leading us to a new period of mass extinctions. *Homo sapiens* may be one more species that ultimately bites the dust.

---

231   Sidney Dekker, *Drift into Failure: From Hunting Broken Components to Understanding Complex Systems* (Ashgate, Surrey, 2011).

232   P. Bak, *How Nature Works: The Science of Self-Organised Criticality* (Oxford University Press, Oxford, 1996).

233   M. Schafer (et al.), "Early Warning Signals for Critical Transition", *Nature*, vol. 461, 2009, pp. 53-59.

234   A. D. Barnosky (et al.), "Approaching a State Shift in Earth's Biosphere," *Nature*, vol. 486, June 7, 2012, pp. 52-58, cited p. 52.

The Mechanisms of Collapse

More will be said below about the environmental crisis as a major mechanism of collapse. Systems collapse can arise from a number of other trigger events and there is a considerable literature covering a number of disciplines from theoretical physics, cosmology, geology and biology. Scenarios include natural events, however unlikely or distant in time, such as time itself "leaking away," collisions of galaxies (e.g. the Milky Way colliding with the Andromeda galaxy); solar collisions (e.g. with a white dwarf), hostile extra-terrestrial alien invasion, the reversal of the Earth's magnetic field leaving the planet vulnerable to cosmic radiation influx, and Hollywood's favorite, asteroid impacts.[235] Other doomsday scenarios are linked to runaway physics and scientific experiments, such as nanotechnology and the "grey goo" problem, and physics catastrophes such as the formation of a small black hole in the lab that swallows the Earth, the formation of negatively charged stable strangelets which convert ordinary matter into strange matter, and the initiation of a phase transition of the vacuum state, destroying the universe. Bioterrorism, cyberwar/cyberterrorism, runaway artificial intelligence (e.g. *Terminator* scenarios of the revolt of the thinking, killing machine), biotechnology and genetic engineering disasters, also present doomsday scenarios. The probability of the occurrence of many of these events is low or unknown (e.g. extra-terrestrial invasion).

Disaster could come from geophysical threats such as the eruption of a supervolcano, which could end the problem of global warming, but confront humanity with the new threat of global "volcanic winter," as temperatures drop, world agriculture production crashes and famine becomes the principal horseman of the apocalypse, the great new Grim Reaper, culler of the human race.

Optimists generally believe that asteroid/comet impacts with the Earth are not a major threat since no large asteroids or comets are on a collision path with the Earth for at least two centuries. Think again.

---

[235] Alok Jha, *The Doomsday Handbook: 50 Ways the World Could End* (Quercus, London, 2011).

There has been a revision of the number of *smaller* asteroids believed to be capable of impacting with the Earth; there are up to 10 times as many *medium*-sized asteroids less than 50 meters in diameter capable of striking the Earth. The Chelyabinsk meteor is estimated to have been less than 20 meters across when it exploded in the atmosphere on February 15, 2013.[236] It had the energy equivalent of 500 (±100) tons of TNT. This rock was about 12,000-13,000 tonnes when it entered the atmosphere from an asteroid belt between Mars and Jupiter in a region of the sky inaccessible to ground-based telescopes. It would only have been visible during the daytime but the sky is too bright to see such small objects.

Bill McGuire, Benfield Professor of Geophysical Hazards at University College London and Director of the University's Benfield Hazard Research Centre, in his book, *Surviving Armageddon*, has discussed another less known geophysical threat.[237] The Cumbre Vieja volcano is on the western Canary Island of La Palma. An eruption in 1949 led to large fractures in the volcano's flank. It is hypothesized by McGuire and others, that the entire flank could separate from the rest of the volcano and slide into the North Atlantic. Measurements by McGuire's research team from 1992-1997 found the landslide at La Palma to still be moving slowly, although the small recorded values are within the range of instrument error. The mass of rock is as large as the UK's Isle of Man and if and when it crashes into the North Atlantic, it will "trash half the planet" with "an enormously destructive mega-tsunami." Much of the modern civilized world is built on coastlines and is vulnerable to mega-tsunamis.

One of the physical scientific arguments advanced by those believing that a global catastrophe may occur is based on anticipated severe space weather events. Here is the problem: in 1859 the "Carrington Event" occurred which involved intense coronal mass ejections (CMEs) from the sun that produced auroras borealis visible

---

[236] P. G. Brown (et al.), "A 500-Kiloton Airburst Over Chelyabinsk and an Enhanced Hazard from Small Impactors," *Nature*, (2013); doi:10.1038/nature2741.

[237] B. McGuire, *Surviving Armageddon: Solutions for a Threatened Planet* (Oxford University Press, Oxford, 2005).

at the equator and caused telegraph lines, towers and stations across the world to catch on fire. The red illumination of aurora borealis was so bright that people in Cuba could read their paper in the early morning by its lights. The energetic particles also altered the chemistry of polar ice.[238] As we will see, another Carrington Event could happen at any time.

Matters will be made worse because NASA's THEMIS satellites discovered a large hole in the magnetosphere, the Earth's magnetic field, which normally defends against such solar blasts.[239] The hole is about four times the size of the Earth and 10 times larger than previously thought. In the past, physicists have observed breaches in the Earth's magnetosphere in response to solar magnetic fields pointing *south*. The present breach occurred with a solar magnetic field aligned *north*. Normally a north-pointing magnetic field impacting with the Earth's magnetosphere directly above the equator, where the Earth's magnetic field points north, would intensify the field preventing solar winds entering – but the opposite has occurred. Such events load the magnetosphere with plasma and when a coronal mass ejection takes place, power outages and other destructive events can occur on Earth. This could result in stronger geomagnetic storms than previously seen, as Jimmy Raeder of the University of New Hampshire has said:

> We're entering Solar Cycle 24. For some reason not fully understood CMEs (coronal mass ejections) in even-numbered solar cycles (like 24) tend to hit Earth with a leading edge that is magnetized north. Such a CME should open a breach and load the magnetosphere with plasma just before the storm gets underway. It's the perfect sequence for a really big event.[240]

---

[238] "Geomagnetic Mega-Storm," Spaceweather.com, September 2, 2009, at http://spaceweather.com/archive.php?view=1&day=02&month=09&year=2009.

[239] "Great Breach in Earth's Magnetic Field Discovered," December 16, 2008, at http://science.nasa.gov/science-news/science-at-nasa/2008/16dec_giantbreach.

[240] As above.

The sun is presently in a period of low activity, so low that some physicists such as Habibullo Abdussamotov, director of the Russian section of the International Space Station, believes that a mini-ice age could develop.[241] However, as will be argued below, this does not rule out the occurrence of a new Carrington Event, and as will be discussed, a coronal mass ejection on July 23, 2012 of near-Carrington Event proportions, narrowly missed the Earth. Lower solar activity only lowers the probability of such an event, but does not eliminate it.[242]

A report by the National Academy of Sciences, *Severe Space Weather Events: Understanding Societal and Economic Inputs* (December, 2008), says that if a Carrington Event occurred today it would cause US \$1-2 trillion in damage to our high-tech society and take four to ten years to completely repair, they rather optimistically predict.[243]

Ex-CIA analyst, Peter Pry has said that an EMP, either natural or via a terrorist and/or military attack, could kill 9 out of 10 Americans.[244] Disaster preparation expert Matthew Stein noted another alarming consequence of geomagnetic disturbances.[245] He observed that all of the world's almost 450 nuclear reactors are critically dependent upon a functioning electric grid to keep their reactor cores cool to avoid meltdowns. In the case of a "grid-down" scenario because of a repeat Carrington Event, only back-up generators would prevent meltdown

---

[241] H. Abdussamotov, "Bicentennial Decrease of the Total Solar Irradiance Leads to Unbalanced Thermal Budget of the Earth and Little Ice Age," *Applied Physics Research*, vol.4, no.1, 2012, pp. 178-184.

[242] P. Farquhar, "Sun Storm to Hit with 'Force of 100 m Bombs," News.com.au, August 25, 2010 at http://www.news.com.au/technology/science/sun-storm-to-hit-with-force-of-100-bombs/story-fn5fsgyc-1225909999465.

[243] National Research Council, National Academy of Sciences, *Severe Space Weather Events: Understanding Societal and Economic Impacts*, (National Academies Press, Washington DC, December 2008), p. 77.

[244] B. Hoffmann, "Ex-CIA Analyst: Attack on US Could Kill 9 Out of 10 Americans," May 12, 2015, at www.newsmax.com/Newsmax-Tv/Peter-Vincent-Pry-power-grid-attack-U-S-/2015/05/12/id/644144/.

[245] Matthew Stein, "Geomagnetic Storms, EMP and Nuclear Armageddon," *Nexus*, February – March, 2012, pp. 21-26, 80; "The Other Electrical Grid Failure Problem," at http://survivalblog.com/letter-re-the-other-electrical-grid-failure-problem/.

occurring. When these generators run out of fuel in a situation of widespread social chaos, or when the back-up generators breakdown, after a few days the water covering the spent fuel rods in the spent fuel ponds will boil away and a meltdown will occur. This, Stein says "will end the industrialized world as we know it, incurring almost incalculable suffering, death and environmental destruction on a scale not seen since the extinction of the dinosaurs some 65 million years ago." How likely is this?

In February 2011 a class x (meaning the strongest type of solar flare, with >10⁻⁴ watts/square meter) flash from a solar flare disrupted short-wave radio communications in South China.[246] In March 1989, a geomagnetic storm knocked out the power over the bulk of Quebec for nine hours. In January 1994 Canada's US $290 million Anik F2 telecommunications satellite was hit by a solar storm; it required six months and US $50-70 million to get the satellite working again. In 1998, a coronal mass ejection hit a communications satellite, causing it to crash in the middle of the United States. Another geomagnetic storm in October 2003 caused blackouts in Sweden and damaged the South African power grid. Storms of greater intensity will severely damage power transformers and the grid. Stein points out that the Fukushima Daiichi nuclear reactor disaster arose not from direct damage from the Tohoku earthquake but because the facility's back-up diesel generators were destroyed by the tidal wave.

On July 23 2012, the most powerful solar storm in 150 years narrowly missed the Earth, but did hit the STEREO-A space craft. One week earlier and it would have struck the Earth, turning civilization back to the 18th century.[247] The emissions of x-rays and extreme UV radiation can produce radio blackouts and errors in GPS navigation and electrons and protons can damage satellites, but the CME magnetized plasma, according to NASA "could cause widespread power blackouts, disabling everything that plugs into a wall socket...

---

[246]   "Is Class X Flash First Warning of 2012 Solar Storm?" News.com.au, February 8, 2011, at http://www.news.com.au/technology/science/solar-flare-jams-radio-satellite-signals/story-fn5fsgyc-1226007817482.

[247]   T. Phillips, "Near Miss: The Solar Superstorm of July 2012," July 23, 2014, at http://science.nasa.gov/science-news/science-at-nasa/2014/23jul_superstorm/.

Most people wouldn't even be able to flush their toilet because urban water supplies largely rely on electric pumps." The CME hit with the energy of a billion hydrogen bombs, but it would also create a southward-orientated magnetic field that could interact with the Earth's northward-orientated magnetic field (magnetic reconnection), rearranging the field and causing even more damage to electronics.

According to one research paper, the probability of another Carrington Event occurring in the next decade is a surprisingly high 12 percent.[248] Although humanity has the technical capability of preparing for such an event and largely mitigating its effects, the political will to do so, by spending money, is lacking.[249]

Another paper hypothesizes that our sun is capable of superflares. A study by researchers at the University of Warwick, using NASA's Kepler space telescope, was made of wave patterns of solar superflares emitted by the star KIC9655129, in the outer edges of the Milky Way galaxy. The flares seen on this star are similar to our own sun's solar flares, probably having the same basic physics, with the main difference being that KIC9655129's flares are more powerful, with the energy of 100 billion megaton bombs. Such a superflare occurring in our solar system would destroy the electronic society (question: what about neural electronics?), but the probability of this is thought to be low.[250] Other though believe that a superflare more powerful than the Carrington event may occur sometime in the next 100 years.[251]

John Kappenman, CEO of electromagnetic damage company Metatech, believes that the prevention of geomagnetic collapse can be done relatively cheaply by adding resistors to the ground connections

---

[248] P. Riley, "On the Probability of Occurrence of Extreme Space Weather Events," *Space Weather*, vol. 10, 2012; S02012; doi:10.1029/2011SW00734.

[249] A. Taggart, "Former CIA Director: We're Not doing Nearly Enough to Protect against the EMP Threat," June 7, 2015, at http://www.peakprosperity.com/podcast/92943/former-cia-director-were-not-doing-nearly-enough-protect-against-emp-threat-.

[250] C. Pugh (et al.), "A Multi-Period Oscillation in a Stellar Superflare," *Astrophysical Journal Letters*, vol. 813, 2015: doi:10.1088/2041-8205/813/1/L5.

[251] Y. Notsu (et al.), "Do *Kepler* Superflare Stars Really Include Slowly Rotating Sun-Like Stars? Results Using APO 3.5 m Telescope Spectroscopic Observations and *Gaia*-DR2 Data," *Astrophysics Journal*, May 1, 2019, 876: 58.

of transformers, as recommended by the US Electromagnetic Pulse Commission's report to US Congress.[252]

The White House in November 2015 recognized these problems, and took the first baby steps of dealing with the EMP threat, by undertaking to prepare a space weather action plan, with emergency management, education and improved prediction technologies.[253] On March 26, 2019 President Trump issued "Executive Order on Coordinating National Resilience to Electromagnetic Pulses" to assess the risks of such an attack to critical US infrastructure, beginning the cycle over again.[254] This is all a good start that should have been undertaken at least a decade ago. My bet is that a geomagnetic apocalypse *does not* occur in the next few years, and that humanity, because of sloth, will continue to fail to implement safeguards with the needed urgency, lulled into complacency and moving at a snail's pace – then, sometime in the near future, our phenomenal and undeserved luck runs out, and it's lights out, forever.[255]

It is also worth noting, relevant to our zombie theme, that there is considerable evidence of the negative effects of geomagnetic storms on human health, affecting sleep, depression levels, mood and thus indirectly, aggression. However, the threat from nuclear disasters remains the gravest health risk.

In May 2012, there was considerable concern about the threat to the world posed by Fukushima reactor No. 4, which could have released 85 times the cesium-137 spewed forth at Chernobyl. Mitshuhei Murata, former Japanese Ambassador to Switzerland said:

---

[252]   J. Kappenman, *Geomagnetic Storms and Their Impacts on the US Power Grid*, (Metatech Corporation, Meta-R-319, January, 2010), at, http://web.ornl.gov/sci/ees/etsd/pes/pubs/ferc_Meta-R-319.pdf.

[253]   Hannah Parry, "White House is Preparing for Catastrophic Solar Flares which Could Wipe Out Power Around the World for Months – Bringing an End to Modern Civilization as We Know It," November 4, 2015, at http://www.dailymail.co.uk/news/article-3302185/White-House-preparing-catastrophic-solar-flares-wipe-power-world-months-bringing-end-modern-civilization-know-it.html.

[254]   https://www.whitehouse.gov/presidential-actions/executive-order-coordinating-national-resilience-electromagnetic-pulses/.

[255]   https://www.dhs.gov/sites/default/files/publications/NIAC%20Catastrophic%20Power%20Outage%20Study_508%20FINAL.pdf.

"It is no exaggeration to say that the fate of Japan and the whole world depends on No. 4 reactor."[256] There are 10,893 spent fuel assemblies at the Fukushima Daiichi plant lying in pools that are vulnerable to destruction from future earthquakes. US Senator Ray Wyden (Democrats, Oregon) visited the Fukushima Daiichi nuclear plant on April 6, 2012 and issued a press release on April 16, expressing alarm at the catastrophic risk the plant posed to humanity and he urged immediate US government intervention.[257] He also sent a letter to Japan's Ambassador to the United States, requesting Japan to accept international assistance to address the crisis. Senator Wyden said that the problem was "worse than reported" with "spent fuel rods currently being stored in unsound structures immediately adjacent to the ocean" and the area was highly susceptible to earthquakes with only a small makeshift seawall of bags of rocks offering protection from a future tsunami. This problem, over six years later, still exists, with radiation at "unimaginable levels."[258] It is worth reviewing the Fukushima disaster as it reveals important lessons about human error, carelessness and corruption.

The worst-case scenario involving a fire at unit 4, igniting the irradiated fuel, could release what some regard as a doomsday dose of radiation that could destroy human civilization, although there is, as we will see, room for the irradiated to debate this issue.

At Chernobyl, after its nuclear disaster, the birds and animals—deer, wild boar, moose, lynx and wolves—have returned, all radioactive. There is controversy about the radiation effects on humans from the Chernobyl disaster. Thus, the report by the UN

---

[256] "An Urgent Request on UN Intervention to Stabilize the Fukushima Unit 4 Spend Nuclear Fuel," May 1 2012, at http://greenaction-japan.org/en/2012/05/press-release-coalition-sends-urgent-request-for-un-intervention-to-stabilize-the-fukushima-unit-4-spent-nuclear-fuel/.

[257] B. Jacobson, "The Worst is Yet to Come? Why Nuclear Experts are Calling Fukushima a Ticking Time Bomb," May 5 2012, at http://carolynbaker.net/2012/05/05/the-worst-is-yet-to-come-.

[258] "New Evidence of Nuclear Fuel Releases Found at Fukushima," February 18, 2018, at https://phys.org/news/2018-02-evidence-nuclear-fuel-fukushima.html; https://www.scientificamerican.com/article/crippled-fukushima-reactors-are-still-a-danger-5-years-after-the-accident1/; https://video.foxnews.com/v/5315777703001/#sp=show-clips.

Scientific Committee on the Effects of Atomic Radiation (2000),[259] found that 134 plant staff and emergency workers suffered acute radiation syndrome. The prevalence of birth defects and leukaemia was allegedly no higher than experienced before the accident with the exception of thyroid cancer in local children, the large cases due to authorities allowing contaminated milk to be used. By the year 2005, there were 6,000 cases of thyroid cancer in children, but thyroid cancer is treatable. Allegedly, only 15 children died by 2005.[260] Other sources see the Chernobyl disaster as having much greater effects, with loses of hundreds of thousands of lives and ill-health effects for generations.[261]

How much radiation was, and may still be released from the Fukushima site is unknown as plant workers were told to lie about radiation readings, being given lead boxes used as shields to block radiation and make readings appear lower than they were in reality. Radiation levels at Reactor 1 in the base water reached levels of 10,300 millisieverts per hour "the equivalent of receiving the maximum annual dose of radiation in just 20 seconds, or enough to become gravely ill in just a few minutes." Whatever the true Fukushima radiation levels, according to scientists from the National Oceanic and Atmospheric Administration's (NOAA) Pacific Marine Environmental Laboratory, computer models simulating ocean currents in the Pacific, indicate that radioactive ocean water will be breaking on the beaches of the US West Coast within five years – but evidence presented at the October 2013, North Pacific Marine Science Organization (PICES) annual meeting indicated that a radioactive plume was detected reaching the shores of Canada and the US by July 2013 both in ocean surface waters and the atmosphere. It took until

---

[259] UN Scientific Committee on the Effects of Atomic Radiation, "The Chernobyl Accident," at http://www.unscear.org/unscear/en/chernobyl.html.

[260] Yuri M Shcherbak, "Ten Years of the Chernobyl Era," *Scientific American*, April, 1996, pp. 44-49.

[261] John Vidal, "Nuclear's Green Cheerleaders Forgot Chernobyl at Our Peril," April 2, 2011, at http://www.theguardian.com/commentisfree/2011/apr/01/fukushima-chernobyl-risks-radiation. Alexey Yablokov (et al.), *Chernobyl: Consequences of the Catastrophe for People and the Environment* (Annals of the New York Academy of Sciences, New York, 2009), volume 1181.

April 2016 for the Japanese to attempt to build a wall of ice around the reactors, in an attempt to contain the massive outpouring of radioactive water into the Pacific Ocean, using underground pipes to freeze the ground. Time will tell if this strategy actually works.[262]

An article in *The Australian* reported that nuclear workers "had received massive undocumented exposures to radiation" and "the danger money supposed to flow to employees from working at Fukushima Daiichi was being creamed off by unscrupulous companies."[263] *The Australian* quoted a nuclear engineer at the plant who said: "What remained intact after the disaster is completely fragile and when the next one comes it's going to collapse," meaning that the Fukushima nuclear plant is vulnerable to a new quake or tsunami. The cooling system is makeshift and the nuclear engineer believes that the next big earthquake will fracture it. He also had doubts about back-up power gear keeping the plant's six reactors cool, because only temporary gear "not proper equipment" is being used. The nuclear engineer also said that earthquake protection measures had not been made. A contractor had identified 20,000 points to be fixed for anti-seismic protection after the 2007 Niigata earthquake; none had been done due to shortages of money. Further, the engineer believes that the reactors were damaged in the 2011 earthquake.

The Australian article mentions the risk of spent fuel in a tank alongside Reactor No. 4 "which must be kept submerged at all times to avoid a catastrophic chain reaction that could render Tokyo uninhabitable." Workers paid to deal with this fuel have had their real wages slashed to as low as 8,000 yen (about US $80) a day, when some workers earned as high as US $5,000 a day for this work in the days before the quake. It is not a proven way to maintain worker morale. Along with this is corruption; after the disaster Japan's mafia (Yakuza) supplied workers who owed them money to work at the plant. These workers violated workplace safety regulations, such as not wearing

---

[262]   https://www.peoplesworld.org/article/eight-years-after-fukushima-nuclear-meltdown-workers-still-facing-radiation-risk/.

[263]   Rich Wallace, "Fukushima Plant 'Set to Collapse' from Another Quake or Tsunami," *The Weekend Australian*, March 9-10, 2013, p. 12.

dosimeters or shielding them inside clothing to minimize exposure recordings. After Yakuza workers left the plant, at least in 2013, these practices continued. *The Australian* article says: "One worker who was in charge of handing out dosimeters to staff in the bunker during the first few months after the disaster said many simply refused to take the devices, saying they would never be able to complete their work if their true readings were recorded."

Tokyo Electric Power Company had initially said that the radiation emitted by the leaking water was about 100 millisieverts an hour, but the equipment used could only record emissions at a maximum rate of up to 100 millisieverts an hour. When more sensitive equipment was used, the correct reading of 1,800 millisieverts an hour, readings 18 times higher than the previous readings, was recorded.[264]

Japanese informants reported that their government had experts on a speaking tour, one of whom told people that radiation wouldn't affect happy people and people smiling. Japanese TV news said that rising radiation levels were due to Chinese atmospheric pollution blowing to Japan!

Singapore-based news outlet AsiaOne reported in April 2013 that 120 tons of radioactive contaminated water, containing about 710 billion becquerels of radioactive materials, had leaked from an underground storage facility at the No. 1 power plant site. Japan's Ministry of Health, Labor and Welfare (MHLW) said in April 2013 that levels of cesium-137 (Cs-137) and cesium-134 (Cs-134), found in tangerines and rice crackers produced in the Shizuoka prefecture, about 225 miles from Fukushima, tested high for both Cs-137 and Cs-134, rice crackers = 3.7 becquerels per kilogram of Cs-137 and tangerines = 1.46 becquerels per kilogram of Cs-134 and 3.14 becquerels per kilogram of Cs-137. The average adult eating such foods at those radiation levels would exceed the safe maximum radiation level of 50 millisieverts of radiation per year in only a few weeks.

---

[264] BBC News Asia, "Fukushima Radiation Level '18 Times Higher' than Thought," September 1, 2013 at http://www.bbc.co.uk/news/world-asia-23918882.

In August 2013 *The Australian* reported that the Japanese Nuclear Regulation Authority was concerned about an "emergency" at Fukushima with the release of tritium-laced groundwater into the sea besides the plant: TEPCO admitted that 20-40 trillion becquerels of radioactive tritium has leaked into the sea since the nuclear disaster.[265] Another report states that 300 tonnes of radioactive water a day has entered the sea since March 2011, also admitted in August 2013 by TEPCO. As well, radioactive ground-water beneath the reactors had breached an underground barrier and was rising towards the surface. High levels of strontium 90 had been detected in the groundwater.[266] The buildings of Reactors No. 1 and 4 receives 400 tonnes of groundwater each day.[267]

Michio Aoyama, senior researcher of the geochemical research department of the Meteorological Research Institute, found 60 billion becquerels of cesium-137 and strontium-90 discharged into the Pacific Ocean every day from a ditch at the northern end of the reactor. Unsurprisingly, there have been rising radiation levels in Japan's seas and prefectures surrounding Fukushima. On January 10, 2014, the Japanese Fisheries Research Agency caught a fish contaminated with 12,400 becquerels per kilogram of radioactive cesium, 124 times higher than the safety standard. Fish catches around Fukushima are mostly destroyed because of dangerous radiation levels.

The Fukushima reactors have melted through the steel vessels into the ground and are continuing fission reactions. To prevent a nuclear explosion, it is necessary to cool this melted core; hence huge quantities of water must be pumped over the core, resulting in radionuclides dissolving in the water and other insoluble radioactive material such as plutonium being held in colloidal suspension. The radioactive water has not been controlled and

---

[265]   Rick Wallace, "Tokyo to Act on Radioactive Leaks," *The Australian*, August 9, 2013, p. 10.

[266]   M. Willacy, "Fukushima Plant Spilling Contaminated Water into Sea 'for Years,'" August 12, 2013, at http://www.abc.net.au/news/2013-08-12/fukushima-plant-workers-raise-safety-concerns/4879960.

[267]   Rick Wallace, "Radioactive Leak at Fukushima," *The Australian*, August 7, 2013, p. 10.

pours into the Pacific Ocean. This will continue forever unless the radioactive material can be removed, but radiation levels are too high to do this. The present attempt to freeze the ground can only be a short-term solution.

David Webb, Chief Executive Officer at Origin Investments AB, is quoted at Voice of Russia.com as saying that the cooling pool of unit 4 at Fukushima is crucial as it contains 400,000 kilograms of hot plutonium: "There is a great danger of a thermo-nuclear reaction if these rods become exposed to the air and the cooling pool itself is just barely containing the temperature levels of the core as it is. . . [O]ne microgram of plutonium could theoretically kill a person. There are a billion micrograms in a kilogram and there are 400,000 hot kilograms in this pool. So, if these rods combust, if the set of rods begins a thermonuclear reaction it will vaporize the water in the pool and the entire pool can become an uncontrolled nuclear reaction open to the air. These particles will be spread through the northern hemisphere. This is perhaps the greatest threat humanity has ever faced."[268] This is known as the "open-air super reactor spectacular." One fuel rod has the potential to kill 2.89 billion people and the number of fuel roads at Fukushima, excluding those in the pressure vessel is 11,421. Some fear a "series of cascading failures with an apocalyptic outcome."[269]

The nuclear risk of Fukushima is dwarfed by the spent fuel rod problem in the United States, the largest store of radioactivity on Earth.[270] The US has 65,000 tonnes of spent fuel of which 75 percent is stored in pools and there are 30 million rods in spent fuel pools. In the pools, the cesium-137 is over 20 times more than that released

---

[268]   E. Sukhoi, "Fukushima Radioactive Leak is "the Greatest Threat Humanity Ever Faced," – Expert," Voice of Russia, September 2, 2013, at http://sputniknews.com/voiceofrussia/2013_09_02/Fukushima-radioactive-leak-is-the-greatest-threat-humanity-ever-faced-expert-3792/.

[269]   "Fukushima Apocalypse: Years of 'Duct Tape Fixes' Could Result in 'Millions of Deaths,'" August 17, 2013, at http://rt.com/news/fukushima-apocalypse-fuel-removal-598.

[270]   T. E. Collins and G. Hubbard, *Technical Study of Spent Fuel Pool Accident Risk at Decommissioning Nuclear Power Plants*, (NUREG-1738, U.S. Nuclear Regulatory Commission, February 2011), pp. x and xi.

from all previous atomic explosions and 15-30 times more than released at the Chernobyl disaster.[271] All of this radioactive material is vulnerable to a 9/11 terrorist attack.[272] The US has 23 reactors the same as the General Electric ones in Fukushima No.1 and also has atomic plants built on fault lines (e.g. Diablo Canyon Nuclear Power Plant's units 1 and 2 near Santa Barbara and the San Onofre Nuclear Generating station, outside of San Clemente, shut down in 2012, but continues in 2018 to leak radioactive material).[273] A quarter of the US's ageing reactors have leaked radioactive tritium-polluted water.[274] There have been nuclear reactor partial meltdowns (Santa Susana Field Laboratory, July 13, 1959) that contaminated surrounding areas, with radiation 300 times the acceptable levels, complete with a cover-up which could have taught the Japanese a thing or two.

The US is also vulnerable to geomagnetic disturbances such as solar flares and EMP events caused by an enemy nuclear attack. Nuclear power plants are not likely, in the US at least, to immediately go "boom," as modern nuclear reactors are designed to shut down if safety limits are reached or exceeded, such as if the electric power shuts down. The problem is in the longer term when diesel runs out, supplying fuel to back-up generators. If the water boils off of the cooling pools and the rods catch fire, massive quantities of radiation would be released, more than in a meltdown. The US Nuclear Regulatory Commission has said that US nuclear power plants affected by a blackout would be able to function without electricity for about eight hours and would be able to keep the reactor and

---

[271] Robert Alvarez, *Spent Nuclear Fuel Pools in the US: Reducing the Deadly Risks of Storage,* (Institute for Policy Studies, Washington DC, 2011).

[272] E. S. Lyman, "Impacts of a Terrorist Attack at Indian Point Nuclear Power Plant," Union of Concerned Scientists, September 2004, at http://www.ucsusa.org/nuclear_power/ making-nuclear-power-safer/keeping-nuclear-plants-secure/impacts-of-a-terrorist-attack. html#.VYfCQImqqko.

[273] C. Wedler, "Defunct Nuclear Power Plant on California Coast is a 'Fukushima Waiting to Happen'" August 17, 2018 at https://www.zerohedge.com/news/2018-08-17/defunct-nuclear-power-plant-california-coast-fukushima-waiting-happen.

[274] Matthew Stein, "Four Hundred Chernobyls: Solar Flares, Electromagnetic Pulses and Nuclear Armageddon," March 24, 2012, at http://truth-out.org/news/item/7301-400-chernobyls-.

spent-fuel pool cool for 72 hours. However, according to an article in the ibtimes.com:

> Nuclear plants depend on standby batteries and backup diesel generators. Most standby power systems would continue to function after a severe solar storm, but supplying the standby power systems with adequate fuel, when the main power grids are offline for years, could become a very critical problem…
>
> If the spent fuel rod pools at the country's 104 nuclear power plants lose their connection to the power grid, the current regulations aren't sufficient to guarantee those pools won't boil over – exposing the hot, zirconium-clad rods and sparking fires that would release deadly radiation…
>
> A report by the Oak Ridge National Laboratory said that over the standard 40-year license term of nuclear power plants, solar flare activity enables a 33 percent chance of a long-term power loss, a risk that significantly outweighs that of major earthquakes and tsunamis.[275]

A solar flare is only one dramatic way for the US power grid to collapse. A study by the Federal Energy Regulatory Commission has concluded that a coordinated terrorist attack on three separate electric systems could collapse the entire US power network.[276] "The U.S. could suffer a coast-to-coast blackout if saboteurs knock out just nine of the country's 55,000 electric-transmission substations on a scorching summer day." The US power grid has been compared to a big pile of sand, stable until a certain "height" is reached.[277] Iranian

[275] S. N. Padala, "Severe Solar Storms Could Disrupt Earth this Decade: NOAA," August 8, 2011, at http://www.ibtimes.com/severe-solar-storms-could-disrupt-earth-decade-noaa-826351.

[276] Rebecca Smith, "U.S. Risks National Blackout from Small-Scale Attack," March 12, 2014, at http://www.wsj.com/articles/SB10001424052702304020104579433670284061220.

[277] M. Koren, "How the U.S. Power Grid is Like a Big Pile of Sand," April 8, 2014, at http://www.nationaljournal.com/tech/how-the-u-s-power-grid-is-like-a-big-pile-of-sand-20140408.

cyberattacks have already breached cybersecurity at dozens of US power plants, and in late January 2016, hackers caused a partial shutdown of the grid in Israel.

And then there is nuclear war. There is continuing debate about the effects of limited and all-out global nuclear war. The really bad news from one study is that nuclear war will "end civilization" with famine, perhaps similar to the movie *The Road* (2009). The study by International Physicians for the Prevention of Nuclear War and Physicians for Social Responsibility, predicted that a limited nuclear war between India and Pakistan (itself hardly a remote probability[278]) could kill up to two billion people through nuclear winter, with black carbon aerosol particles reducing food production across the world.[279] An all-out nuclear exchange between the US and Russia, or even a threesome with China, could possibly lead to the extinction of the human race. "Let us eat and drink, for tomorrow we shall die": Isaiah 22:13.

Nothing to Sneeze at: Plagues, Pandemics and Social Breakdown

In the 14th century, the Black Death (the bubonic plague) killed between one third and two thirds of Europe's population. The Spanish flu, between September and November 1918, killed over 20 million people, almost twice as many as died in World War I. This flu affected about one third of all people on the planet, and as scientific philosopher Quentin Smith has noted, if the infection/death ratio of the Spanish flu (actually from China) was higher (e.g. the Ebola virus kills around 90 percent of those affected, the bubonic plague,

---

[278] "Nuclear Weapons Risk Greater than in Cold War, Says Ex-Pentagon Chief," January 8, 2016, at http://www.theguardian.com/world/2016/jan/07/nuclear-weapons-risk-greater-than-in-cold-war-says-ex-pentagon-chief.

[279] Ira Helfand, *Nuclear Famine: Two Billion People at Risk?* 2nd edition, (International Physicians for the Prevention of Nuclear War and Physicians for Social Responsibility, November, 2013) at, http://www.psr.org/assets/pdfs/two-billion-at-risk.pdf.

50 percent) "the human race would have become extinct in late 1918 or 1919."[280] This, however, is probably incorrect, as it presupposes an unrealistic infection/death ratio of 100 percent. Nevertheless, human death rates would have been high enough to collapse civilization.

There is some evidence that new variants of avian influenza have, and are incorporating genetic material from other avian influenza strains, so that the viruses may be evolving to become better adapted to infecting humans with a potential pandemic. Ian MacKay, a virologist at the University of Queensland, has said:

Each new strain could be one that is better genetically equipped to transmit from person to person. Without contemporary sequence analysis, such a strain could emerge from among the 'noise' of human infection by less efficient strains, to begin spreading rapidly and with pandemic potential.[281]

A pandemic flu may not naturally arise from viruses with an infection/death ratio approaching or exceeding that of Ebola's, but a genetically engineered viral bioterrorist weapon perhaps could. In December 2011, there were concerns about the journals *Science* and *Nature* publishing details of a genetically altered H5 N1 bird flu virus that was likely to be highly contagious among humans. The US National Science Advisory Board for Biosecurity was concerned that terrorists could replicate the experiments and unleash the virus, leading to a pandemic killer flu.[282]

A pandemic with a high mortality globally would be capable of producing civilizational collapse.[283] Some indications that a high

---

[280] Quentin Smith, "Critical Note of John Leslie, *The End of the World*," *Canadian Journal of Philosophy*, vol. 28, no. 3, 1998, pp. 413-434.

[281] "Pandemic Potential Seen in Gene Changes of Bird Flu," at http://www.bloomberg.com/news/articles/2014-02-13/pandemic-potential-seen-in-gene-changes-of-bird-flu; E. Tsang, "Doctor Warn of Pandemic Potential of the New H10 N8 Bird Flu Virus," February 5, 2014, at http://www.scmp.com/news/china/article/1421212/china-scientists-reveal-second-case-h10n8-raising-alarm-about-bird-flus.

[282] R. A. Langlois (et al.), "MicroRNA-Based Strategy to Mitigate the Risk of Gain-of-Function Influenza Studies," *Nature Biotechnology*, (August 11, 2013); doi: 10.1038/nbt.2666.

[283] D. MacKenzie "Why the Demise of Civilisation May be Inevitable," *New Scientist*,

mortality pandemic could do this are the loss of personnel in key industries and the death of technicians. A severe pandemic could hypothetically threaten the nuclear industry. The death of key service personnel in the transport, fuel and energy industries could have a knock-on effect leading to some of the nightmare scenarios discussed in the previous section. However, even if the nuclear industry is protected, shops and supermarkets will run out of food due to "just-in time" delivery methods, which do not involve having stockpiles of goods beyond a few days' use on hand. If coal-fired power plants cannot get supplies of coal because of chaos in the transport sector, there could be a destructive ripple effect throughout society causing breakdown. With a breakdown in sewage systems, diseases would spread. The crippling of the financial system will make it difficult to re-establish social order and there could be a downward spiral into chaos, what can be called "the great spiral down."

Ecological Collapse and Looming Resource Shortages

So far, we have considered collapse/disorder scenarios that may or may not occur. However, there are other threats that are occurring right now. For example, environmental degradation and climate change may also drive social and civilizational collapse.[284] Professor John Beddington, chief science advisor to the UK government said in March 2009 that the world was facing a "perfect storm" of "food shortages, water scarcity, and costly oil by 2030. These developments, plus accelerating climate change and mass migration across national borders could lead to major upheavals."[285] Jonathon Porritt, former

---

April 2, 2008, at http://www.newscientist.com/article/mg19826501.500-why-the-demise-of-civilisation-may-be-inevitable.html.

[284] H. Weiss and R. S. Bradley, "What Drives Societal Collapse?" *Science*, vol. 291, 2001, pp. 609-610.

[285] J. Beddington, Speech to the GovNet Sustainable Development UK Conference, March 19, 2009, at http://www.gren.org.uk/resources/Beddington'sSpeechatSDUK09.pdf

chair of the UK Sustainable Development Commission, agreed with Beddington, but put the time of the crisis closer to 2020 than 2030, being a "perfect storm" of environmental and economic collapse.[286] Lester Brown of the Earth Policy Institute says in his preface to his book *World on the Edge*,[287] that he does not know how much time civilization has left on a business-as-usual scenario but "the time is more likely measured in years than in decades. We are now so close to the edge that it could come at any time."

Our civilization may already be approaching its demise, as the late theoretical physicist Professor Stephen Hawking has said: "We are entering an increasingly dangerous period in our history. Our population and our use of the finite resources of the planet earth are growing exponentially along with our technological ability to change the environment for good or ill ... It will be difficult enough to avoid disaster in the next 100 years, let alone the next thousand or million."[288]

In the first section of this chapter some of our interconnected environmental problems were mentioned including the depletion and/or degradation or water, soil and food resources. Many other such problems can be mentioned. For example, the sustainability of world food production is threatened not only by global climate change (discussed below), but also by more, seemingly humble problems such as "peak phosphorus."[289] Phosphate supplies are becoming increasingly scarce. Phosphorus is a limiting nutrient in agricultural plant growth; it can be recycled (i.e. returned to the soil through the use of sewage sludge composted), but in modern agriculture it is wasted and becomes too dissipated to recycle. Patrick

---

[286] J. Porritt, "Perfect Storm of Environmental and Economic Collapse Closer than You Think," *The Guardian*, March 23 2009, https://www.theguardian.com/environment/2009/mar/23/jonathon-porritt-recession-climate-crisis.

[287] L. Brown, *World on the Edge: How to Prevent Environmental and Economic Collapse*, (Earth Policy Institute/W. W. Norton, New York, 2011).

[288] Stephen Hawking, "Stephen Hawking: Asking Big Questions about the Universe," TED Talk Series, at http://www.ted.com/talks/stephen_hawking_asks_big_questions_about_the_universe?language=en.

[289] D. Cordell (et. al.), "The Story of Phosphorus: Global Food Security and Food for Thought," *Global Environmental Change*, vol. 9, 2009, pp. 292-305.

Déry applied the linearization depletion analysis devised by M. King Hubbert (applied in Hubbert's case to oil[290]), to phosphorous. It was concluded that the peak of US phosphorous occurred in 1988, and for the world in 1989.[291]

Financial analyst Jeremy Grantham has said about the coming shortage of phosphorous (phosphate) and potassium (potash):

These two elements cannot be made, cannot be substituted, are necessary to grow all life forms, and are mined and depleted. It's a scary set of statements. Former Soviet states and Canada have more than 70 percent of the potash. Morocco has 85 percent of all high-grade phosphates. It is the most important quasi-monopoly in economic history. What happens when these fertilizers run out is a question I can't get satisfactorily answered and, believe me, I have tried. There seems to be only one conclusion: their use must be drastically reduced in the next 20-40 years or we will begin to starve.[292]

Peak fertiliser, along with other interacting and compounding problems such as water shortages, land degradation (peak soil), climate change and peak fuel is producing a world food crisis Grantham argues, and this food crisis is unlikely to disappear until global population peaks and considerably declines.[293] Already grain productivity has fallen each decade since 1970 from 3.5 to 1.5 percent. Genetic engineering could result in more efficient genes being inserted in plants such as rice and wheat in 20-30 years' time, which could increase outputs by up to 50 percent. However, to feed 9+ billion people by 2050 will require an increase in food production by

---

[290] M. King Hubbert, "Degree of Advancement of Petroleum Exploration in United States," *AAPG Bulletin*, Nov. 1967, vol. 51, no. 11, pp. 2207-2227.

[291] Patrick Dery and Bart Anderson, "Peak Phosphorus," *Energy Bulletin*, August 13, 2007, at http://www.energybulletin.net/node/33164.

[292] Jeremy Grantham, "Be Persuasive. Be Brave. Be Arrested (If Necessary)," *Nature*, vol. 491, 2012, p. 303.

[293] Jeremy Grantham, "Welcome to Dystopia! Entering a Long-Term and Politically Dangerous Food Crisis," *GMO Quarterly Letter*, July 2012, at http://f2cfnd.org/wp-content/uploads/2012/09/GMOQ2Letter.pdf

60-100 percent of present day levels. Grantham concludes: "If food pressures recur *and are reinforced by fuel price increases*, the risks of social collapse and global instability increase to a point where they probably become the major source of international confrontations."[294] Further: "[i]n the longer term...energy costs and absolute shortage in the case of oil form a serious problem second only to food shortages and will result in prices so high they will impact global growth and even the viability of modern, rather fragile, economies."[295] There will be "soaring commodity prices and impending shortages" because humanity is simply running out of raw materials.

In conclusion, Grantham believes, as do many environmentalists, that the world human population is now unsustainable and that the Earth can only sustainably support 1.5 billion people, not 7 + or 9 + billion – hence most people are, in the future, going to starve to death.

There are looming shortages of many metal stocks. Gordon (et. al.) concluded that "virgin stocks of several metals appear inadequate to sustain the modern 'developed world' quality of life for all Earth's peoples under contemporary technology."[296] Global supplies of platinum are diminishing and there is no synthetic alternative for this chemical element.[297] China produces 97 percent of the world's rare earth metal such as indium (used in making LCDs for flat-screen TVs) and gallium (used in indium gallium arsenide semiconductors), and these and other rare earths are used in a wide-range of high tech devices, from giant electromagnets in wind turbines to satellite components. Shortages of these "alternative energy minerals" may trigger a trade war or even a shooting war, if military hardware still works.[298]

---

[294]   As above, p. 3.

[295]   As above, p. 4.

[296]   R. B. Gordon (et al.), "Metal Stocks and Sustainability," *Proceedings of the National Academy of Sciences*, vol. 103, 2006, pp .1209-1214.

[297]   D. Cohen, "Earth's Natural Wealth: An Audit," May 23 2007, at http://www. sciencearchive.org.au/nova/newscientist/027ns_005.htm.

[298]   "Shortages of Alternative Energy Minerals May Trigger Trade Wars," November 1 2010, at   http://www.tgdaily.com/sustainability-features/52283-shortage-of-alternative-energy-

Alice Friedemann has observed that "computers are the top card in the house-of-cards complex civilization we built with coal and oil, and computers will be the first to go when supply chains fail."[299] Further:

> [a]s global shipping, factories, and countries have a hard time keeping the lights on, computers will stop being made as supply chains breakdown. If even one of the dozens of types of single-sourced equipment or pure chemical supplies goes out of business, the assembly line stops.[300]

Human knowledge is increasingly being preserved using computer technology, with libraries often getting only electronic versions of scientific journals, and e-books. Computers are too vulnerable for the preservation of knowledge as they,

> are the top cards in the civilization house of cards. Knock out any below and it all crumbles. Computers have too many complex, energy intensive inputs and dependencies.[301]

Some human knowledge could be preserved on archival paper, which at ideal temperatures can last up to 500 years and words can be etched into metallic substances to preserve knowledge for a coming Dark Age, but since the status quo is "comfortably numb," convinced that our present society is invulnerable, little will be done to save human knowledge. When the spiral down to chaos happens, much of the knowledge, which we now take for granted, will be lost. Welcome to the new Dark Age of barbarism.

---

minerals-will-trigger-trade-wars.

[299] Alice Friedemann, "Peak Oil and the Preservation of Knowledge," *Energy Bulletin*, January 7, 2006 at http://www2.energybulletin.net/node/18978.

[300] As above.

[301] Friedemann, as above; Thomas E. Hecker, "The Twilight of Digitization is Now," *Journal of Scholarly Publishing*, vol. 35, no. 1, October, 2003, pp. 52-65.

Peak Energy

The American Left, especially the Progressive movement, is the most delusional, ineffective, and compromised political worm ball I have experienced, past and present. I view the entire American political and economic system as broken and corrupt, subservient to corporate/financial interests and an economic paradigm (based on fiat currency, fractional reserve banking, and debt-based expansion) which demands infinite growth. That economic pyramid scheme—that mandate for infinite growth—is the beast which has driven us headlong into the unyielding steel wall of Peak Oil and the edge of the cliff lying just beyond.[302]

Jeremy Leggett, a former faculty member of the Royal School of Mines, London, said in his 2005 book *The Empty Tank: Oil, Gas, Hot Air, and the Coming Global Financial Catastrophe*,[303] that he believed that a change to a renewable energy infrastructure was possible, given the political will, but "the shortfall between current expectation of oil supply and actual availability will be such that neither gas, nor renewables, nor liquids from gas and coal, nor nuclear, nor any combinations thereof, will be able to plug the gap in time to head off the economic trauma resulting from the oil tipping point."[304] Consequently, economic collapse looms:

The price of houses will collapse. Stock markets will crash. Within a short period, human wealth—little more than a pile of paper at the best of times, even with confidence about the future high among traders—will shrivel. The inescapable consequences of the crisis will then roll out in slow motion. Companies will go bankrupt by the hundreds and then thousands. Workers will

---

[302] Michael C. Ruppert, *Confronting Collapse: The Crisis of Energy and Money in a Post Peak Oil World*, (Chelsea Green Publishing, White River Junction, Vermont, 2009), p. 13.

[303] Jeremy Leggett, *The Empty Tank: Oil, Gas, Hot Air, and the Coming Global Financial Catastrophe*, (Random House, New York, 2005).

[304] As above, pp. 141-142.

fall into unemployment by the hundreds of thousands and then millions. Once affluent cities with street cafes will have queues at soup kitchens and armies of beggars on the streets. The crime rate will soar. The Earth has always been a dangerous place, but now it will become a tinderbox.[305]

This position can be contrasted with that of Matt Ridley in *The Rational Optimist*,[306] who dismisses such fears and expresses (with little evidence and argument) a common optimistic view about humanity's energy future: "Oil, coal and gas are finite. But between them they will last decades, perhaps centuries, and people will find alternatives long before they run out."[307] Such claims – that technology will save humanity just in time, and that substitutes for depleting resources will *always* be found—are not rationally justified claims—and are undermined by the unsolved problem of induction.[308] To explain: technology may have solved our problems in the *past,* but how can that supply a non-circular justification for believing that it will do so in the *future*? Substitutes have been found for many depleted resources *so far,* but that is no basis for believing that substitutes will *always* be found: our "luck" may run out. Further, it takes at least 30 years to change an energy infrastructure; society cannot be rebuilt overnight, especially our trucking infrastructure.[309]

The issue of peak oil has been debated for almost 20 years and has generated its own technical books, articles and websites.[310] The argument for peak oil has been summarized as follows:

---

[305] As above, p. 191.

[306] Matt Ridley, *The Rational Optimist: How Prosperity Evolves*, (Fourth Estate, London, 2010).

[307] As above, p. 238.

[308] On the unsolved problem of induction see: "The Problem of Induction," at http://www.princeton.edu/~grosen/puc/phi203/induction.html.

[309] Alice Friedemann, *When the Trucks Stop Running: Energy and the Future of Transport*, (Springer, New York, 2016).

[310] J. Murray and D. King, "Oil's Tipping Point has Passed," *Nature*, vol. 481, 2012, pp. 433-435; Ugo Bardi, *Extracted: How the Quest for Mineral Wealth is Plundering the Planet*, (Chelsea Green Publishing, White River Junction, 2014).

- "The peak of oil discoveries was reached in the 1960's.
- This peak in discoveries has to be followed by a peak in production, since we can only produce what has been found before.
- The production peak of individual fields is a historical fact [and] almost all large oil fields have already passed their production maximum and are in decline.
- The aggregation of the production profiles of individual fields (with their individual peaks) sums up to a production peak of individual oil regions. Historically, peak production was reached in Austria in 1955, in Germany in 1968, and in the USA in 1971, and in Indonesia in 1977. Recent regions joining the club of countries with declining production rates are Gabon (1997), UK (1999), Australia (2000), Oman (2000) and Norway (2001).
- The aggregate decline of mature regions is getting steeper with every "new member of the club." In order to keep over-all production just flat, ever fewer regions have to increase their production.
- This pattern [has been observed for] more than thirty years."[311]

Owen (et al.), have said that they support "the contention held by many independent institutions that conventional oil production may soon go into decline... and it is likely that the era of plentiful, low cost petroleum is coming to an end."[312] Further: "[r]eserves that provide liquid fuels today will only have the capacity to service just over half of BAU (business as usual) demand by 2023."[313]

Although the International Energy Agency (IEA) sees the peak of world oil production as some time off, Aleklett (et al.) reanalysed IEA data and concluded that peak oil occurred in 2008.[314] To repeat: this

---

[311] W. Zittel and J. Schindler, "Future World Oil Supply," L-B System tecnik, January 2003, at http://www.peakoil.net/files/International-Summer-School_Salzburg_2002.pdf, quoted from R. Heinberg, *Powerdown*, cited above.

[312] N. Owen (et. al.), "The Status of Conventional World Oil Reserves - Hype or Cause for Concern?" *Energy Policy*, vol. 38, 2010, pp. 4743-4749, cited p. 4743.

[313] As above, p. 4749.

[314] K. Aleklett (et. al.), "The Peak of the Oil Age: Analysing the World Oil Production

follows from IEA's own data. Indeed, the International Energy Agency in its *World Energy Outlook* (WEO) (2010), said that by 2035 global oil production "reaches 96 mb/d, the balance of 3 mb/d coming from processing gains." Crude oil output "reaches an undulating plateau of around 68-69 mb/d by 2020, but never regains its all-time peak of 70 mb/d reached in 2006, while production of natural gas liquids (NGLs) and unconventional oil grows strongly."[315]

Unconventional oil has been said to be generating what Alan Kohler enthusiastically describes as a "new global oil rush" and to have led to the "death of peak oil."[316] Matt Ridley has proclaimed that when the shale revolution goes "global," "oil and gas in tight rock formations will give the world ample supplies of hydrocarbons for decades, if not centuries." Ever the "rational optimist."[317] However, some establishment sources are not as optimistic. Brian Walsh in his April 9, 2012, *Time* magazine article "The Truth about Oil,"[318] says that new technological breakthroughs are increasing global supplies but "the era of cheap oil may be gone forever." Unconventional oil includes pre-salt and deep-water (50-100 billion barrels), oil shale (800 billion barrels) and oil sands (169 billion barrels). However, these sources "are often dirtier, with higher risks of accidents. The decline of major conventional oil fields and the rise in demand mean the spare production capacity that once cushioned prices could be gone, ushering in an era of volatile market swings. And burning all this leftover oil could lock the world into dangerous climate change."

Energy researcher Jean Laherrére believes that the deep-water oil reserve figures are too optimistic and that most discoveries will

---

Reference Scenario in World Energy Outlook 2008," *Energy Policy*, vol. 38, no. 3, 2010, pp. 1398-1414.

[315] International Energy Agency, "Executive Summary," *World Energy Outlook 2010*, (OECD/IEA, Paris, 2010), p. 6.

[316] Alan Kohler, "The Death of Peak Oil," March 28, 2012, at http://www.businessspectator. com.au/article/2012/2/29/commodities/death-peak-oil.

[317] Matt Ridley, "Fossil Fuels are Here to Stay," *The Australian*, March 24, 2015, p. 11.

[318] Brian Walsh, "The Truth about Oil," *Time*, April 9, 2012; A. B. Lovins, "A Farewell to Fossil Fuels," *Foreign Affairs*, vol. 91, 2012, pp. 134-136.

be made before 2025.[319] The US Legislative Peak Oil and Natural Gas Caucus concluded that "oil shale cannot compensate in a timely way for loss of conventional oil production and cannot meet sustainable productions at a rate that will offset high oil prices."[320] On the subject of shale oil, or organic marlstone, the Caucus concluded:

> The US contains massive amounts of oil shale but it is a low grade material with about the equivalent energy proud for pound of a baked potato. Regardless of its low EROEI [Energy Returned on Energy Invested] oil shale production appears to be feasible at some scale. That scale, however, appears not to be significant enough to alter oil supply trends in coming years. It is clear that limiting factors such as water, safe deposits of spent process material and other issues remain unanswered.[321]

The comprehensive assessment of the sustainability of unconventional oil given by Kjell Aleklett in *Peeking at Peak Oil*[322] agrees with the Caucus conclusion cited above: "Oil production from oil shale is insignificant." And: "There is nothing to indicate that the United States will become self-sufficient in oil production or even become an oil exporter despite enthusiastic reportage in the news media." For example, the average Bakken well makes use of horizontal drilling to get to the layer of rock containing the oil that does not flow and then fracturing or "fracking," involving pumping down a chemical mixture at high pressure to allow the oil to be pumped out. There has been observed to be a rapid decline in oil output from shale oil drilling in Montana, part of the Bakken Field and at the Eagle Ford play in Texas; of the 16 wells completed between December 2005 and November 2009, only seven remain productive, and US officials have

---

[319]   http://www.theoildrum.com/node/9169.

[320]   US Legislative Peak Oil and Natural Gas Caucus, *Peak Oil Production and Implications to the State of Connecticut: Report to the Legislative Leaders and the Governor. Addendum: Tar Sands and Shale Oil*, (December, 2007), at http://www.housedems.ct.gov/backer/pubs/TSandOSfina.pdf.

[321]   As above, p. 13.

[322]   Kjell Aleklett (with Michael Lardelli), *Peeking at Peak Oil*, (Springer, New York, 2012).

reduced by 96 percent the estimated recoverable oil from California's Monterey shale deposits.[323]

Michael Klare has pointed out that there are environmental limits to shale oil mining as well.[324] Hydraulic fracturing uses millions of liters of water and creates a problem of disposal of toxic water, which can contaminate other water resources. These vast quantities of water may not be available because of droughts, arguably due to climate change. In July 2012 in Pennsylvania, some drillers suspended operations after the Susquehanna River Basin Commission suspended permits for water withdrawals from the Susquehanna River. According to Chris Faulkner, the president and CEO of Breitling Oil and Gas: "Without water, drilling shale gas and oil wells is not possible. A continuing drought could cause our domestic production to decline and derail our road to energy independence in a hurry."

Deep-water drills are another example of "extreme oil" and dangers of large-scale mishaps are always present. The 2010 BP Deep-water Horizon disaster in the Gulf of Mexico is an example, but Shell Oil's drilling in the Alaskan Artic was suspended until 2013 (and plans resumed in 2015), due to a series of accidents. In any case, total oil production from all existing deep-water wells by 2020 is thought to be 8.4 mb/d and as Aleklett puts it "not even 10% of the necessary increase can be provided by production from deep water."[325] Aleklett concludes: "[d]eep water is the last output of global oil production. The production journey that began in the United States and Russia in the 1850s has now reached the end of the road."[326]

[323]   https://www.forbes.com/sites/arthurberman/2017/03/01/the-beginning-of-the-end-for-the-bakken-shale-play/#69096dde1487; https://energypost.eu/bakken-shows-us-tight-oil-production-limits/.

[324]   Michael Klare, "The New 'Golden Age' of Oil that Wasn't: Extreme Oil Means an Extreme Planet," October 5, 2012 at http://www.carolynbaker.net/2012/10/05/the-new-golden-age-of-oil-that-wasnt-extreme-energy-means-an-extreme-planetby-michael-klare.

[325]   Aleklett, as above, p. 165.

[326]   As above. On the limitations of supply of Canadian Oil Sands see B. Söderbergh (et al.), "A Crash Programme Scenario for the Canadian Oil Sands Industry," *Energy Policy,* vol.35, 2007, pp.1931-1947.

Proponents of the peak oil hypothesis are allegedly in "disgrace," according to Steven F. Hayward, visiting professor at Pepperdine University's Graduate School of Public Policy, Los Angeles, as all "of the recent projections forecast that the age of hydrocarbon dominance (including coal) will last several decades longer than previously thought."[327] This in itself is an admittance that peak energy will eventually be reached, albeit "several decades longer than previously thought." However, as J. David Hughes points out, the Energy Information Administration (EIA) sees US domestic crude oil production, including "tight oil (shale oil), peaking at 7.5 million barrels per day in 2019/2020." By 2040, the percentage of US domestically produced crude oil of total US crude oil used will be only 32 percent, lower than today's share of 34 percent.[328] Thus, the idea of a century of US energy independence, based on *in situ* unconventional oil resources, is a myth. Hughes summarizes: "although resources such as oil shale, gas hydrates, and in situ coal gasification have very large in situ potential, they have been produced at only miniscule rates if at all, despite major expenditures over many years on pilot projects. Tar sands similarly have immense in situ resources, but more than four decades of very large capital inputs and collateral environmental impacts have yielded production of less than two percent of world oil requirements."[329] Shale gas wells, for example, have a high rate of production decline – conventional gas wells usually decline by 25-40 percent in the first year of production, whereas shale wells decline by 63-85 percent, and then require re-fracking, hence generating the need to drill faster and faster.

Richard Heinberg in *Snake Oil: How Fracking's False Promise of Plenty Imperils Our Future*, reaches this conclusion on unconventional oil: "Rather than a century of plenty, we face the

---

[327] Steven F. Hayward, "Obama's Carbon War Running Out of Gas," *The Australian*, June 3, 2013, p. 7.

[328] J. David Hughes, *Drill, Baby, Drill: Can Unconventional Fuels Usher in a New Era of Energy Abundance?* (Post Carbon Institute, Santa Rosa, February, 2013), at http://www.postcarbon.org/drill-baby-drill/.

[329] As above, p. i.

likely recommencement of declines in US oil and gas production *before 2020*. We've purchased a few years of respite from the relentless and inevitable erosion of our nation's oil and gas production rates, but at what cost?"[330]

The US shale oil boom had also had a question mark placed over it by the recent instability of oil prices. The world oil market is artificial, not economically free, with supply regulated by the Organization of Petroleum Exporting Countries. The Saudis have not reduced supply, as they have done in 1977, 1985, 1991 and 2008. Some speculate that this is an attempt to slow down the US's unconventional oil industry; others, that it is a strategy to visit economic pain on regimes that the Saudis are in conflict with such as Iran and Russia (an ally of Syria's Bashar al-Assad), or maybe both. In any case, the instability of oil prices has nothing to do with any vast new oil reserves suddenly being discovered in Saudi Arabia and everything to do with geopolitics.

The frantic scramble to secure what is left of declining world oil resources, Michael Klare has argued, raises the likelihood of resource wars through the 21st century—if nation states even survive the threat of peak energy.[331] China is already driving up global oil prices with its consumption rising by 0.5 m/bpd each year—this being 9.2 m/bdp in a world market of 90 m/bpd. David Greely, "oil guru" of Goldman Sachs has said: "It is only a matter of time before inventories and OPEC spare capacity become effectively exhausted, requiring higher oil prices to restrain demand."[332]

Other energy resources are fast approaching their peak. In 2006, the Energy Watch Group predicted that the peak of world uranium

---

[330] Richard Heinberg, *Snake Oil: How Fracking's False Promise of Plenty Imperils Our Future* (Post Carbon Institute, Santa Rosa, 2013), p. 79.

[331] M. Klare, *The Race for What's Left: The Global Scramble for the World's Last Resources*, (Metropolitan Books, New York, 2012); M. Klare, "Oil Wars on the Horizon," *Counterpunch*, May 10, 2012, at http://www.counterpunch.org/2012/05/10/oil-wars-on-the-horizon/.

[332] Ambrose Evan-Pritchard, "Peak Cheap Oil is an Incontrovertible Fact," August 26, 2012 at http://www.telegraph.co.uk/finance/comment/ambroseevans_pritchard/9500667/Peak-cheap-oil-is-an-incontrovertible-fact.html.

production would occur in 2040,[333] but there are more pessimistic predictions of peak uranium such as 2016, that the peak has already been reached. Even coal reserves are depleting faster than previously thought, with one study concluding that the peak occurred in 2011,[334] and other studies putting peak coal at 2026.[335] Peak coal will lead to the "blackout" of industrial society as Richard Heinberg predicts:

> Grid failure becomes the norm; lights are on only occasionally and electricity is strictly rationed. Communication networks are drastically reduced in scope and are continually strained. Industrial activity contracts and gradually disappears.[336]

Both Richard Heinberg[337] and Ted Trainer[338] have put the case that no combination of alternative energy options would enable the consumer society to continue on a business-as-usual basis, let alone grow exponentially. Further, many conventional economists, who reject the peak oil hypothesis, also believe that alternative energy resources will not fuel our bubbling global consumer society. For example, wind turbines face a "ballooning cost" compared to the cheapest fossil fuel.[339] Alternative energy sources such as solar have been cut back throughout the world because of economic conditions. There was a push in Spain

---

[333] Energy Watch Group, *Uranium Resources and Nuclear Energy*, (EWG-Series No. 1/2006, December 2006), at http://energywatchgroup.org/wp-content/uploads/2014/02/EWG_Report_Uranium_3-12-2006ms1.pdf.

[334] T. W. Patzek and G. D. Croft, "A Global Coal Production Forecast with Multi-Hubbert Cycle Analysis," *Energy*, vol. 35, 2010, pp. 3109-3122.

[335] S. H. Mohr and G. M. Evans, "Forecasting Coal Production Until 2100," *Fuel*, vol. 88, 2009, pp. 2059-2067. See generally R. Heinberg and D. Fridley, "The End of Cheap Coal," *Nature*, vol. 468, no. 7322, pp. 367-369.

[336] R. Heinberg, *Blackout: Coal, Climate and the Last Energy Crisis*, (New Society Publishers, Gabriola Island, 2009), p. 155.

[337] R. Heinberg, *Searching for a Miracle: "Net Energy" Limits and the Fate of Industrial Society*, (International Forum on Globalization and Post Carbon Institute, False Solutions Series No.4, September, 2009), at http://ifg.org/v2/wp-content/uploads/2014/04/Searching-for-a-Miracle_web10nov09.pdf.

[338] T. Trainer, "Can the World Run on Renewable Energy? A Revised Negative Case," *Humanomics*, vol.29, 2013, pp. 88-104.

[339] B. Lomborg, "Ballooning Cost is Blowing in the Wind," *The Australian*, March 22, 2012, p. 12.

for the nation to become the world leader in renewable energy. In 2008 Spain accounted for about half of the world's new solar power installation re wattage due to generous government subsidies. Now, however, due to poor economic conditions and the need to curb the public deficit, these subsidies have been temporarily suspended and a dark cloud has passed over solar optimism.[340]

Safety concerns continue to be an issue with nuclear power, as we have seen from the discussion given previously in this chapter.[341] Claims by Lockheed Martin to have made a breakthrough in nuclear fusion, and to have a working nuclear fusion reactor by about 2017 (it does not seem to have happened by 2019, but some media reports say 2020), have been greeted with skepticism by the scientific community. The project lead at Lockheed Martin has said that a commercial application would take about a decade. However, others see this as optimistic, with domestic fusion unlikely before 2050.

Richard C. Duncan has seen peak energy leading to the end of industrial society by 2025-2030, with a Malthusian catastrophe and global population crash culling the human population to two billion by 2050.[342] An "Olduvai" die off will occur everywhere, and large cities will be very dangerous (and sources of disease from rotting corpses), when the lights of modernity go out. C. Stager, *Deep Future: The Next 100,000 Years of Life on Earth*, writes:

We're already near the limits of economically viable petroleum production, and the decline of cheap oil will have swift and severe consequences for those who will inherit the full measure of that problem. If and when the prices and availability of petroleum-based fuels, fertilizers, plastics, pharmaceuticals, cosmetics, synthetic fabrics, and even roadway pavement go haywire, the

---

[340] *The Australian*, February 13, 2012, p. 13.

[341] See further, "Nuclear Power: The Dream that Failed," *The Economist*, March 10, 2012, at http://www.economist.com/node/21549936.

[342] R. C. Duncan, "America: A Frog in the Kettle Slowly Coming to a Boil," *The Social Contract*, Fall, 2007, pp. 3-13.

scale of human suffering could outstrip anything in the works for us from climate [change].[343]

But, peak energy is not humanity's only existential problem.

The Climate Cataclysm

The best-known doomsday predictions arising from the issue of global climate change were made by James Lovelock, known for his Gaia hypothesis that the Earth ("Mother Earth") behaves like an organism, exhibiting systems-self-regulation. Lovelock in his various books on the topic used metaphors which transcended normal science and essentially involved philosophical speculation and metaphysics in my opinion. Nevertheless, at a minimum, he saw the world as a non-linear system, subject to chaotic effects. In 2006, he said: "Before this century is over, billions of us will die and the few breeding pairs of people that survive will be in the Arctic where the climate remains tolerable."[344] In his 2009 book, *The Vanishing Face of Gaia: A Final Warning*, Lovelock said "global warming may all but eliminate people from Earth."[345]

Lovelock recanted from his doomsday predictions, describing his own predictions as "wrong" and others as "alarmist" – although only holding to the complete annihilation of life would be more alarmist than Lovelock's earlier predictions. At no point did he examine the survival rates of past extinction episodes involving climate change and human survival. Surprisingly enough, Lovelock himself accepted a non-linear model of climate change, described as follows: "Do not expect the climate to follow the smooth path of slowly but sedately rising temperatures predicted by the IPCC [Intergovernmental Panel

---

[343] C. Stager, *Deep Future: The Next 100,000 Years of Life on Earth* (Scribe, Melbourne, 2011), p. 235.

[344] "Scientist Cools on Climate Alarmism," *The Australian*, April 26, 2012, p. 11.

[345] James Lovelock, *The Vanishing Face of Gaia: A Final Warning* (Allen Lane, Camberwell, Victoria, 2009), p. 4.

on Climate Change], where change slowly inches up and leaves plenty of time for business as usual. The real Earth changes intermittently with spells of constancy, even slight decline between jumps to greater heat." Lovelock's recanting was produced because he believes that climate change has not proceeded as fast as the Gaia model would predict. But, so much the worst for his model.

The earlier, pessimistic Lovelock though was on the right track, and saw the gravest dangers to humanity arising from "starvation, competition for space and resources, and tribal war." He also said that to survive in the harsh world of the future we need "to prepare ourselves to fight a barbarian warlord out to seize us and our territory." So, he seems to be *logically* committed to the thesis of this book.

Journalists skeptical of the very existence of global climate change have made much of the claims of Kaufmann (et al.) that "global surfaces temperatures did not rise between 1998 and 2008."[346] These journalists should have read the entire paper, which does not support climate change skepticism. The title of the paper is "Reconciling Anthropogenic Climate Change with Observed Temperature 1998-2008." It presents evidence that the rapid increase in sulfur emissions, primarily by China's coal consumption, has been so vast as to mask the increase in radiative forcing (the rate of change of energy or net irradiance per unit area of the Earth relative to the top of the atmosphere) that would have otherwise occurred from rising greenhouse gas concentrations (global dimming). When the sulphur emissions are reduced by technological improvements in the Chinese coal industry, global warming will allegedly return with a vengeance. A paper by Solomon (et al.)[347] puts the position that man-made pollutants may have slowed global warming as aerosol particles from burning coal may reflect sunlight back into space. More will be said about the issue of "the pause" shortly.

---

[346] R. K. Kaufmann (et. al.), "Reconciling Anthropogenic Climate Change with Observed Temperature 1998-2008," *Proceedings of the National Academy of Sciences*, www.pnas.org/cgi/doi/10.1073/pnas.1102467108.

[347] S. Solomon (et. al.), "The Persistently Variable 'Background' Stratospheric Aerosol Layer and Global Climate Change," *Science*, vol. 333, 2011, pp. 866-870.

Climate change skeptics maintain that there is no direct evidence that 20th and 21st century warming (if such warming did occur – the skeptic teams are divided on this), was caused by carbon dioxide increases, as ice ages have occurred when the atmosphere carbon dioxide levels were higher than at present.[348] The causes of an ice age are complex and involve more factors than just the atmospheric concentration of greenhouse gases. Factors include Milankovitch cycles (variations in the Earth's orbit), sunspot cycles, volcanism and other factors. It is possible for an ice age to occur even with a higher than present-day concentration of atmospheric greenhouse gases relative to these other factors.[349] However, there are various "signatures" of human-caused climate change, rather than natural variability, such as cooling in the upper atmosphere, with lower-level warming, nights warmer than days, winters warmer than past summers and land warming more than oceans.

The Earth has also experienced a number of past mass extinctions, such as the Cambrian extinction of 490 million years ago and the more recent Paleocene thermal event of 55 million years ago. These were caused by increased carbon dioxide in the atmosphere, leading to changes in ocean currents and circulation patterns, via the disruption of ocean conveyer currents. This disruption led to the massive growth of green sulfur-producing bacteria and other bacteria producing hydrogen sulphide. The gas enters the atmosphere, and over millions of years builds up to such a high concentration that the Earth's protective ozone layer is destroyed. The influx of ultraviolet radiation and high concentrations of hydrogen sulphide in the atmosphere kills off most of life on Earth.[350] According to University of Washington paleontologist, Professor Peter Ward, "[t]he present rise in carbon dioxide levels seems to eclipse any other rate of increase

---

[348] Ian Plimer, "Basic Sciences is the Answer, Not Blinding Ideology," *The Australian*, January 4, 2012, p. 13.

[349] R. A. Muller and G. J. MacDonald, *Ice Ages and Astronomical Causes: Data, Spectral Analysis and Mechanisms*, (Springer-Verlag, London, 2000).

[350] Peter P. D. Ward, *Under a Green Sky: Global Warming, the Mass Extinctions of the Past and What They Can Tell Us about Our Future*, (Smithsonian Books/Collins, New York, 2007).

from the past" and once CO_2 levels rise above 450 parts per million (ppm) (May 15, 2019 atmospheric CO_2 levels are at 415.64 ppm, NOAA-ESRL data) "we head irrevocably toward an ice-free world, which will lead to a change in the thermohaline conveyer belt currents [which] will lead to a new greenhouse extinction."

Professor David Battisti of the University of Washington, however, sees CO_2 levels reaching 800 ppm by the end of the 21st century and rising to 1,100 ppm shortly after that, melting the world's ice sheets and setting in motion the next greenhouse extinction.[351] Some authorities believe that adding CO_2 levels from other greenhouse gases means that we may already be at the tipping point of 450 ppm, so that humanity is already on the highway to extinction.[352]

While climate change skeptics maintain that global temperatures have not risen since 1997,[353] other climate scientists have said that the past decade is the warmest on record. For example, Professor Richard A. Muller was once one of the world's leading climate change skeptics, and was a skeptic because of the poor quality of data from temperature stations, with temperature uncertainty of 2-5 C or more. This margin of error is due to the stations being in cities, which are typically hotter than rural areas (known as the "heat island effect"). Muller chaired the Berkeley Earth Surface Temperature Project, which obtained over 1.6 billion measurements from over 39,000 temperature stations across the world. The urban-heating bias was avoided by using rural locations. It was concluded that: "The changes at the locations that showed warming [⅔ showed warming, ⅓ did not] were typically between 1-2°C much greater than the IPCC's average of 0.64°C."[354] Muller concluded that global warming is real.

---

[351] As above, p. 194.

[352] Foundation for the Future, *Humanity Three Thousand: Anthropogenic Climate Destabilization: A Worse-Case Scenario*, (Executive Summary), at http://www.futurefoundation.org/documents/HUM_ExecSum_ClimateDestabilization.

[353] J. Leake, "Warming Data Shows Shades of Grey," *The Australian*, February 7, 2012, p.13; B. Stephens, "Climate Zealots, the End Isn't Nigh," *The Australian*, November 30, 2011, p. 10.

[354] R. A. Muller, "The Case Against Global-Warming Scepticism," 21 October, 2011 at http://www.wsj.com/articles/SB10001424052970204422404576594872796327348.

James E. Hansen, director of NASA's Goddard Institute for Space Studies has said that his predictions in 1988 about increasing global temperature have been proved true, but he was too optimistic about the speed at which temperature changes would result in an increase in extreme weather.[355] His research team's analysis of six decades of global temperature statistics found a statistically significant increase in the frequency of extremely hot summers. The analysis shows "that, for the extreme hot weather of the recent past, there is virtually no explanation other than climate change."[356] Plotting the temperatures of the world over time on a Gaussian or bell curve, showed that the extremes of unusually cold and unusually hot are changing, so that they *both* become more severe and more common. Thus, in the period of 1951 to 1980, extremely hot temperatures covered 0.1-0.2 percent of the Earth, but since that time the extremes now cover around 10 percent of the Earth.[357] The European heat wave of 2003, the Russian heat wave of 2010, the droughts in Texas and Oklahoma in 2011, the extremely hot 2012 US summer, and perhaps the 2018 droughts across the US, all have probably been caused by climate change, or the intensity of these events influenced by climate change.[358]

In 2013 the Intergovernmental Panel on Climate Change (IPCC) released its latest scientific report from Working Group I, which is said to constitute the "consensus" view on climate change.[359] The report states that the atmospheric concentrations of greenhouse gases such as carbon dioxide, methane and nitrous oxide are at an

---

[355]   J. Hansen, "Climate Change is Here – and Worse than We Thought," *The Washington Post*, August 4, 2012, at http://www.washingtonpost.com/opinions/climate-change-is-here--and-worse-than-we-thought/2012/08/03/6ae604c2-dd90-11e1-8e43-4a3c4375504a_story.html.

[356]   As above.

[357]   J. Hansen (et al.), "Ice Melt, Sea Level Rise and Superstorms: Evidence from Paleoclimate Data, Climate Modeling, and Modern Observations that 2° C Global Warming is Highly Dangerous," *Atmospheric Chemistry and Physics*, vol. 15, 2015, pp. 20059-20179.

[358]   Q. Schiermeier, "Droughts, Heat Waves and Floods: How to Tell when Climate Change is to Blame," *Scientific American*, July 30, 2018, at https://www.scientificamerican.com/article/droughts-heat-waves-and-floods-how-to-tell-when-climate-change-is-to-blame/.

[359]   T. F. Stocker (et al., eds.), *Climate Change 2013: The Physical Science Basis. Contribution of Working Group I to the Fifth Assessment Report of the Intergovernmental Panel on Climate Change* (Cambridge University Press, Cambridge, 2013).

unprecedented level compared to other times over the past 800,000 years.[360] A 5,000 year long-term cooling trend has been reversed; the period 1982-2012, for example, in the northern hemisphere was *very likely* the warmest 30 year period in the past 800 years and *likely* the warmest 30 year period for 1,400 years.[361] The average temperature for the 20th century was approximately 0.4 C higher than the average temperature of the past five centuries.[362]

From 1901 to 2012, almost the entire planet experienced warming.[363] There was a warming trend of 0.85 C for 1880 to 2012, with respect to the globally averaged combined ocean and land temperature. The total increase between the average of the 1850-1900 period and the 2003-2012 periods is 0.78 C. Most of the Earth's heating has been in the oceans; the 1971-2010 estimate of energy gain being 199×10^{12} W, equivalent to 0.42 Wm^{-2} of heating over the Earth's surface and 0.55 Wm^{-2} warming over the ocean's surface. Such warming has led to both an annual multi-year and perennial decrease in Arctic sea ice extent from 1979-2012 of about 3.5 and 4.1 percent per decade. In the period 1971-2009, the total mass loss from all glaciers (except those on the periphery of ice sheets) was very likely 226 gigatonnes/ year (range, 91 to 361 gigatonnes/per year). The Greenland ice sheet has lost ice at an accelerating rate since 1992 and it is very likely that the increase is 34 (- 6 to 72) gigatonnes/per year for 1992-2001. Earthquakes of magnitude 4.6 to 5.2 have occurred in Greenland due to large icebergs breaking off from tidal glaciers, forcing the glaciers backwards. There has been an increase of seven-fold of such earthquakes since the 1990s.[364]

Most ice loss in the Antarctic ice shelf has been in the northern Antarctic Peninsula and Amundsen Sea, from the melting of outlet

[360] As above, p. 1.

[361] As above, p. 41.

[362] M. Ahmed (et. al.), (PAGES 2K Consortium), "Continental-Scale Temperature Variability During the Past Two Millennia," *Nature Geoscience*, vol.6, 2013, pp. 339-345, cited p. 339.

[363] Stocker (et al.), as above, p. 37.

[364] T. Murray (et al.), "Reverse Glacier Motion During Iceberg Calving and the Cause of Glacial Earthquakes," *Science*, vol. 349, 2015, pp. 305-308.

glaciers, with the average rate of ice loss increasing from the 1992-2001 period of 30 gigatonnes/per year to 147 gigatonnes per year in the period 2002-2011.[365] However, in 2015 sea ice in Antarctica averaged 14.93 million square kilometres, and in June 2015, this was the third highest June extent in the records. This was thought to be due to strong atmospheric wave-3 patterns, rather than from a reversal of climate change impacts.[366]

The IPCC accepted that there has been something of a "pause" or "hiatus" in global mean surface temperatures from 1998 to 2012. As already mentioned, this "pause" has been taken by climate change skeptics as showing that global warming is not occurring, or has ceased. The rate of warming from 1998 to 2012 is smaller than the trend from 1951 to 2012; the 1998-2012 trend was 0.05 C (-0.05 to 0.15 C) per decade, compared to the 1951-2012 trend of 0.12 C (0.08 to 0.14 C) per decade.[367]

Even granting the reality of the "pause," the decade of the 2000s is the warmest decade in the record of global mean surface temperatures.[368] The World Meteorological Organization regarded the period 2001-2010 as the warmest since records began in 1850.[369] The World Meteorological Organization said that 2014 was tied with 2010 as the hottest year on record, with the global average temperature for January to October being 0.57 C above average, and in their January 18, 2018 statement, this claim was also revised to claim that 2016 was the warmest on record, 1.2 C above the preindustrial era.[370] Average global temperatures were the highest in 136 years in July 2015 due to record warming of the oceans. The combined sea and land

[365]   As above.

[366]   M. Wegmann (et al.), "Arctic Moisture Source for Eurasian Snow Cover Variations in Autumn," *Environmental Research Letters*, vol. 10, 2015; doi:10.1088/1748-9326/10/054015.

[367]   Stocker (et al.), as above, p. 37.

[368]   As above, p. 61.

[369]   World Meteorological Organization, *The Global Climate 2001-2010: A Decade of Climate Extremes*, Summary Report, (World Meteorological Organization, Geneva, 2013), p.3.

[370]   "WMO Confirms 2017 Among the Three Hottest Years on Record," January 18, 2018, at http://www.latimes.com/science/sciencenow/la-sci-sn-global-temperatures-2017-20180118-story.html.

temperature in July 2015 was 16.61 C, 0.81 C above the 20th century average of 15.8 C.[371]

There is considerable scientific controversy about the cause of the "pause" and even if it really existed. The IPCC, for example say that it is real but due to natural variability, with reduced radiative forcing because of volcanic eruptions and a less-active phase of the sun.[372] However, if a time series of unweighted 11-year average temperatures is used, with a removal of year-to-year variations caused by volcanic eruptions, a global warming trend exists.[373] The alleged "pause," based on a short time frame, may not be statistically significant.[374] Others believe that the "pause" may indicate that estimates of climate sensitivity (the equilibrium temperature in response to a doubling of CO_2) needs to be revised down,[375] but many authorities disagree.[376] There is debate about the idea that the deep oceans have absorbed the "missing heat," with one research team at the Lawrence Livermore National Laboratory, claiming to have identified an "anthropogenic warming signature" in the upper (0-700 meters) of the ocean, with one third of the accumulated heat occurring below 700 meters.[377] Evidence of an increase in the acidity of the oceans from pre-industrial times, is but one argument for CO_2 being absorbed by the oceans.[378]

---

[371] "Global Summary Information – July 2015," at https://www.ncdc.noaa.gov/sotc/summary-info/global/201507.

[372] Stocker (et. al. eds.), as above, p. 63; Y. Kosaka and S.-P. Xie, "Recent Global-Warming Hiatus Tied to Equatorial Pacific Surface Cooling," *Nature*, vol. 501, 2013, pp. 403-407.

[373] K. Cowtan and R. G. Way, "Coverage Bias in the HadCRUT4 Temperature Series and its Impact on Recent Temperature Trends," *Quarterly Journal of the Royal Meteorological Society*, vol. 140, 2014, pp. 1935-1944.

[374] D. R. Easterling and M. F. Wehner, "Is the Climate Warming or Cooling?" *Geophysical Research Letters*, vol.36, 2009, L08706; doi: 10.1029/2009GL037810 cited p. 1.

[375] A. Otto (et al.), "Energy Budget Constraints on Climate Response," *Nature Geoscience*, vol. 6, 2013, pp. 415-416.

[376] The Geological Society, *An Addendum to the Statement on Climate Change: Evidence from the Geological Record*, (December, 2013), at http://www.geolsoc.org.uk/climaterecord.

[377] P. J. Gleckler (et al.), "Industrial-Era Global Ocean Heat Uptake Doubles in Recent Decades," *Nature Climate Change*, (2016); doi:10.1038/NCLIMATE2915.

[378] J-P. Gattuso (et al.), "Contrasting Futures for Ocean and Society from Different CO_2 Emissions Scenarios," *Science*, vol. 349, 2015, pp. aac4722-1 – aac4722-10.

Scientists, including those of NOAA's Pacific Marine Environmental Laboratory, see ocean warming from climate change as "unstoppable."[379] Recent research also refutes the notion that it will take decades for the climate system to respond to an increase in CO_2 – maximum warming may occur in as little as one decade.[380] The evidence from ocean heating has led to some climate researchers, such as Kevin Trenberth of the National Center for Atmospheric Research, to believe that the "pause" is now over and that a period of rapid warming is now beginning.[381]

Victor and Kennel have proposed that the measure of global average temperature is not a good measure of climate stress.[382] It is beyond the scope of this book to evaluate this debate further, but – none of the scientists believe that global warming is not occurring. Indeed, there is weighty opinion that the IPCC consensus on climate change is far too conservative.

In August 2008, the former chair of the IPCC Bob Watson, said that the world should work on mitigation and adaption strategies for a 4 C warming, as the world has probably surpassed CO_2 limits.[383] Sea levels could rise by one meter per century, destroying land now occupied by 145 million people. Abrupt climate change, triggered by positive feedback mechanisms, such as tundra methane release, could melt the ice of Greenland and Antarctica, ultimately leading to a catastrophic sea level rise.[384]

---

[379] S. Goldenberg, "Warming of Oceans Due to Climate Change is Unstoppable, Say US Scientists," July 17, 2015, at http://www.theguardian.com/environment/2015/jul/16/warming-of-oceans-due-to-climate-change-is-unstoppable-.

[380] K. L. Ricke and K. Caldeira, "Maximum Warming Occurs about One Decade after a Carbon Dioxide Emission," *Environmental Research Letters*, vol. 9, 2014, 124002.

[381] M. Le Page, "Earth Now Halfway to Warming Limit," *New Scientist*, August 1, 2015, pp. 8-9.

[382] D. G. Victor and C. F. Kennel, "Ditch the 2°C Warming Goal," *Nature*, vol. 514, 2014, pp. 30-31.

[383] J. Rockstrom (et. al.), "A Safe Operating Space for Humanity," *Nature*, vol. 461, 2009, pp. 472-475; https://www.theguardian.com/environment/2013/may/10/carbon-dioxide-highest-level-greenhouse-gas.

[384] R. E. Kopp (et al.), "Temperature-Driven Global Sea-Level Variability in the Common Era," *Proceedings of the National Academy of Sciences*, February 22, 2016, at www.pnas.org/

James Hansen (et al.) note that ice sheets in contact with the ocean face non-linear disintegration from ocean warming and they predict a sea level rise of up to 3 meters by the end of the 21st century, rather than the 0.9 meters predicted by the IPCC. A sea level rise of + 5-9 meters occurred in a prior interglacial period less than 1 C warmer than the present and human-caused climate change forcing is stronger than this.[385] Hansen (et al.) concluded that "[i]t is not difficult to imagine that conflicts arising from forced migrations and economic collapse might make the planet ungovernable, threatening the fabric of civilization."[386]

The OECD's *Environmental Outlook to 2050*, hardly a radical "green" publication, predicts that global greenhouse emissions will rise by 50 percent by 2050 on a business-as-usual scenario, and CO_2 emissions by 70 percent, leading to a rise in global average temperatures of 3-6 C by 2100.[387] These changes are likely to exceed tipping points, leading to abrupt climate change and runaway greenhouse effects. This "catastrophic climate change" will lead to 2.3 billion people facing severe water stress, and air pollution alone is likely to mean that 3.6 million premature deaths occur in China and India. A global average temperature rise of 4 C would see the "lungs of the world," the Amazon rainforest, shrinking by 85 percent, which in-itself could constitute a positive feedback mechanism accelerating even further climate change.[388]

---

cgi/doi/10.1073/pnas.1517056113.

[385] J. Hansen (et al.), "Ice Melts, Sea Level Rise and Superstorms: Evidence from Paleoclimate Data, Climate Modeling, and Modern Observations that 2° C Global Warming is Highly Dangerous," *Atmospheric Chemistry and Physics*, vol. 15, 2015, pp. 20059-20179.

[386] See M. Le Page, "Superstorms Possible Even with 'Safe' 2 ° C Rise," *New Scientist*, August 1, 2015, p. 9.

[387] P. Love, "OECD Environmental Outlook to 2050: We're All Doomed," *OECD Insights*, March 19, 2012, at http://oecdinsights.org/2012/03/19/oecd-environmental-outlook-to-2050-were-all-doomed.

[388] D. Adam, "Amazon Could Shrink by 85% Due to Climate Change, Scientists Say," *The Guardian*, March 11, 2009, at http://www.guardian.co.uk/environment/2009/mar/11/amazon-global-warming-trees.

BP in its *Energy Outlook 2030*[389] predicts that by 2030 there will be 15 percent more oil, 26 percent more coal and 46 percent more natural gas being consumed than at present, leading to 4 C warming in the 21st century. The International Energy Agency (IEA) in *Redrawing the Energy-Climate Map* (2013),[390] sees growing use of fossil fuels, such as coal, leading to global temperatures rising in this century from 3.6 C to 6 C; 3.5 C, over pre-industrial levels by 2040; 4 C by 2050 and 6 C by 2100. After 2017, (and it is now 2019), it may be impossible to reverse trends because "our energy system—power plants, the industry sector, the transport sector—will be locked into the capital investments in a way they will use fossil fuel energies."[391] The International Energy Agency believes that the development of low-carbon energy systems will be too slow to stop this extreme global warming.[392]

Pricewaterhousecoopers' report, *Too Late for Two Degrees?* (2012), doubts that warming can be held to 2 C and may reach 4 C or even 6 C. Leo Johnson says in the foreword to this report: "Even doubling our current rate of decarbonization, would still lead to emissions consistent with 6 degrees of warming by the end of this century. To give ourselves a more than 50% chance of avoiding 2 degrees will require a six-fold improvement in our rate of decarbonisation."[393] The 2 C carbon budget requires world cuts in carbon intensity by 5.1 percent each year from now until 2050, but as Johnson says, this "required rate of decarbonisation has not been seen in a single year since the mid-20th century when these records began."[394] Hence,

---

[389] BP, Energy Outlook 2030, (January, 2013) at http://www.bp.com/content/dam/bp/pdf/statistical-review/BP_World_Energy_Outlook_booklet_2013.pdf.

[390] International Energy Agency, *Redrawing the Energy-Climate Map: World Energy Outlook Special Report* (International Energy Agency, Paris, 2013).

[391] F. Montaigne, "An Influential Global Voice Warns of Runaway Emissions," June 11, 2012, at http://e360.yale.edu/feature/fatih_birol_iea_economist_on__risk_of_climate_change/2537.

[392] "Clean Energy Process too Slow to Limit Global Warming – Report," April 17, 2013, at http://www.reuters.com/article/2013/04/17/carbon-energy-warming-idUSL5NoCX3I020130417.

[393] Pricewaterhousecoopers LLP, *Too Late for Two Degrees? Low Carbon Economy Index 2012*, (PricewaterhouseCoopers, November, 2012), p. 1.

[394] As above, p. 2.

it is unlikely that global warming will be limited to 2 C.[395] Climatic doomsday is inevitable.

The assessments just considered are highly pessimistic, "doomsday" of course, yet they are not from environmentalist groups, but from respectable business organizations. Those who dismiss climate change as a "conspiracy" (conservatives, many Christian groups, Big Business groups) should hesitate to do so, because the support for climate change comes from a wide range of sources, while opposition is largely from Big Business groups who have the most to lose. Cult-like Christian conservative groups, who oppose climate change because of "New World Order" concerns, are strangely silent on most other NWO-like issues that are way too difficult for their over-spiritual worldview. Don't tell anyone, but there has been a globalized world, a rule of the corporate elite, more constraining than any world government, for some time, a spawn of the liberal/conservative's cherished capitalism.

We can also mention the report by the World Bank, *Turn Down the Heat* (2012),[396] the National Research Council, *Climate and Social Stress* (2012)[397] and the National Intelligence Council, *Global Trends 2030*,[398] all of which give a much more alarming view of climate change than the more conservative IPCC. In other words, there is weighty Establishment opinion supporting a climate disaster thesis. In general, these reports assume a "business-as-usual" approach, where fossil fuel use increases, primarily through the use of "dirty" sources such as unconventional oil and gas.

One critique of this is that such large temperature increases are unlikely as there is too little oil/fossil fuel left.[399] Thus, peak oil

---

[395] G. A. Jones and K. J. Warner, "The 21st Century Population-Energy-Climate Nexus," *Energy Policy*, vol. 93, 2016, pp. 206-212.

[396] World Bank, *Turn Down the Heat: Why a 4° C World Must be Avoided*, (World Bank, Washington DC, 2012).

[397] National Research Council, *Climate and Social Stress: Implications for Security Analysis* (National Academy of Sciences, Washington DC, 2012).

[398] National Intelligence Council, *Global Trends 2030: Alternative Worlds* (Central Intelligence Agency, Washington DC, 2012).

[399] J. D. Ward (et. al.), "High Estimates of Supply Constrained Emissions Scenarios for

theorist K. Alexlett predicts a 21st century temperature rise of 1.5 to 2 C.[400] However, even at the upper end of this prediction, extreme climate change could still occur.

The idea that peak oil will save us from climate change is wrong. There are still abundant masses of hydrocarbons, not sufficient to sustain the global consumer society for much longer, but enough to cause, if all or most are used, the worst-case climate catastrophe.[401] Carbon-based fuel, according to most authorities, will continue to meet world energy demands.[402] China is building coal-fired power plants like there is no tomorrow – because there is not likely to be. An average global temperature increase of 2 C is considered to constitute dangerous climate change where tipping points are reached, such as the complete loss of Arctic summer sea ice and the melting of the Greenland ice sheet. A 4 C change will make many already hot regions of the world simply unlivable, and lead to events such as extensive melting of the West Antarctic ice sheet and a global sea level rise of up to 5 meters. A 6 C rise will melt all polar ice[403] and could spell by itself the end of human civilization, with a massive die off of the world's population.[404]

The other argument against the idea that peak oil will save us from climate change (even though it would itself lead to a collapse of civilization perhaps more catastrophic in the short-term than climate change), is that positive feedback mechanisms which accelerate climate change are already beginning to act; such mechanisms include vegetation changes, ice sheet changes, ocean circulation and

Long-Term Climate Risk Assessment, *Energy Policy*, vol. 51, 2012, pp. 598-604.

[400] K. Aleklett, *Peeping at Peak Oil* (Springer, New York, 2012), p. 253.

[401] Richard Heinberg, *Snake Oil*, as above, pp. 123-124.

[402] I. Cronshaw, "The Current and Future Importance of Coal in the World Energy Economy," Energy Policy Institute of Australia, Public Policy Paper No. 5/2014, at http://www.energypolicyinstitute.com.au/images/Policy_Paper_Jan2014_Ian_Cronshaw_5-2014.pdf.

[403] K. Anderson, "What They Won't Tell You about Climate Catastrophe," November 12, 2012, at http://www.ecoshock.info/2012/11/kevin-anderson-what-they-wont-tell-you.html.

[404] J. R. Schramski (et al.), "Human Domination of the Biosphere: Rapid Discharge of the Earth-Space Battery Foretells the Future of Humankind," *Proceedings of the National Academy of Sciences*, vol. 112, 2015, pp. 9511-9517.

biogeochemical cycling and other mechanisms.[405] For example, a study by Eric Rignot of the retreat of ice in the Amundsen Sea sector of West Antarctica has concluded that the collapse of the Western Antarctic Ice Sheet has already begun and is now "unstoppable."[406] Glacier grounding lines are retreating by kilometers each year. A sea level rise of one meter worldwide from this will trigger the loss of the rest of the ice (over a period of two centuries) and a sea level rise of between three and five meters. However, there are some positive feedback mechanisms that may reduce the two-century period.

Of particular concern is the so-called "methane bomb" where in the relatively shallow East Siberian Arctic Shelf, methane fields have been detected, with plumes of a kilometre or wider, with a methane concentration up to 100 times higher than normal.[407]

Can technologies such as geoengineering save us? Carbon-capture and storage methods are costly and take decades to implement and proposals such as the stratospheric injection of sulphate aerosols could lead to ozone loss and changes to rainfall patterns particularly in Asia.[408] Rainfall in the tropics could be cut by 30 percent.[409] Kleidon and Renner, based on their climate model, have concluded that even if geoengineering succeeded in reducing surface warming, "it cannot undo differences in hydrologic cycling and convective mass exchange at the same time."[410]

---

[405]   M. S. Tom and J. Harte, "Missing Feedbacks, Asymmetric Uncertainties, and the Underestimation of Future Warming," *Geophysical Research Letters*, vol. 33, 2006, L10703; doi: 10.1029/2005GL025540.

[406]   https://www.jpl.nasa.gov/news/news.php?release=2014-148.

[407]   S. Connor, "Vast Methane 'Plumes' Seen in Arctic Oceans as Sea Ice Retreats," at http://www.independent.co.uk/news/science/vast-methane-plumes-seen-in-arctic-ocean-as-sea-ice-retreats-6276278.html. N. Shakhova (et. al.), "Extensive Methane Venting to the Atmosphere from Sediments of the East Siberian Arctic Shelf," *Science*, vol. 327, 2010, pp. 1246-1250.

[408]   Z. Carpenter, "Scientists: We Cannot Geoengineer Our Way Out of the Climate Crisis," February 10, 2015, at http://www.thenation.com/blog/197521/scientists-we-cannot-geoengineer-our-way-out-of-climate-crisis.

[409]   A. J. Ferraro (et al.), "Weakened Tropical Circulation and Reduced Precipitation in Response to Geoengineering," *Environmental Research Letters*, vol. 9, 2014, 014001; doi: 10.1088/1748-93/26/9/1/014001.

[410]   A. Kleidon and M. Renner, "A Simple Explanation for the Sensitivity of the Hydrological

Clive Hamilton is right in my opinion in seeing climate change as signalling the end of orthodox social sciences, humanities and philosophy, which in itself is a good thing. He quotes US climate scientist Kevin Trenberth who has said: "The answer to the oft-asked question of whether an event is caused by climate change is that it is the wrong question. All weather events are affected by climate change because the environment in which they occur is warmer and moister than it used to be."[411] The separation of the "Human" and "Nature," taken to be the defining quality of modernity, is thus an illusion Hamilton says, as climate change "shatters the self-contained world of social analysis that is the terrain of modern social science, and explains why those intellectuals who remain within it find it impossible to "analyse" the politics, sociology or philosophy of climate change in a way that is true to the science. They end up floundering in the old categories, unable to see that something epochal has occurred, a rupture on the scale of the Industrial Revolution or the emergence of civilization itself."[412]

Or, the coming collapse of civilization, the zombie apocalypse.

Conclusion

Guillaume Faye in *Convergence of Catastrophes*,[413] predicts a collapse of global civilization by around 2020, which is already too late to stop, although he has probably jumped the gun slightly on the early time frame. Nevertheless, even if the evil date of collapse is a more likely 2030, societies will return to a state similar to the Middle Ages, but more destructive. This is due to converging forces of environmental destruction and climate change, global financial collapse, world

Cycle to Surface Temperature and Solar Radiation and its Implications for Global Climate Change," *Earth System Dynamics*, vol. 4, 2013, pp. 455-465.

[411] Clive Hamilton, "Climate Change Signals the End of the Social Sciences," February 7, 2015, at http://www.carolynbaker.net/2015/02/07/climate-change-signals-the-end-of-the-social-sciences-by-clive-hamilton.

[412] As above.

[413] Guillaume Faye, *Convergence of Catastrophes*, (Arktos Media, 2012), originally published as *La Convergence des catastrophes*, (Diffusion International Edition, Paris, 2004).

pandemics, the depletion of fossil fuels, the destruction of agricultural land, the depletion of fishing resources, the undermining of Western societies through mass immigration, civilizational clashes with Islam, the ageing of Western populations, terrorism and nuclear proliferation, and ultimately, nuclear war. He says:

> ... war is coming and announcing itself with unheard-of violence: war in the streets, civil war, widespread terrorist war, a generalised conflict with Islam and very probably, nuclear conflicts. This will probably be the face of the first half of the twenty-first century. And we have never been less prepared: invaded, devirilised, physically and morally disarmed, the prey of a culture of meaninglessness and masochistic culpability.[414]

Western societies, Faye concludes, believe in "miracles," seduced by egalitarian, humanitarian and liberal dogmas, believing that no matter what, an "invisible hand" will continue to produce harmonious equilibrium. Miraculous beliefs include: the sustainability of unlimited economic growth and development; that the permissive society will produce social harmony, that mass immigration will not erode the social fabric and that cultures can be preserved and nurtured without widespread social conflict. But, there are no miracles in this cold (or, rather, hot) brutal world; hence the planet faces a series of converging ecological, economic, cultural, and religious crises. Facing so many threats means that one or more is almost certain to nail us, and polish us off.

In a nutshell, the collapse of techno-industrial civilization is inevitable. It is possible that the human race itself, if not most life on the planet, faces extinction in the more distant future, but that is less probable than the end of the world as we know it. The zombie apocalypse, a world of violence, disease, bloody death and heat (if not radioactivity) is just around the corner. What now?

---

[414]   As above, p. 198.

I am an archaeologist. I have spent my career attempting to make sense of the past, and I find a world completely at odds with popular misconceptions. Not only is the past I observe not peaceful and pristine, but, cruel and ugly as it may be, it provides great insight into the present [...] Humans have been destroying their environments for a long time and continue to do so for the same reasons they did in the past. Much of today's warfare reads just like the warfare of tens of thousands of years ago – the same causes, the same tactics, the same attitudes.

- Steven A. LeBlanc and Katherine E. Register[415]

Whatsoever therefore is consequent to a time of Warre, where every man is enemy to every man; the same is consequent to the time, wherein men live without other security, than what their own strength, and their own invention shall furnish them withall. In such condition, there is no place for Industry; because the fruit thereof is uncertain; and consequently no Culture of the Earth; no Navigation, nor use of the commodities that may be imported by Sea; no commodious Building; no Instruments of moving, and removing such things as require much force; and no knowledge of the face of the Earth; no account of Time; no Arts; no Letters; no Society; and which is worst of all, continuall feare, and danger of violent death; *And the life of man, solitary, poor, nasty, brutish, and short.*

- Thomas Hobbes (1588-1679)[416]

In my mind. I'm never going to die in no ghetto. Absolutely never. If a man tries to punch me in the head, the fight is on. If he cuts me, the fight is on. If I'm shot the fight is on. I'm not losing no fight to no scumbag out there in no ghetto. Period. That's it. No son-of-bitch out there is going to get me. The only way he gets me is to cut my head off, and I mean that. I'll fight you while I got a breath left in me... You don't lose the fight.

- Jim Phillips[417]

If you must journey to mountains and firths, take food and fodder with you.

- Odin[418]

[415]   S. A. LeBlanc and K. E. Register, *Constant Battles: The Myth of the Peaceful, Noble Savage* (St. Martin's Press, New York, 2003), pp. xi-xii.

[416]   Thomas Hobbes, *Leviathan, or the Matter, Forme, and Power of a Commonwealth, Ecclesiasticall and Civil* (1651), chapter 13, paragraph 9, emphasis added.

[417]   Jim Phillips, *Surviving Edged Weapons,* (Calibre Press Video, 1988), cited by Lt. Col. Dave Grossman and Loren W. Christensen, *On Combat: The Psychology and Physiology of Deadly Conflict in War and Peace* (PPCT Research publications, 2004), p. 134.

[418]   "Words of the High One," in W.H. Auden and P.T. Taylor, *Norse Poems* (The Athlone Press, London, 1981), p. 161.

CHAPTER

CHAPTER

4

ALL YOU NEED IS LEAD AND A FEW OTHER THINGS :
SURVIVALISM, TEOTWAWKI AND ZOMBAGEDDON

Introduction: Dare to Prepare... for the End

CONOMIST AND financial advisor Barton Biggs in *Wealth, War and Wisdom* (2008)[419] says in chapter 16 of his book, entitled "Barbarians at the Gate," that those who have wealth should recognize that the "four horsemen will ride again, and... someday, suddenly *the barbarians* will be at your gate."[420] This threat is usually posed by war but today the greatest danger he believes "will be some form of total breakdown of civilized society and the social and financial infrastructure as we know it."[421] Here is Biggs' advice:

> Another, much smaller part of your diversification strategy should be to have a farm or a ranch somewhere far off the beaten track but which you can get to reasonably quickly and easily. Think of it as an insurance policy, and for rich people in the

---

[419] Barton Biggs, *Wealth, War and Wisdom*, (John Wiley, New York, 2008).

[420] As above, p. 331

[421] As above.

developed economies a farm is a fine diversifier and probably an excellent long-term investment. Perhaps its purchase price should amount to five percent of your net worth. The control of food-producing land is a basic instinct of mankind, and landowners seem to find considerable psychic satisfaction just from the knowledge of possession. There are few things as fulfilling as having a drink in the sunset and looking at your field and cows… You should assume the possibility of a breakdown of the civilized infrastructure. Your safe haven must be self-sufficient and capable of growing some kind of food. It should be well-stocked with seed, fertilizer, canned food, wine, medicine, clothes, etc. Think Swiss Family Robinson. Even in America and Europe there could be moments of riot and rebellion when law and order temporarily breaks down. A few rounds over the approaching brigand's heads would probably be a compelling persuader that there are easier farms to pillage. Brigands tend to be cowards.[422]

This sensible "survivalist" or "prepper" attitude can be contrasted with the generally less-than-prepared position of most characters in apocalypse movies, especially those dealing with the zombie apocalypse. Of course, the unrealistic attitudes, carelessness, stupidity and screw-ups in many such films is necessary to create dramatic tension and viewer interest. Nevertheless, it is still valid to study film to examine what survivalist lessons can be learnt from the general folly of these characters.

For example, the film *The Road* (2009) tells the story of a man and his son trying to survive in a post-apocalyptic world, as they journey along a road/roads, to the coast to hopefully find a more sustainable place. This is likely to be a nuclear winter world: cold, grey and dying. The man, narrating at the beginning of the film says: "The clock stopped at 1:17. There was a long shear of bright light then a series of low concussions." Tramping on he then laments:

---

[422]   As above, pp. 332-333.

each day is more grey than the one before… it is cold and growing colder… [as] the world slowly dies… no animals have survived. All the crops are long gone. Soon all the trees in the world will fall.

Such is the savagery of nuclear winter.

We ignore the logical point that in such a devastated world, humans outside of underground high-tech facilities would not be likely to survive. The man, has a revolver, but only two bullets, one to kill his son and one for himself, in the worst-case scenario that they are cornered by cannibals. A flash-back to a scene with his late wife indicates that they never prepared for catastrophe; they did not stockpile guns, ammunition and food, so consequently they lived in fear of becoming food themselves for cannibals as they slowly starved. Formerly, he and his wife lived in a comfortable suburban home and enjoyed art, culture and sex. But, a flash-back indicates that the man's wife was not too keen about enduring in a post-apocalyptic world: tired of living, she walks out from the house to die in the cold of the night (her body to be eaten by cannibals), or to be gang raped and *then* eaten by cannibals. The wife contrasts with another wife seen at the end of the film who has two children, a husband and a dog. This group takes the man's boy after the man dies of blood poisoning from an arrow fired at him by an attacker, armed with a crossbow, fired from the second story of a house, in one of the man's many mistakes. The classic foul-up was the scene where the man and the son reach the coast with a cart which they have, luckily enough, been able to fill with food, scavenged from someone's survival stockpile. The pair see a wrecked ship, a little way out to sea. The man leaves his son (who has a fever), on the beach with the food cart while he strips off, and naked swims out to the ship to see what he can find. But all that he finds in the ship is a flare gun with only one round. However, the man comes back to find that someone has stolen the cart while the sick son slept; fortunately, he wasn't raped and/or throat-cut. The man is deeply angry about this, and having his clothes still left, manages to catch up with the thief, a poor old black guy who has, as his sole weapon, a carving knife. The man, under protest from his son, takes back the cart and makes the thief strip, and leaves him naked in Post Apocalyptica, to freeze to death.

The Road is a story of survivalist mistakes by an ordinary person who more by good luck than good management, initially survives a catastrophe. It is likely that the world has experienced an all-out nuclear war but not an *On the Beach* (1959) type of die-off. The man regularly coughs blood, which may be due to respiratory disease; he has no other visible symptoms of radiation poisoning, and nor does the son. Nuclear war survival preparation skills could have been acquired before the catastrophe from books such as Bruce D. Clayton's *Life after Doomsday*;[423] Cresson H. Kearny, *Nuclear War Survival Skills*[424]and Dick Couch, *The U.S. Armed Forces Nuclear, Biological and Chemical Survival Manual*.[425] At an absolute minimum, more revolver ammunition could have been obtained with just a little bit less of the pre-apocalypse good life. Even a Ruger 10/22 with a wheelbarrow load of bricks of bullets would have been better than a revolver with only two rounds. Going up a few prepper levels, if a more secure retreat was obtained before the catastrophe and stockpiled with guns, ammunition, other weapons and provisions (especially long-life food) and seeds, then the journey would not have been needed in the first place. One could have sat back and greeted human extinction in comfort.

Likewise, in the film *The Day* (2011), a party of five survivors in the same grey post-apocalyptic world as *The Road*, seek refuge in a decaying farmhouse as they prepare to battle a ZMB band of roaming cannibals who want them as fresh meat. The survivors are better armed than the man in *The Road*, having shotguns, what looks like a Mini-14, an AK-47 and a M1A1 battle rifle, a couple of combat knives, an axe, but a very limited supply of ammo. Genuine survivalists would have done their best to avoid being in this situation in the first place.

---

[423] Bruce D. Clayton, *Life After Doomsday: A Survivalist Guide to Nuclear War and Other Major Disasters* (Paladin Press, Boulder, 1992).

[424] Cresson H. Kearny, *Nuclear War Survival Skills* (Updated and expanded, 1987 edition), at http://www.oism.org/nwss/s73p904.htm.

[425] Dick Couch, *The U.S. Armed Forces Nuclear, Biological and Chemical Survival Manual* (Basic Books, New York, 2003).

Amc's *The Walking Dead* derives its drama, suspense and entertainment value primarily from mistakes. Indeed, in episode 5, season 2 ("Chupacabra"), after an initial meeting with Hershel, the former veterinarian and farmer expresses amazement that Rick's motley band of survivors have made it this far. These are folk who (for a few seasons) avoid picking up military assault weapons (that seem to be everywhere around dead soldiers), but who risk zombification in season 1 by going back to Atlanta's CBD to recover a bag of shotguns and bolt action rifles. Zombies and MZB (such as the band of thugs Daryl had joined, the "Claimers," led by Joe) always sneak up on them because no guards are posted, or if they are, they are "blind," or, as in the case of episode 8, season 6, they walk or drive right into a trap. Thus, Daryl, Abraham and Sasha take a truck, which no doubt belongs to a band of bad guys, members of which they have just fought, and merrily drive along the road, right into a road block by warlord Negan's band of MZB, saved only by Daryl's "convenient" rocket launcher. And, way back in season 1, the group has an enjoyable dinner with plenty of wine and no guard; Amy needs to do a cute pee and is the first to get her throat torn open by a party-crashing zombie, toilet paper tragically in her hand. Zombies overran Hershel's farmhouse in season 2 and the group drives around in cars trying to shoot them, Hershel having a pump action shotgun with endless rounds. There was, again, no fortification, or thought of just fleeing the horde, and coming back later.

Heading to the prison definitely had many security advantages for team Rick,[426] but it is debatable whether there would be enough farmland (water seemed to come from a stream) for a long-term survival via agriculture. Further, the prison's wire mesh fences ultimately started to fall apart. There was no attempt made at further perimeter fortification, using nearby trees. In fact, a belt of trees surrounding the prison gave cover to the Governor in season 4 to sneak right up to the prison perimeter and capture Hershel and Michonne who were burning the dead. Later, after this warning of

---

[426] See Angry Vikingman, "Prison: Fortress or Folly?" At http://web.archive.org/web/20140420060601/http://www.zombiesarecoming.com/2012/08/01/prison-fortress-or-folly/.

imminent attack, the Governor and his gang plus a tank are able again to come right up to the prison perimeter fence. Then the tank driver leans outside of the tank, an easy target for a sniper. But, no shot comes, although Rick's son Carl contemplates it. Rick delivers a speech about us all living together, though they have seen from the battles of season 3 the Governor is a psychopath even by raised-bar psychiatric standards of Post Apocalyptica.

Better yet, in season 4 and 5, team Rick enter "Sanctuary" (a place advertised by signs saying that it offered refuge: believe everything you read), but this time make a small security concession of burying some of their guns, just in case it is a trap. Good – but wouldn't you leave at least one good fighter outside just in case Sanctuary was really populated by a band of cannibals and everybody got trapped? It seems that team Rick are slow learners because in season 6, episode 2, ("Just Survive Anyhow" (2015)) Rick, now at the Alexandria Safe Zone (which is anything but safe), takes all of his fighters, except Carol, to drive a herd of walkers away from Alexandria (what stops them from eventually wandering back?). While they are doing this, Alexandria is attacked by the "Wolves," a group of gunless, melee weapon-wielding (knives, machetes, sharpened sticks etc.), hacking, hyper-psycho-MZB, and a group with a surprisingly large number of women, perhaps former Women's Studies or sociology/cultural studies graduates. Carol, the only good fighter there, is baking a casserole and is not on combat alert until the hacking begins. She doesn't even have an assault rifle (the rifles seem to be M4A1s) with her, although she has a handgun with limited ammo. So – leave a group of defenceless people, a group about which Rick has said *ad nauseam*, can't fight – alone, while conducting a mission that would be difficult to do with sheep, let alone the walking dead: go figure.

As for plans, Team Rick in episode 8, season 6 ("Start to Finish"), plan to escape a house that is surrounded by zombies by using a tried and proven method of camouflaging themselves with zombie guts. Fine, but somehow, they forget about a little boy Sam, who is scared shitless by "monsters," and they fail to even cover his head, as they did with the baby, Judith. He, of course, says "mom" right in the middle

of a big crowd of zombie shoppers. But, that's show business. Oh…
then in the next episode, "No Way Out," (2016, season 6, episode 9),
the continuity problem occurs of him not saying "mom" at that time
at all. Rather, although the team start walking with their zombie guts
suits in daylight, by nightfall, the kid is freaking out, taking all day
to walk a few meters, leading to him to then speak and getting eaten
by zombies, and his mom (Jessie) freaking out, and getting eaten
by even more zombies, and the older brother (Ron), freaking out,
and aiming his gun at Rick, and Michonne skewering him with her
katana, leading to his gun going off (which wouldn't have happened
if she beheaded him) and taking out Carl's eye with a dying shot.
The foolishness of it all would lead a real survivalist to eating the TV
remote, or not watch at all.

And then there is Morgan, a born-again Buddhist-style pacifist
(complete with quarterstaff), who previously was outrightly crazy
(e.g. season 3, episode 12, "Clear" involving ritualistic burning of
walkers), but now thinks that all human life is to be saved, due to
his meeting with Eastman (season 6, episode 4, "Here's Not Here"),
a former forensic psychiatrist, turned mystic via the martial art of
Aikido. Yes, a psycho has the luck of running into a professional
who specialized in treating people just like him. He aids Morgan
in recovering from his PTSD madness through use of, among
other things, jō staff-katas/forms, and Morihei Ueshiba's Aikido
philosophy. Thus, while the Wolves are running around Alexandria
hacking people to death, he wastes valuable time binding up Wolves
that he has captured, much like a spider. His pacifist sins of omission
kill people "just as dead" as if he shot them himself. Paradoxically,
his attitude of "all life is precious" does not extend to the living dead;
dead they may be as ordinary humans, but walkers seem to have
interests (eating people), and can "die another day."

Morgan's philosophically incoherent pacifism leads to him letting
a group of Wolves escape, one of which, red-headed and wearing
a battered blue denim jacket, picks up a gun and in a real zom poc
would have ended his Buddhism with a bullet (even though Morgan
had a holstered gun, which he made no attempt to draw). Then in

the very next episode, season 6, episode 3, "Thank You," that same MZB uses that gun to almost kill Rick, who is parked in his recreation vehicle, with the doors conveniently unlocked and oblivious to possible attacks, even though he is aware that Alexandria is under attack and the whole area is teeming with walkers. And it gets even kookier, where in episode 8, season 6, Morgan defends his captured "Wolf" from Carol who is seeking to kill him, leading to them both getting knocked out and the Wolf getting a gun. The Wolf knocks out Morgan, who has just knocked out Carol, and then puts a knife to Denise's throat, hostage-siege-style. Tara and Rosita come, and although they could easily shoot this crazy, decide to lay down their guns at the command of the Wolf with just a knife, so that the Wolf gets a gun (oddly leaving the rest of the guns), and makes off with Denise as a hostage! Any psycho killer worth his meds would have put them all out of their politically correct misery, then and there. This gets my vote for the most stupid scene ever to appear in an action film, and Carol in any case shoots this Wolf in the mid-season premiere, "No Way Out" (season 6, episode 9), so it is all for nothing. Yet, the episode, despite being ridiculous, was entertaining, once, like with superhero movies, belief is suspended, and one believes in fairies. Or zombies.

Finally, should one mention that in season 6, episode 1, ("First Time Again" (2015)), Morgan, who is wiping zombie-goo off of his quarterstaff, takes baby Judith to hold without washing his hands, and makes skin contact with her hands, as if a baby is not going to suck or lick her hands? In fact, although walker bites are deadly, the characters are seemingly swimming in zombie goo and blood almost every episode, yet never get infected. Apparently, they don't have cuts and cracks on their skin.

And, we shouldn't be too hard on team Rick in the dumb decision category in the light of all of the above. In season 6, episode 10 ("The Next World" (2016)), Rick and Daryl go on a scavenging mission, as everyone is getting pretty hungry – Rick is seen in one scene putting a new hole in his belt. The pair find a truck loaded with goodies, which miracle after miracle, has gas to go. But, rather than getting the goods home fast, as common sense would dictate, they decide to go on a frolic after more goods, and after meeting new character "Jesus," in a Benny Hillesque chase, lose it all, as the truck takes a swim in a lake.

Only the script writers save team Rick from oblivion each episode, and in the end, the supposed death episode where Rick leaves the series (season 9, episode 5, "What Comes After," November 4, 2018), Rick's "death" while blowing up a bridge is not a real death, since he is whisked away by helicopter to start in a movie versions of *The Walking Dead*, may the Gods help us. Yet in a real zombie apocalypse, the one we are now going into, we need to do better. None of *The Walking Dead* characters would have enough street wisdom to survive a real collapse situation, for even a day. To get the ball rolling we start with some considerations about the philosophy of survivalism; for we all love the smell of (burning) philosophy in the morning.

The Philosophy of Survivalism

Some of the politically inclined have expressed opposition to survivalist ideas and its core philosophy, even while accepting that a collapse of techno-industrial civilization is coming. American ecological writer and former Grand Archdruid of the Ancient Order of Druids in America, John Michael Greer, has been critical of survivalism in his books *The Long Descent: A User's Guide to the End of the Industrial Age*[427] and *The Ecotechnic Future: Envisioning a Post-Peak World*[428] and other writings. As a caveat, Greer's more recent book *Dark Age America*,[429] is more along the lines of this present work being more pessimistic than his previous works in this genre.

---

[427]   John Michael Greer, *The Long Descent: A User's Guide to the End of the Industrial Age* (New Society Publishers, Gabriola Island, 2008).

[428]   John Michael Greer, *The Ecotechnic Future: Envisioning a Post-Peak World* (New Society Publishers, Gabriola Island, 2009), and *Not the Future We Ordered: Peak Oil, Psychology, and the Myth of Progress* (Karnac Books, London, 2013). Further references to this note are to *The Ecotechnic Future*.

[429]   J. M. Greer, *Dark Age America: Climate Change, Cultural Collapse, and the Hard Future Ahead* (New Society Publishers, Gabriola Island, 2016).

Greer starts from the plausible enough position that at this point "it's almost certainly too late to manage a transition to sustainability on a global or national scale, even if the political will to attempt it existed – which clearly it does not." Consequently, "we are headed at breakneck pace toward a future of narrowing options, dwindling resources and faltering technology." For Greer, there will be no crash or a massive catastrophe, but rather a gradual process of decline, a "slide down statistical curves that will ease modern industrial civilization into history's dumpster." This process of decline and fall will take between one to three centuries and end in a Dark Age.

The West will be subject to epic migrations (or invasions) as the industrial age ends and military forces dependent on fossil fuels, fail. Mass migration will occur by sea and will result in the English language itself "only [being]spoken in a few enclaves in the Pacific Northwest."

The *Mad Max/Road Warrior* society scenario is dismissed by Greer, even though the very thesis of *The Long Descent* is that in the long march to a Dark Age most of the technology and knowledge of today will be lost. But, he also inconsistently says that even if a mass die-off of humanity occurred the survivors could still use today's culture and resource base, and before long the internet would be working! He also says: "Everyone alive after the collapse would have grown up in the pre-collapse world and learned the skills needed to operate a modern society." This is certainly wrong because a society of the technical sophistication and complexity of ours requires millions of specialized technicians to function and after the death of these technicians, society grinds to a halt, as has been said previously. Most people lack the skills and know-how to be able to repair even relatively simple electronic or mechanical devices, or even light a fire using only sticks.[430]

Greer has a comic book view of survivalists as generally lone madmen hiding in a cabin in the woods with stockpiles of food and firearms, while the outside world burns. This is the same view held

---

[430] Lewis Dartnell, *The Knowledge: How to Rebuild our World from Scratch* (The Bodley Head, London, 2014); Leonard Read, "I, Pencil," *The Freeman*, December 1958.

by the founder of the transition town initiative, Rob Hopkins, who believes that cities such as the mega-developed Sunshine Coast, Queensland, can make a transition away from fossil fuel use and become sustainable ecocities.[431] No, they are not pulling our greens. Greer criticizes survivalists for believing in the myth of apocalypse, but the real myth-makers are those who believe such communitarian fairy tales. A few people planting "community gardens" and holding hands and chanting, or praying, does not a revolution make. Nevertheless, the opposition to survivalism is made clear by Hopkins in his article "Why the Survivalists Have Got it Wrong,"[432] which makes the misguided critique that survivalists seek to live in isolation while, "peak oil and climate change, and the challenge that they present, are a call to return to society" and that most beloved of entities, "community." All of this assumes, of course, that a *Mad Max/ Road Warrior* die-off situation will not occur, and that a rapid collapse is not going to happen, assumptions which we have seen are questionable.

Greer also makes specific and weak criticisms of survivalism: "Isolated survivalist enclaves with stockpiles of food and ammunition would be a tempting prize and could count on being targeted" by roaming brigands. That, of course is if they find them. Perhaps the attention of these roaming gangs will be taken up targeting the anti-weapon "communities" who have plenty of food, but no guns and no will to resist. *The Walking Dead* TV series gives good examples of this, especially Alexandria. To this challenge it could be said: "However many you kill, there will always be more – and eventually your ammo will run out." All the more need for truly massive stockpiles of guns and ammo and the use of melee weapons, going medieval, using weapons that won't run out, as will be discussed later in book 2. Call it "sustainability."

---

[431]   Rob Hopkins, *The Transition Handbook: Creating Local Sustainable Communities Beyond Oil Dependency* (Finch Publishing, Sydney, 2009), p. 79, and p. 224.

[432]   Rob Hopkins "Why the Survivalists Have Got it Wrong," September 4, 2006 at http://transitionculture.org/2006/09/04/why-the-survivalists-have-got-it-wrong. The article is a response to Zachary Nowak, "Preparing for a Crash: Nuts and Bolts," *Energy Bulletin*, at http://www.resilience.org/stories/2006-08-31/preparing-crash-nuts-and-bolts.

Hopkins says that survivalism is a distinctly anti-social and irresponsible creed. However, the survivalist movement has never strictly been about *lone* people or even *isolated* families preparing for disaster in all its forms and retreating to safer ground.[433] Safety in numbers, as far as that is possible, is accepted by survivalists. Survivalists though, by contrast to back-to-the-landers, (deep) ecologists, and preparedness retreaters, are robust and rugged individualists who are ready, willing and able to go it alone if necessary, come what may, even if the sewers of hell are opened and flood the earth. The spirit of self-reliance, self-sufficiency, independence and overall toughness, is repugnant to both the socialized communitarian Left and the globalized economic Right. Survivalism is about raising a defiant "rude finger" up to the Establishment's modernist way of life, that of urban helplessness and dependence upon the crusty teat of Big Sister, the modern boss of Big Brother.

Kurt Saxon, who coined the term *survivalist*,[434] also notes that survivalists, generally unlike back-to-the-landers, (deep) ecologists and preparedness retreaters, are ready, willing and able to fight if necessary, because self-protection is taken to be a primary component of self-reliance.[435] Kurt Saxon was not anti-community by the way; because of insurmountable problems of the future survival in cities, he thought that the most reasonable survival strategy was for people wanting to live, to get out of the cities and head to small rural towns and "become part of community."[436]

Rawlesian survivalists, followers of the survival philosophy of James Wesley, (comma intentional) Rawles,[437] although also

[433] Meg Raven, "What is Survivalism?" At http://www.aussurvivalist.com/whatissurvivalismmeg.htm; Douglas Good, "What is Survivalism?" at http://www.aussurvivalist.com/whatissurvivalismgood.htm.

[434] "Survivalism," at http://en.wikipedia.org/wiki/Survivalism.

[435] Kurt Saxon, "What is a Survivalist? (1980), at http://www.aussurvivalist.com/whatissurvivalismsaxon.htm.

[436] As above.

[437] James Wesley, Rawles, *How to Survive the End of the World as we Know It*, (Plume/Penguin Books, New York, 2009); "Precepts of Rawlesian Survivalist Philosophy," at http://

concerned with self-defense, believe that survivalists by stockpiling resources are in a position during a crisis to dispense charity to people in need; hardly an anti-social and irresponsible creed, contrary to Hopkins. Rawles sees it as practical Christianity in action. My view of Christianity is detailed in the next book, and it has no monopoly on kindness and charity.

In a debate/dialogue with Richard Heinberg, Hopkins was asked whether a focus on emergency planning should be made just in case dire things happen during the "transition."[438] Hopkins response was that "in terms of visioning, there isn't a positive potential outcome to use to inspire and engage people. Transition is very deliberately designed to be non-threatening, to be inviting and engaging."[439] A vision of collapse preparations could make the movement look like a "survivalist cult" – a politically incorrect fate-worse-than-death. However, just when it seems that all hope is lost, Hopkins says that there is merit in putting together bushcraft training, bioregional studies, biointensive horticulture, traditional allotment gardening and emergency response organisation.[440] Even in terms of "positive thinking," as Peter Sandman has said, it is calming for people to prepare, giving a sense of control which builds confidence and hopefully gives a greater capacity to cope with fear.[441]

Chris Martenson in *The Crash Course*, argues that personal preparation is not selfish because it is one less person drawing on community resources, so putting one's survival affairs in order, is the best thing an individual can do for the community:

---

www.survivalblog.com/precepts.html.

[438] Richard Heinberg and Rob Hopkins, "To Plan for Emergency, or Not? Heinberg and Hopkins Debate," May 28, 2009, at http://www.postcarbon.org/article/40535-to-plan-for-emergency-or-not.

[439] As above.

[440] As above.

[441] Peter Sandman, "The Government is Preparing for the Worst While Hoping for the Best – Now it Needs to Tell the Public to do the Same Thing," at http://www.psandman.com/col/WashPost.htm.

If you do, you'll have a stable foundation to utilize, and you'll be in a better position to add valuable resources and skills to community efforts. A strong community begins with strong household.[442]

Surviving the Zombie Apocalypse 101: The Coming Collapse of Civilization

Apart from a number of excellent books dealing explicitly with the zombie apocalypse,[443] where zombies are conceived as the living/walking dead, little has been written about surviving the coming collapse of civilization, the multi-generational scenario.

Christ Lisle, a former US Army Ranger in an often cited online article "Prepare for Peak Oil on a Budget,"[444] saw peak oil leading to billions of people dying and leaving large quantities of stuff behind. He adopted a minimalist approach and recommended not buying survival items (bar one item), but that one should "pick up off the ground when others leave it behind." For many lacking wilderness survival skills, such a minimalist approach could guarantee a place among the billions dying. Nevertheless, Lisle recommends purchasing a high-quality synthetic (not down) sleeping bag, rated down to -20 C. The synthetic bag, unlike the down, can still keep you warm when wet, and is a "mobile shelter." Lisle said:

> I've slept comfortably in the snowy Italian Alps and Alaska with no fire, no tent, and no ground pad – all I had was a good sleeping bag. I've spent many nights outside, and I am here to say that a

---

[442] Chris Martenson, *The Crash Course: The Unsustainable Future of Our Economy, Energy and Environment* (John Wiley and Sons, New Jersey, 2011), pp. 258-259.

[443] See: Max Brooks, *The Zombie Survival Guide: Complete Protection from the Living Dead* (Three Rivers Press, New York, 2003); Roger Ma, *The Zombie Combat Manual: A Guide to Fighting the Living Dead* (Berkley Books, New York, 2010).

[444] Chris Lisle, "Prepare for Peak Oil on a Budget," at http://ebookbrowse.com/how-to-plan-for-peak-oil-on-a-limited-budget-pdf-d230019877.

good sleeping bag can keep you cosy warm in any climate under any conditions, be it rain, sleet or snow.

Well, maybe, but a tarp, ground sheet and tent/swag would be an improvement – and why not treat yourself, for this is TEOTWAWKI! Put a good synthetic sleeping bag on the shopping list, and if you haven't got one, get one soon. Or, buy two.

James Ballou's *Long-Term Survival in the Coming Dark Age*[445] is an excellent introduction to new Dark Age collapseology. The foreword is by Ragnar Benson, a leading survivalist author. Neither Ballou nor Benson speculate about the most likely cause of The Great Collapse and the book plunges straight into strategies and tactics for long-term survival. Long-term survival differs from shorter-term disaster preparedness insofar as there is going to be nobody coming to rescue you because there is *no rescue*. All has been lost. Cites will become "violent slum areas for the most part plagued with disease,"[446] as with no government and no government support services, human waste, and human violence will not be contained. Hence, there is a need to retreat/bug out from cites to rural areas, and ultimately live much simpler lives, with tribal living for protection. There will be stalking, killing and butchering game (what is left) for meat, along with gathering wild foods, with horticulture and agriculture the main food sources. Until, or while, such practices are being put in place, short-term survival will be by drawing on food stockpiles, accumulated before the Great Collapse.

Ballou's book discusses bugging out (also discussed below[447]), but the most important sections of the book deal with life in the post-collapse world. Pre-collapse there is an urgent need for people to acquire extensive self-defence skills (with firearms and other weapons) as well as practical skills e.g. medicine over arts, blacksmithing over the humanities, mathematics and philosophy,

---

[445] James Ballou, *Long-Term Survival in the Coming Dark Age: Preparing to Live After Society Crumbles* (Paladin Press, Boulder, Colorado, 2007).

[446] As above, p. 3.

[447] See James Ballou, *The Poorman's Wilderness Survival Kit: Assembling Your Emergency Gear for Little or No Money* (Paladin Press, Boulder, Colorado, 2013).

woodworking skills over law. The world of paper and computer work, the world of talking, chattering and whinging, will be replaced by a practical, hands-on, can-do world – or death. A survival workshop, using hand tools as was done in the 19th century, needs to be established at one's retreat, and I will discuss the issue of tools later in this chapter.[448] Survivors will recycle and salvage everything, because as Chris Lisle noted, the great die off of the bulk of humanity will leave a mountains of resources (e.g. scrap metal, timber and other materials) that can be used by salvaging parties, once the formerly-populated areas are no longer a disease and security threat. Nevertheless, the consumer society itself supplies many useful items that people throw away each day, such as containers to use for storage during the Dark Age. Rubbish dumps are a source for scrap timber and building materials which can be scavenged from the trash.[449] Indeed – on "hard rubbish days," consumers throw out great treasures for scroungers, such as old tools and scrap material that could be used for clothing. And, taking clothing as an example, in the "short-term," for about 50 years, I estimate, stockpiled clothing and clothes made from stored cloth and scavenged materials will sustain the survivors, but in the longer-term clothes and footwear will need to be made first hand from fibers, animal hides and leather.

Ballou's *Long-Term Survival in the Coming Dark Age*, and related books, are a useful starting point for one's survival framework of knowledge. I suggest that it can be supplemented by further books and information organized under the following topics:

1. Bug out and survival retreats.
2. Wilderness and backwoods survival philosophy.
3. Disaster preparedness philosophy.
4. Self-reliance and self-sufficiency philosophy.
5. Tools and the craftsman.
6. Zombie apocalypse preparation and survival philosophy.

---

[448] See further James Ballou, *Makeshift Workshop Skills for Survival and Self-Reliance* (Paladin Press, Boulder, Colorado, 2009) and *More Makeshift Workshop Skills* (Paladin Press, Boulder, Colorado, 2011).

[449] As above, p. 68.

Bug Out and Survival Retreats

Although some survivalists believe that urban survival is possible in situations of much less severity than a collapse, in general, survivalists such as Ragnar Benson, Bruce D. Clayton, Jeff Cooper, Cresson Kearny, James Wesley Rawles, Kurt Saxon, Joel Skousen and Mel Tappan, have favoured bug-out locations (BOLS) or survival retreats.[450]

Piero San Giorgio in *Survive the Economic Collapse*,[451] writes of the need to find a "Sustainable Autonomous Base" (SAB), a "secure space" with "rootedness, autonomy, permanence," "where one cannot merely survive, but hopefully thrive, living perhaps more simply, but well."[452] SAB is based on seven fundamental principles discussed in their own chapters in his book and are (1) water; (2) food; (3) hygiene and health; (4) energy: (5) knowledge; (6) defense and (7) the social band, creating a tribe (a genuine "community" rather than a socialist hippy commune) for genetic and socio-cultural reproduction. Some of the basic aspects of the SAB will be discussed in this chapter and in this book.

Mel Tappan in *Tappan on Survival*[453] argued that population density is a major factor in choosing a retreat because retreats less than a tank of gas away from population centers face the real risk of being overrun by systems-dependent people. Apart from the problems of hungry mobs and roaming bands of looters, there is the problem of disease. Tappan listed other factors affecting retreat locations such as whether nuclear power plants are in the vicinity (in case they are abandoned and not shut down and go into meltdown). Locating near military bases or National Guard armories may prove problematic, in case the troops ultimately decide to be the new warlords in a collapse, or maybe worse, they desert to be with their

---

[450] "Retreat (Survivalism)," https://en.wikipedia.org/wiki/Retreat_(survivalism);" Ragnar Benson, *The Modern Survival Retreat: A New and Vital Approach to Retreat Theory and Practice* (Paladin Press, Boulder, Colorado, 1998).

[451] Piero San Giorgio, *Survive the Economic Collapse: A Practical Guide* (Radix/Washington Summit Publishers, Whitefish, 2013).

[452] As above, p. 250.

[453] Mel Tappan, *Tappan on Survival* (Janus Press, Rogue River, 1981).

families leaving the ghouls and associated scum to feast on highly destructive weapons that will ultimately be unleashed against you.

Nuclear war targets are also another matter of concern. Radiation fallout patterns need to be considered. The site also needs to be farmable with good soil and water, and ideally hunting, trapping and or fishing should be available. It is a matter though of trade-offs and balancing factors in decision making, and single-family retreats were not regarded by Tappan as desirable given that if the retreats are found by looters, the superior force will win. Thus, he believed that long-term survival in a post-collapse world, especially in the light of the problem of facing organized gangs of vicious looter, murders, rapists and cannibals—MZBS—would come from living in a small rural community up to about a population of 5,000 people, engaged primarily in agriculture, not industry.

Tappan felt, and I agree with him, that many people think that they can live, say, in a city and work, and when really stinky, lumpy excreta hits the fan, bug out to their retreat, just in the nick of time. The series *Doomsday Preppers* was full of these feet-in-both-camps bug out types. He said that there may be no clear warning at all and unless one is already living at one's retreat, the odds are that one will never reach it. Living in such a "community" (that word again) has clear advantages over bug out options such as boat or mobile land retreats or isolated wilderness retreats, insofar as it is no longer necessary to guess correctly when the collapse will occur (the timing-problem) and it avoids the problems and dangers of bugging out travel e.g. safely getting to your retreat though the "zombies." It also means that there is adequate time to prepare for the post-collapse world, stockpiling food, clothing, tools, seeds, firearms, ammunition, bladed and bludgeon melee weapons and other supplies. There is time to settle into the "community" and perhaps when confidences and trust are reached, begin preparing defenses ready for when TSHTF.

It takes considerable time to convert an existing farm into a self-reliant post-apocalypse retreat, so having as much lead time as possible before the end is important. For example, it may take a number of years to get fruit trees and crops established. The last thing that a survivalist wants is to be in a post-apocalyptic situation and find crop failure (because of pests, diseases or personal incompetence), or find that soils are lacking in fertility. That is not the time to fail. Rick and co, in one edition of the graphic novel *The Walking Dead*, after fighting zombies for about two years, find that their tin food supply is starting to run out and he thinks it is time to find seeds and grow crops. The folk at Alexandria in AMC's *The Walking Dead*, season 6, episode 2, are also beginning a vegetable garden, at a time also of around two years into Post Apocalyptica, and only have it flourishing in season 9. Good luck fictional folks, you'll need it. In reality all of them would have starved to death long ago.

Fernando "Ferfal" Aguirre in his excellent book *The Modern Survival Manual*,[454] has presented a survival treatise based on his first-hand experience of living through the 2001 economic collapse in Argentina. He differs from survivalists such as Tappan and Saxon in being critical of the approach of retreating to the country side.[455] Aguirre argues against this based on surviving Argentina's economic collapse. He sees governments surviving and coming to the countryside to confiscate food. As well, most people can't bug out and live off the land given large population numbers, so they will stay in cities. A similar position has been taken by "Survival Mom."[456] And isn't "Mom" always right? Well, no.

To this much can be said in reply, due respect to motherhood and all that. It is true that governments may survive a partial economic collapse as Argentina periodically has done, but a complete collapse where the army and police do not get paid and hence desert their posts, is one where the government *does not survive*. Further, there is no reason why, if a government survives, it won't confiscate food from people *in* the city: it has and will. Season 1 of *Fear the Walking*

---

[454] Fernando "Ferfal" Aguirre, *The Modern Survival Manual: Surviving the Economic Collapse* (The Author, 2009).

[455] "4 Things Doom-And-Gloomers Got Totally Wrong," June 2, 2014, at http://ferfal. blogspot.com.au/2014/06/4-things-doom-and-gloomers-got-totally.html.

[456] Survival Mom, "13 Reasons a Rural Retreat May Not be the Safe Refuge You Might Think," September 26, 2015, at http://thesurvivalmom.com/rural-survival-retreats-not-safe-refuge/.

Dead gives a dramatic illustration of this with the US Army becoming essentially a barbarian gang. Further, as described in *The Modern Survival Manual*, cities become highly dangerous places during an economic collapse, with gangs conducting block-by-block home invasions, and although violent crime in the US had gone down in the past few years, 2019 has seen a surge of homicides in several US cities, with some cities' homicide rates, such as Baltimore's, "exploding."[457]

Thus, almost everywhere becomes dangerous in a collapse, but the larger number of people in the city makes the probability of attack greater than in the country. Those considerations are based solely on an economic collapse scenario, and consideration of pandemic disease spread makes a general case against city-based survivalism, although, of course, circumstances could dictate otherwise if terrorists decided to attack rural areas first. The terrorist group Boko Haram, for example, has attacked rural targets in Nigeria, (killing 86 people in late January, 2016, with children being burnt alive), but most of its attention has been on city targets, such as with its bombing of the United Nations office in Abuja. Ferfal in his book does not consider the possibility of a more general collapse involving ecological variables, as discussed here and in Piero San Giorgio's equally as admirable treatise *Survive the Economic Collapse*.

While Ferfal is critical of "off grid," presumably isolationist survivalism, he does say:

> I recommend basically what I later learned Mel Tappan recommended as well: live in a small town or community. This community or subdivision should be close enough to a moderately-sized city with enough job opportunities, education and entertainment.[458]

However, there can be a case made even for isolationist survivalism in the classic lone family/tribe or even individual sense. A global

---

[457] https://www.usatoday.com/story/news/2018/02/19/homicides-toll-big-u-s-cities-2017/302763002/, J. LaFond and J. J. Bowie, *Letters from the Fall; Civilization Decomposes* (Independently Published, April 18, 2019).

[458] Aguirre, as above, p. 37.

pandemic, a "zombie apocalypse" disease of a flu with a high mortality, will spread quickly in a large city where people live like hens in a chicken coop. A small town could more easily practice quarantine and an isolated doomster essentially exists in perpetual quarantine. Consequently, context decides everything; in some desperate survival situations, there is merit even in an isolationist approach. Certainly, in a classic *The Walking Dead* zombie apocalypse, where even in a small town an infection could occur, isolation, like silence would be golden.[459] And it can be done—Soichi Yokio, a Japanese WW II solider who refused to surrender after the end of the war, lived in a cave in the jungles of Guam from 1945-1972—alone, and with much less resources than we have.[460]

There is a large quantity of literature available about bug out locations for the United States, Canada, Europe, New Zealand and Australia, but relatively less for Asia, and South America.[461] Joel M. Skousen has published respected books in this field, including *Strategic Relocation: North American Guide to Safe Places*,[462] which in its third edition gives a comprehensive guide to the threats that North Americans and Canadians face, from economic collapse to nuclear war, with associated strategic analyses. For example, there are considerations of the most dangerous areas for earthquakes, the top ten most economical US states to live in, and states with no sales tax and so on. Skousen also offers paid consultation for those seeking special contingency retreat plans.[463] Joel Skousen has also published *The Secure Home*,[464] which tells you how to construct high security, fortified retreats, both in terms of construction of such retreats as

---

[459] For a general discussion and criticism of alleged problems with the American redoubt concept see, "The Problem with the American Redoubt Concept," December 24, 2014, at http://ferfal.blogspot.com.au/2014/12/the-problem-with-american-redoubt.html.

[460] C. Nyergen, "Thirty Years in the Jungle! Could You do It?" At www.primitiveways.com/jungle_30_years.html.

[461] "Survivalist Retreat," at http://www.conservapedia.com/Survivalist_retreat.

[462] Joel Skousen, *Strategic Relocation: North American Guide to Safe Places*, 3rd edition, (Joel Skousen Designs, 2011).

[463] See http://www.joelskousen.com; joel@joelskousen.com.

[464] Joel Skousen, *The Secure Home*, 3rd edition, (Swift, 1999).

well as remodelling existing retreats. He has also produced Special Reports, such as *How to Implement High Security Shelter in the Home* (1996)[465] and *How to Fortify a Closet*, for those on a budget who cannot afford to build a vault room.

James Wesley, Rawles has published the excellent *Rawles on Retreats and Relocation*[466] and there is some discussion of retreatism in his survivalist novel, *Patriots: A Novel of Survival in the Coming Collapse*,[467] although a more detailed discussion is given on the fortification of retreats, reinforcing houses, constructing anti-vehicular ditches, obstacles, and so on. Of course the ballistically-protected house can also integrate a fallout shelter as well. Rawles' Survival Blog.com has a superb discussion of recommended retreat areas in North America, favouring Idaho, Montana, Oregon, Washington and Wyoming, as the top five US retreat states, and Kalifornication as the worst. Interestingly enough, Alaska is not an ideal retreat location because although it is the US state with the lowest population density, it has the second highest crime rate of the US states per capita and most goods, even food, are transported in. Those most likely to survive are seasoned backwoodsmen and native tribal folk having outdoors skills and able to live self-sufficiently, from hunting and fishing. Much of the land is covered with ice and snow at least half of the year. By contrast, California has a mild climate and long growing seasons, but an appalling post-white socio-political climate and draconian gun control laws, massive illegal and "legal" immigration and most other factors that will make, post-collapse, California the zombie apocalypse capital of America. One contributor to SurvivalBlog.com's discussion of retreat areas said that when TSHTF in California "it will make Katrina's aftermath look like a kindergarten dance."[468]

---

[465] See http://www.joelskousen.com/Secure/reports.html.

[466] James Wesley, Rawles, *Rawles on Retreats and Relocation* (Clearwater Press, 2007).

[467] James Wesley, Rawles, *Patriots: A Novel of Survival in the Coming Collapse* (Ulysses Press, Berkeley, 2009) (4th expanded edition, originally published in 1990).

[468] See http://www.survivalblog.com/retreatareas.html

By way of summary: there is no easy answer to the question of where do you go, if anywhere, when TSHTF. Beyond generalizations, such as leaving large population centres, each person will need to make informed decisions on the basis of their own personal circumstances and what resources are available. It therefore may not be possible to follow Tappan's advice and move to an ideal location now. In Australia, there may be no ideal location at all; properties meeting the standard conditions of being an ideal survival retreat in the sense of having adequate water and good soils, could still be overrun in a type of "condition 4" doomsday zombie apocalypse (with either Hollywood zombies or your unfriendly neighbourhood types).[469] Bugging out, getting out of Dodge, always needs to be considered as a Plan B option.

A good place for beginning survivalists to start in exploring the theory and practice of bugging out is Scott B. Williams' *Bug Out: The Complete Plan for Escaping a Catastrophic Disaster before It's Too Late* (2010).[470] Williams is not primarily concerned with the situation of the "lost hiker" (although the advice in his book would clearly help such a person), but rather with shit hitting the fan and TEOTWAWKI scenarios. Fixed position survivalism is not pursued, as most people lack the financial resources to invest in a retreat, he argues. But even so, for a collapse of civilization scenario, ultimately one will need to find such a retreat to grow food. Owning the land is now ideal, but not essential in my opinion, given coming high mortality rates. One could attempt to bug out to that location post-apocalypse after the death of the masses. Williams is right in saying that there are dangers in putting all of one's resources in one location because of the difficulty in hiding and defending stockpiles. Agreed: but there will be clear limits in stockpiling resources which will be bugged out as well. What one needs, if at all possible, is a pluralistic response: a fixed, defendable position as Tappan advocated, plus resources cached securely, safely and sustainably underground, as well as

---

[469] Max Brooks, *The Zombie Survival Guide: Complete Protection from the Living Dead* (Three Rivers Press, New York, 2003), pp. 154-181.

[470] Scott B. Williams, *Bug Out: The Complete Plan for Escaping a Catastrophic Disaster before It's Too Late* (Ulysses Press, Berkeley, 2010).

putting into place a bug out procedure to deal with the worst case scenario: that is, fleeing your retreat post-collapse. Williams rightly notes that there is enough land in the US for survivalists to bug out and thrive, but not for the entire US population. But, most people are not survival-minded and will wait for Big Sister Government to save them. They will die and rot, producing epidemic disease in the cities.

Williams gives a comprehensive discussion of bug out locations right across our great and wonderful United States, and in my opinion the material is accurate. Certainly, any serious US survivalist should study this material and make up his/her own mind.[471] Williams, for example, gives a very comprehensive outline of the bugout bag, which covers the major survival bases of clothing, shelter and fire, food and water, hunting and fishing, and tools. By way of summary, the *bugout bag and clothing* comprise: an internal frame backpack, fanny pack, lightweight mesh bag, leather and Gore-Tex waterproof hiking boots to wear, river shoes, moisture wicking socks and wool outer socks, wool cap, Tilley sun hat, three bandanas, pants, long underwear, Gore-Tex rain pants, heavy-duty belt, two T-shirts, long underwear shirt, polar fleece long sleeve, Gore-Tex parka, gloves and cammo poncho. For specific survival categories:

Shelter and Fire: camping hammock, paracord, synthetic sleeping bag, disposable butane lighters, Fire Steel Scout x2, fire sticks, cotton balls soaked in Vaseline for tinder.

Food and Water: three-day supply of lifeboat rations or MREs, trail mix, protein bars/power bars, beef jerky, bag of oatmeal, seasonings, water bottles, Polar Pure water disinfectant, filter straws.

Hunting and Fishing: takedown .22 rifle, 200 rounds .22 LR ammo, .357 magnum revolver + holster + speed loaders + 100 rounds ammo, .357 lever action rifle, fishhooks and fishing line, spool of line for drop hooks, wire shares for small game.

---

[471]   As above pp. 101-269.

Tools: machete with sheath, Bowie knife, multitool, small mill file, diamond sharpener, hand-bearing compass, GPS, cooking pot, stainless-steel spoon, sewing needles [and thread].

Miscellaneous Items: include maps, insect repellent, 50+ sunblock, sunglasses and case, sailmaker's thread and needles, first-aid supplies, extractor snakebite kit, cortisone cream, Benadryl, EpiPen, Imodium, ibuprofen, field guide to edible plants in region, passport/driver's licence, cash, gold and silver coins, tooth care (tooth-brush, toothpaste/salt, dental floss), toilet paper, comb, LED torch, duct tape, gun oil, gun-cleaning tool. William also lists a number of optional items (e.g. water purification filter and reverse-osmosis desalinator).

Along with Williams' book, Fernando "Ferfal" Aguirre has produced another extremely good book which is well worth consulting: *Bugging Out and Relocating: What to Do When Staying in Not an Option.*[472] This book is a comprehensive overview of all of the main aspects of bugging out and relocating and has a sensible and balanced view of the relative advantages and disadvantages of overseas locations for relocation. The author has relocated to Ireland from Argentina (and then to Spain) because of the violence and poor quality of life in Argentina.

For my generalist purposes, the most relevant part of the bug out literature book is the discussion of the bug out bag, which one will need wherever one goes. All survivalists in the know recommend that people not buy generic survival kits but tailor a survival kit to suit their personal circumstances.[473] All items should be essential, durable and dependable, because whether the bugging out is by foot, horse or a vehicle, space and weight are principal concerns. For example, there is no point taking with one in emergency situations, survival and preparedness books. This material *must be* absorbed into your very being long before the collapse. It is what you should

---

[472] Fernando "Ferfal" Aguirre, *Bugging Out and Relocating: What to Do When Staying is Not an Option* (The Author, 2014).

[473] As above, p. 23.

be doing now. It would be insane to suppose that say, one will begin to learn how to light a campfire without matches, fire starters or any modern technology, by consulting a wilderness survival book when the time comes. Hello hyperthermia. No doubt, pages of the book would be useful for fire-starting purposes, and specialist books, such as an illustrated guide to a region's edible plants are an exception and could be taken.

The bug out bag should be rugged and easy to carry long distances – hence a backpack big enough to take "everything." And what is "everything"? Cody Lundin, an American teacher of aboriginal survival skills says that the bug out bag or survival kit "is a distillation of the most simple and effective means of staying alive. It's your lifeline in terms of need, the components within possibly being your only chance of living through your present crisis."[474] The bug out bag should therefore address fundamental human needs: (1) *shelter*, including clothing; (2) *water* and the means of purifying water; (3) the technology for making *fire*; (4) *food* and items for *cooking* it (e.g. a cast iron cooking pot, a plate, cups and utensils); (5) *clothing* to deal with a range of environments; (6) a *sleeping* system including perhaps a swag (eliminating the need for a tent) and definitely a good synthetic sleeping bag; (7) *health, medical and hygiene* beginning with a basic first aid kit and hygiene (e.g. toothpaste or even salt, toothbrushes and dental floss); (8) *basic tools*, beginning with a knife at a minimum and arguably including much more such as paracord, duct tape, and a machete/hatchet and/or saw and (9) *weapons and security*, firearm(s), and a bladed weapon. All of the specific items are subject to debate because individual circumstances, climate and environmental resources vary. Nevertheless, the correct approach to take to preparing a bug out/ survival kit is to address the areas of fundamental human need: without backup, what do *you* need to survive *your environment*?

The difficulties of surviving without adequate equipment are well illustrated by two enjoyable survivalist reality TV shows. In *Naked and*

---

[474]   Cody Lundin, *98.6 Degrees: The Art of Keeping Your Ass Alive!* (Gibbs Smith, Salt Lake City, 2003), p. 14.

Afraid (2013-2019, *Discovery*), or what could be better called *Tease Adam and Eveing*, two survivalists, one male and one female have to survive naked for 21 days. The locations are generally those where this unrealistic scenario would allow survival without hypothermia, such as the Costa Rican jungle, by contrast to the Simpson Desert of Australia. Even so, the program is well worth a look. If only it had hard-core sex, but alas, even the interesting bits are blurred out.

In *Alone* (2015-2019, *History Channel*), season 1, 10 survival "experts" battled to last the longest on Vancouver Island, British Columbia, taking with them 10 survival items. Although Vancouver Island has the mildest climate in Canada, the Island is constantly wet and contestants struggled to make fire. The island also has a large number of black bears, wolves and cougars, which in the early episodes, freaked out at least one contestant, causing him to tap out. This was done even though contestants were supplied with flares and bear spray for "wild life emergencies." Life would have been easier with fire starter and fuel. However, one contestant who had a fire going, but who lost his striker, tapped out even though he could, like the Australian Aborigines and Amerindians, have kept the fire continuously burning. This illustrates the importance of mental toughness in survival situations and the need for a "can do" attitude.

There are many excellent books which give insightful "shopping list" approaches to preparing a bug out bag, rather than starting with a general human needs approach. The authors of these books have already done the hard thinking for you. I would suggest that people who for one reason or another do not want to think all of this through from first principles consult these texts and make up their own "shopping list" by a process of mixing and matching.

To begin, former light weight champion of Ultimate Fighting Championship (UFC), Forrest Griffin (with Erich Krauss) in *Be Ready When Shit Goes Down*,[475] a joyful masculine book of ribald humour and absurdity, presents a sound, but basic bug out bag of : (1) canned food (could be a possible weight issue for loner treks); (2) tent; (3)

---

[475] Forrest Griffin and Erich Krauss, *Be Ready When the Shit Goes Down: A Survival Guide to The Apocalypse* (itbooks, Harper Collins, New York, 2011).

sleeping bag (rated to minus 20 C) and wool blankets (wool retains heat when wet); (4) a propane stove; (5) guns (a semi-auto rifle or a pump action shotgun); (6) machetes; (7) books on native plants; (8) first aid kit; (9) pick and shovel (presumably a small army folding version); (10) axe; (11) fishing line/gear; (12) boots.[476] Forrest has a "go pack" for getting out quick, consisting of: (1) pistol; (2) ammo for said pistol (50 rounds); (3) multitool; (4) Meals Ready to Eat (MREs) (three per day plus some spares); (5) peanut butter (an excellent, sustaining survival food); (6) water; (7) water purifier; (8) map of bug out area; (9) compass; (10) waterproof matches; (11) goggles; (12) gloves; (13) wool socks; (14) boots; (15) wool blanket; (16) flashlight and (17) toothpaste (brush and dental floss).[477] This is the tough, hairy-scrotum man's approach to the apocalypse: grab the basics and piss-off fast. I would add that a good manual can opener should be in every bug out bag even if you don't take any canned food. You may get lucky and find the odd unopened can of baked beans, clutched in the hands of a decaying corpse. As well, for both sunny and snowy environments, good sunglasses should be added, but occur on few survival lists. They should, because in some environments glare will make your eyes feel like they are popping out of your idiot head. A pair of strong leatherwork gloves could also prove useful to minimise cuts to one's hands, and possible infections.

Along the same lines, this time from Australia, we have dinky di bushman Bob Cooper, who in his distinctly Aussie approach to survival *Outback Survival*,[478] has put together a survival kit light enough that you actually take it with you wherever you go. The dimensions are 13 x 8 x 5 cms, allowing for the addition of a basic medical kit comprising: antibiotics, diarrhoea tablets, anti-nausea tablets, antihistamines, ear/eye ointment and any personal medications.[479] Bob's Mark-III survival kit, which has saved his hide in the tough Aussie outback is: (1) plastic container; (2) compass; (3)

---

[476]   As above, pp. 53-55.

[477]   As above, pp. 61-63.

[478]   Bob Cooper, *Outback Survival* (Hachette Australia, Sydney, 2016).

[479]   As above, pp. 50-51.

flint and striker; (4) hacksaw blade; (5) cotton pad (first-aid, tinder); (6) whistle; (7) knife; (8) mirror; (9) tweezers; (10) large plastic bags (for obtaining water); (11) needle; (12) fishing line; (13) fishing hooks; (14) brass swivel (stop fishing line twisting); (15) sinkers; (16) trace wire; (17) stock cubes (soup and fishing lure); (18) paracord; (19) tea bags; (20) coffee; (21) glucose tablets; (22) water purifying tablets; (23) Condy's crystals (potassium permanganate, antiseptic, antifungal, fire-making); (24) plasters; (25) scalpel blade; (26) sewing kit (clothes repairs) (27) alcohol swabs; (28) antiseptic wipes; (29) magnifying glass; (30) torch; (31) multitool; (32) playing cards (amusement); (33) pencil; (34) instruction sheet.[480] Note that toilet paper is not on the list – Forrest and Bob are so tough that they don't need it! Toilet paper takes up a lot of space and will quickly run out. Even as a kid I found that wiping the shit off my arse with soft vegetation (that wasn't too thorny) did the job fine. Poor people in South East Asia still use their hand (one of them) to wide their ass, plus water. In the longer term, post-apocalyptic bum cleaning will be done as people did before toilet paper, using either a cloth and water, or one's hand and water. You too will get used to it.[481]

Les Stroud in *Survive!*[482] states that one should have for survival situations a personal survival kit carried with you at all times, on your person, so that it is not separated from you or lost, as well as a complete survival kit. The personal survival kit comprises: a sharp belt knife, bandana, small LED flashlight, two large garbage bags, a butane lighter, strike-anywhere matches in a waterproof case, a magnesium flint striker, metal cup, multitool and/or a Swiss Army knife, painkillers, parachute cord, protein bar/snack bar, space blanket and Ziploc bag.[483] The complete survival kit comprises: a sharpening stone for the knife, a candle, dried food, duct tape ("can repair just about any outdoor equipment), fire-starting devices and

---

[480] As above.

[481] The classic "shitting in the woods book" is Cathleen Meyer, *How to Shit in the Woods: An Environmentally Sound Approach to a Lost Art*, 3rd edition (Ten Speed Press, Berkeley, 2011).

[482] Les Stroud, *Survive! Essential Skills and Tactics to Get You Out of Anywhere – Alive* (William Morrow, New York, 2008).

[483] As above, p. 28.

tinder, fishing lures, hooks, sinkers, a leader and fishing line, flares, small LED flashlight, GPS, map, compass, garbage bags, small hand lens, marker tape (bright colors), money, multitool, needle and thread, Personal Locator Beacon (PLB), Emergency Position Indicating Radio Beacon (EPIRB), parachute cord, pencil and notebook, safety pins, folding saw, signal mirror, snare wire, space blanket, SPOT satellite messenger, water purification tablets, water purifying straw, whistle and Ziploc bags.[484] A basic first aid kit includes: antidiarrheal tablets, pain killers, antihistamines, bandages, antiseptic ointment, butterfly sutures, any prescription medicine, surgical blades and triangle bandages. Stroud does not mention dental gear (toothbrush, toothpaste/salt, dental floss) all of which could be improvized, but the thought of toothache in the field justifies the inclusion of a dental kit, especially toothache drops. In summary, Stroud presents an excellent selection of survival items, as one would expect from a leading wildness survival expert.

The US army has survival kits for cold climates, hot climates and over water.[485] The basic items are as follows.

1. *Cold Climate Kit* – food packets, snare wire, smoke illumination signals, waterproof match box, saw/knife blade, wood matches, first-aid kit, MC-1 magnetic compass; pocket knife, saw-knife-shovel handle, frying pan, illuminating candles, compressed trioxane fuel, signalling mirror, survival fishing kit, plastic spoon (metal would be better), *Survival Manual (AFM 64-5)*, poncho, insect head net, ejector snap, attaching snap, kit - outer case, kit - inner case, shovel, water bag, packing list, sleeping bag.

2. *Hot Climate Kit* – canned drinking water, waterproof matches, plastic whistle, smoke illumination signals, pocket knife, signalling mirror, plastic spoon, food packets, compressed trioxane fuel, fishing tackle kit, MC-1 magnetic compass, snare wire, frying pan, wood matches, insect head net, reversible

---

[484]   As above (Stroud), pp. 21-38, 354.

[485]   *US Army Survival Manual FM 21-76*, at http://www.equipped.org/.

sun hat, tool kit, kit - packing list, tarpaulin, *Survival Manual* (AFM 64-5), kit - inner case, kit - outer case, attaching strap, ejector snap.

3. *Overwater Kit* - packing list, raft boat paddle, *Survival Manual* (AFM 64-5), insect head net, reversible sun hat, water storage bag, MC-1 magnetic compass, boat bailer, sponge, sunburn-preventive cream, wood matches, first-aid kit, plastic spoon, pocket knife, food packets, fluorescent sea marker, frying pan, seawater desalter kit, compressed trioxane fuel, smoke, illumination signals, signalling mirror, fishing tackle kit, waterproof match box, raft repair kit.

Items in the various medical packets include: a surgical razor, tweezers, insect repellent, sun screen lotion, soap, surgical adhesive tape, aspirin tablets, adhesive bandage, gauze, elastic bandage, diphenoxylate hydrochloride and atropine sulphate tablets, sulfacetamide sodium ophthalmic ointment and iodine water purification tablets.

Zombie apocalypse writers have also put together some good, basic survival packs. F. Kim O Neill, in *The Ultimate Guide to Surviving a Zombie Apocalypse*,[486] has the following zombie bug out bag: (1) maps and compass; (2) a gun and at least 100 rounds of ammo, magazines and maybe a cleaning kit; (3) multitool; (4) utility knife; (5) short sword-kukri or sheathed gladius; (6) flashlight, batteries and spare bulbs; (7) food rations; (8) small quantity of water (weight problem) plus water purification tablets; (9) fire making gear; (10) first-aid kit; (11) warm clothes; (12) space blanket; (13) rope/paracord; (14) radio; (15) personal hygiene kit (sunblock, toothpaste, dental floss, towel); (16) shovel and for zom poc, armor such as gauntlets.[487]

A similar sound list is given by Michael Thomas and Nick Thomas in *Zompoc: How to Survive a Zombie Apocalypse*:[488] (1) drinking

---

[486] F. Kim O'Neill, *The Ultimate Guide to Surviving a Zombie Apocalypse* (Paladin Press, Boulder, Colorado, 2010).

[487] As above, pp. 86-87.

[488] Michael Thomas and Nick Thomas, *Zompac: How to Survive a Zombie Apocalypse* (Swordworks, United Kingdom, 2009).

water; (2) first-aid kit; (3) antibacterial wipes; (4) antibacterial hand sanitizer; (5) toilet paper; (6) feminine hygiene products (for the ladies and wound dressing); (7) clean towels and face cloths: (8) fuel stove and cooking pot; (9) toothpaste, toothbrush and dental floss; (10) hydrogen peroxide; (11) isopropyl alcohol; (12) flashlight and batteries; (13) candles; (14) green emergency glow sticks; (15) survival whistle; (16) compass; (17) signal mirror; (18) flint fire starter, waterproof matches, lighter; (19) waterproof containers and bags; (20) warm jacket (also waterproof and breathable); (21) multitool/ knife; (22) working gloves; (23) nylon rope, at least 45 feet; and (24) gaffer tape.

Max Brooks' bestselling book, *The Zombie Survival Guide: Complete Protection from the Living Dead*,[489] also contains items, which by now we are seeing as standard: (1) backpack; (2) hiking boots; (3) two pairs of socks; (4) water bottle; (5) water purification tablets; (6) waterproof matches; (7) bandana; (8) maps of area; (9) compass; (10) flashlight; (11) poncho; (12) signalling mirror; (13) bedroll or sleeping bag; (14) sunglasses; (15) first-aid kit; (16) Swiss Army knife or multitool; (17) radio; (18) knife; (19) binoculars; (20) firearm, rifle, 50 rounds of ammo; (21) cleaning kit; (22) pistol (Brooks favors a .22 rimfire, 25 rounds); (23) hand weapon and (24) signal flares.[490] Brooks recommends for a group, that one person carry maps, a compass, radio, binoculars, cleaning kit and signal flares.[491] He recommends for groups: (1) silent ballistic weapon e.g. crossbow or silenced firearm plus ammo (a good thing to have even without Hollywood zombies); (2) telescopic sight; (3) medical kit; (4) two-way radio; (5) crowbar; and (6) water-purification pump.[492] Again, all sound ideas.

Be sure that your bug out bag/survival kit has multiple means of starting a campfire including waterproof matches, flint and steel

---

[489]   Max Brooks, *The Zombie Survival Guide: Complete Protection from the Living Dead* (Three Rivers Press, New York, 2003).

[490]   As above, pp. 101-102.

[491]   As above, p. 102.

[492]   As above.

and a number of magnesium block fire-makers, Swedish fire steels and even cigarette lighters. Learn how to start a fire in wet weather.[493] Embers could be carried to start the next fire as the Australian Aborigines did, and survivalists could do this using their cast iron cooking pots. A short-term supply of tinder could come from cotton wool soaked in petroleum jelly, but torn-up philosophy and sociology books, soaked in petroleum jelly, a classical genitalia lubricant, burn with a politically correct warmth. One can even see a halo over the books as they burn.

There are two excellent disaster preparedness books by women that give detailed bug out/survival kits: Kathy Harrison, *Just in Case: How to be Self-Sufficient When the Unexpected Happens*[494] and Peggy Layton, *Emergency Food Storage and Survival Handbook: Everything You Need to Know to Keep Your Family Safe in a Crisis*.[495] Apart from these being overall good books, especially in the area of food storage and preparation, the flavor of the books and writing style appeals to women and gifts of these books to your female partner and daughters should be considered. Both books also have discussions of emergency kits, and some important information can be found, not explicitly mentioned in most of the books written by those with testicles, such as dealing with children or babies. Harrison, for example, mentions that cast iron is the only cookware material able to withstand the high temperatures of wood fire cooking and most other cookware material will not last as long.[496] This is an important consideration for apocalyptic bugging out, as a cooking pot will be essential for boiling water as part of your water purification rituals, as well as carrying embers.[497]

---

493 "How to Start a Fire in the Rain: An Illustrated Guide," November 5, 2015, at http://www.artofmanliness.com/2015/11/05/how-to-start-a-fire-in-the-rain-an-illustrated-guide/.

494 Kathy Harrison, *Just in Case: How to be Self-Sufficient When the Unexpected Happens* (Storey Publishing, North Adams, 2008).

495 Peggy Layton, *Emergency Food Storage and Survival Handbook: Everything You Need to Know to Keep Your Family Safe in a Crisis* (Three Rivers Press, New York, 2002).

496 Harrison, as above, p. 45.

497 For further bug out/survival kit lists see Albert Bates, *The Post-Petroleum Survival Guide and Cookbook: Recipes for Changing Times* (New Society Publishers, Gabriola Island, BC, 2006); "Thoughts on Disaster Survival," at http://www.frfrogspad.com/disastr.htm.

Earlier I mentioned Cody Lundin, US Aboriginal skills expert. His two must-read books are *98.6 Degrees: The Art of Keeping Your Ass Alive!*[498] and *When All Hell Breaks Loose: Stuff You Need to Survive When Disaster Strikes.*[499] Both books are written with an earthly humour; Lundin cites a note from Col. Jeff Cooper who refused to endorse *98.6 Degrees*: "Sorry, but Anglo-Saxon vulgarisms give evidence of lack of imagination and limited vocabulary, and are not to be taken seriously." On the contrary, the literary device of "vulgarisms," the zany drawings, especially of hot babes with big tits, gets Lundin's message across to his intended audiences; the books are "blokey," but in no way show limited knowledge. Lundin exhibits considerable knowledge of human physiology and biochemistry, as he clearly explains the dangers of hypothermia and hyperthermia, for example. He shows how hypothermia, the drop of one's core body temperature below 98.6 F (37 C) and hyperthermia, the raising of core body temperature above these base temperatures, can be prevented by use of clothing, shelters and making a fire, for the case of hypothermia. It is not the point of the present book to examine all of these details and reinvent the wheel. Regarding, for example, hypothermia prevention, he gives a fine outline of the modern layering system for cold environments (base layers, insulation layers and environmental layers). Stated simply the *base layer* is worn against the skin and must wick away sweat, but in cold weather, keep you warm. The mid-base layer provides basic insulation and warmth when conditions are mild. The insulation later supplements the mid and base layers for colder conditions. The outer or environmental layer is breathable to allow sweat and heat to escape, but provides a waterproof barrier against wind, rain and snow. Having faced the prospects of hypothermia once myself on a hunting trip, I greatly appreciated these books.[500]

---

[498]   Cody Lundin, *98.6 Degrees: The Art of Keeping Your Ass Alive!* (Gibbs Smith, Salt Lake City, 2003).

[499]   Cody Lundin, *When All Hell Breaks Loose: Stuff you Need to Survive When Disaster Strikes* (Gibbs Smith Publishers, Salt Lake City, 2007).

[500]   See further, L. McCullough and S. Arora, "Diagnosis and Treatment of Hypothermia," *American Family Physician*, vol. 7, no. 12, 2004, pp. 2325-2332.

Specific details about clothing, sleeping bags and tents can be found in a classic backpacker's book such as Chris Townsend's *The Backpacker's Handbook*, which is now in its fourth edition.[501] Townsend is an experienced backpacker and has travelled across the world, and experienced all matter of climates. His book goes into detail about the best brands of hiking books, sleeping bags, tents and so on. This is another must-get, must-read book by an author who is a world expert on this topic.

The basics: as you do not know where you will end up, a person bugging out after a collapse will need to have a synthetic sleeping bag rated to at least -20 C and adequate warm clothing in the layer system to survive if and when it snows. One should have sound wet wear-pants and a jacket or poncho, waterproof and breathable and a snow parker, also waterproof and breathable and when not in use, it can be rolled up, and a cotton work shirt can be put over it to make a pillow. Clothing systems need also to be able to deal with hot weather, and while cotton is a "death cloth" for cold wet weather, the fabric works fine in hot, dry climates, wicking moisture.

Headgear is essential: a waterproof, wide brimmed hat for winter travel, plus a woollen cap or balaclava for sleeping. In the summer, especially areas with a diminished ozone layer, such as Australia and Chile, a wide-brimmed sun hat plus bandana is reasonable. However, as the sun gets "lower" on intensive UV days, one can still get burnt even if wearing a hat and bandana. Here in Texas, I usually stitch cotton side protection to a hat that can be clipped in the front to resemble Arab head gear. When I was working in the Australian bush, I have worked outdoors in 43 C + heat with eye-frying UV radiation, and with good wrap around glasses, have not gotten sunburnt. I have fashioned sun hats with cotton side and front covers from cheap straw hats (two or three placed over each other creates strength and resistance from moderate strikes from vegetation/light tree branches when cutting) and in the winter I take off the covers and put duct tape on the surface of the hat to make a rain hat for less than US $6.

---

[501] Chris Townsend, *The Backpacker's Handbook*, 4th edition (McGraw Hill, New York, 2012).

Lightweight tents will not see out the distance in any longer-term survival event. Usually zips fall apart, or the fabric tears. Tarps are a good fall-back when the tent ultimately dies. Otherwise bugging out could become a form of buggery by Nature.

There are other things to be said about equipment that I leave to the section below on wilderness and backwoods survival philosophy. Rounding off this discussion on bugging out, it is important to note that all of the discussions in bugout/survival kits are heavily influenced by "lost in the woods/bush/desert" scenarios. Not much thought has been given to "bugging out forever" where one takes all that one can carry, and like the first settlers, our pioneering ancestors, makes a new home from scratch. The reason for this is that most preppers are not preparing for the zombie apocalypse. Indeed, it would be extremely difficult for one person or a small survival group to survive with just the gear on their backs. We are assuming here the worst-case scenario of say evacuation from one's retreat because of climate change, disasters or a range of other factors. Eco-refugees, we assume as well, will travel on foot, perhaps because of the presence of real zombies, cannibals, predators and associated ZMB scum and filth on the roads, as in the movie and book, *The Road*, or if roads are simply clogged with the debris of cars. In the alternative, bugging out may occur in the distant future because of climate change and other ecological disasters, long after cars have deteriorated.

In the worst-case scenario, assuming again that one has at least enough time to bug out, an individual or group needs a survival cart with tires that are from a mountain bike, with a repair kit and bike pump, or solid rubber tyres. Each person can carry a basic survival backpack with their cloths and personal items in case they get separated from the group. Thus, each person has everything they need for bugging out on an individual basis. The survival cart will be a small version of the pioneers' covered wagon. Waterproof, extra-large duffel bags will be arranged to a human's needs survival theme. One bag can be full of *medical, surgical and health supplies*; another, small hand *tools*; another to *self-defense*, with spare parts to guns (if you have any left), cleaning kits and ammunition. There should be at least one large food bag with compact, nutritious, long-life foods. MRE's are a possibility, although there are problems for many people with long-term use, such as digestive issues, as MRE's have ingredients similar to most highly processed food, being high in salt and low in fiber, and they are not light weight.[502] But, perhaps one could have dried goods, beans, legumes, grains, powdered milk, protein powder, multivitamins, powdered "superfood" supplement, and freeze dried foods, to construct one's own healthy MRE's.[503] Tin food would be unsatisfactory because of the weight of the tin and liquid content. Food to be taken must have a high nutrition energy to weight ratio, and one can't eat the tin. It is true that tin foods in having water already in the food do not need to have water added, but you are simply not going to be able to carry sufficiently more than a few days' supply of water, so obtaining water will become, along with preventing hyper- and hypothermia and security, your main concerns in bugging out.

We will discuss wilderness survival shortly. My view on "living off the land" is that if what is meant by this phrase is heading into the woods or outback scrub with no bushcraft skills, or poor ones, you will probably starve to death, or get eaten by predators. Much depends on what wild food is in the environment where you choose to make your, perhaps, last stand. If game is available and you have a firearm, your chances of survival improve. Living entirely on gathered wild foods is difficult. This is well illustrated by the documentary *Alone in the Wild* (2009, Channel 4), where the likeable bloke Ed Wardle attempted to last three months in the wild at Dog Pack Lake and Tincup Lake, Yukon, Canada. He lasted a respectable 50 days, breaking down because of loneliness ("I miss people too much") and lack of food. Although he had a rifle and a pump action shotgun, Canadian socialist law prevented him from shooting game, which

---

[502] Sergeant Survival, "Best Bug Out Bag Survival Foods: The Ultimate Guide to Picking the Perfect Food for Your BOB," at http://besurvival.com/guides/best-bug-out-bag-survival-foods-the-ultimate-guide-to-picking-the-perfect-food-for-your-bob.

[503] Tess Pennington, "Do It Yourself: How to Make Nutritious Homemade Meals-Ready-To-Eat (MREs)," February 23, 2016, at http://www.shtfplan.com/headline-news/do-it-yourself-how-to-make-nutritious-homemade-meals-ready-to-eat-mres_02232016.

was available. He reflected, in one segment of the documentary, while hungrily eyeing a juicy moose, that if he could have shot the beast, hunger would be gone.

However, long-term survival will involve more than just hunting and gathering. Simple agriculture will need to be practiced. This means that a survival bag needs to be devoted to non-hybrid seeds for vegetables (and fruit trees that can be grown realistically from carried seeds rather than nursery-prepared seedlings, which as pot plants will not be practical to carry), with adequate stocks to prepare for a possible failed first or even second crop. Some basic hand tools will need to be taken. I have planted gardens on the family farm by hand since the age of six, growing my own food, as my alcoholic father drunk most of the food money. I was able to grow melons, potatoes, corn and other vegetables just using seeds which I got from the wasted food, collected from supermarket waste, before it was fed to the pigs and cows. If I could grow my own food, using only hand tools as a grade school kid, nothing should hold you back. I planted crops using a mattock and a heavy "chipping hoe." These tools are your basic ones. To clear scrub, it would be useful to have a cutting-edge mattock or bushhook, which by the way can double-up as an excellent zombie melee weapon. It would be nice to have, a "slasher"—an old-style tool which is essentially an agriculture version of a pole axe weapon (or vice-versa)—a thick blade on a pole (say a long shovel handle), for scrub clearing. You will probably need to make one if you have black smithing skills or get one made up before the collapse. A long-handled spade, with a flat rather than curved blade, can also be sharpened on the edges for scrub clearing, and as we will see later in book 2, zombie clearing as well.

Wilderness and Blackwood's Survival Philosophy: Live Off the Land or Die Trying

Bear Grylls' series (2006-2011) *Man vs. Wild* (and more recently *The Island with Bear Grylls* (2014-2018) and *Running Wild with Bear Grylls*, (2014- 2018), has taken wilderness survival into the lounge room and made this aspect of survivalism respectable for the TV watching, pizza chomping crowd. Bear is famous for tasting truly disgusting survival "foods" such as thick juicy bugs and describing the taste sensations, along the lines of: "It's like eating lukewarm pus mixed with snot…" As well, he has drunk his own urine, and squeezed elephant turds to put water his mouth, to hell with disease transmission. If you think about drinking your own urine, while theoretically this seems reasonable, in a survival situation when you are desperate enough for moisture to drink your own urine, the urine is likely to be concentrated with salts and toxins and not suitable for drinking anyway. Likewise, for water in shit. Bear's urine was not likely to be very concentrated, so he was able to do it because he was not in a real survival situation. Most survival literature recommends against drinking one's urine (along with sea water of course), but both can yield drinking water if distilled.[504] Securing water is a vital wilderness skill that I will say more on shortly.

Bear is also a superb climber, having made it to the summit of Mount Everest,[505] and he did this after he recovered from breaking his back in three places from a parachute accident. Good for him! In one episode, he was in Montana, and climbed about 150 feet up a ladder on a railway bridge. At the top he found that there was a protruding cement lip preventing his climb onto the bridge. He threw a chain with some piece of metal fitting on the end over the cement protrudement, which caught. He pulled on it and it held, then he swung out into space and pulled himself up. It was breathtaking

---

[504] Les Stroud, *Survive! Essential Skills and Tactics to Get You Out of Anywhere - Alive* (William Morrow, New York, 2008) p. 86; J. Hunter, "The Worst Bear Grylls Survival Advice," December 16, 2015, at www.primalsurvivor.net/worst-bear-grylls-survival advice/.

[505] Bear Grylls, *Two All-Action Adventures* (Macmillan, London, 2012).

television. However, in a genuine survival situation such high-risk movements should never be attempted even if you are an excellent climber, as you can always slip: maybe at that moment you pull a muscle and it goes into spasm? Or a bee decides, in its wisdom, to sting you in the eye. The same can be said about many of Bear's attempts to quickly get down cliffs (e.g. by swinging over trees) and his journeys into caves to find abandoned items. It is better to take the long way around and be in one piece. He seldom found anything of any value in the caves and entering them was a high risk move. Caves, like civilizations, do collapse.[506]

> Les Stroud's *Survivorman* (2005, 2007-2016), was an earlier excellent TV program, where this Canadian survival expert survived alone in remote locations with no backup crew, no production crew with him and a minimum of gear, apart from the camera equipment.

Apocalypse Man (2010) (History Channel), hosted by former US marine Rudy Reyes, took survivalism even further, explicitly exploring post-doomsday themes. The program had some good tips about urban apocalypse survival, except it was not explained why one would be in a city at all at such a time, or why no snipers had shot him whilst he was running around in plain daylight. Like Bear Grylls, there was a climbing episode involving Reyes swinging by a rope over what he said was probably a contaminated river, a high risk move. He also exited a building via an elevator shaft: good TV but crazy for most of us to try in a survival situation where an injury could mean death. As well, much of the episode involved getting electricity (from a hospital back-up diesel generator), to power a car battery, so that the survivor could meet other survivors, whom he contacted via a CB radio broadcast. Although he mentioned that one should take the precaution of getting to the meet site a day earlier

---

[506]   Bear Grylls, *Great Outdoor Adventures* (4 Books, London, 2008), *Man vs. Wild: Survival Techniques from the Most Dangerous Places on Earth*, (Hyperion, New York, 2008), *Born Survivor* (4 Books, London, 2007), *Living Wild: The Ultimate Guide to Scouting and Fieldcraft* (4 Books, London, 2011).

to conduct surveillance, ZMBS may do the same, and either take you out, and any good guys who also come.

Wilderness survival has been exhaustively covered in two broad genres of books. First, there are army/navy/air force survival guilds such as the *US Army Survival Manual* FM 21-76;[507] the Royal Australian Navy, *The Survival Manal*[508] and the Royal Canadian Air Force Survival Training School, *Down but Not Out.*[509] This school of thought has flourished into a large number of SAS and commando-type books which cover the same basic topics of: the psychology of survival (can-do positive attitude and all that), shelter, water, food and dangerous animals and poisonous plants. These books outline primitive skills to help one live off the land (or maybe even the sea), including hunting, trapping and fishing. The classic book in the field is John Wiseman's *SAS Survival Handbook.*[510] But, more recently there have appeared a number of other superb texts,[511] with the *SAS and Elite Forces Guild* series by Chris Mc Nab being particularly good.[512] The second genre of wilderness survival is the backwoods, or for Australia, bushman traditions.[513] The great American magazine *The Backwoodsman* ("The Magazine for the 21st Century Frontiersman") has been published for over 30 years and all of this

---

[507] *US Army Survival Manual FM 21-76*, at http://www.equipped.org/fm21-76.htm.

[508] Royal Australian Navy, *The Survival Manual* (Navy Office, Canberra, 1968).

[509] Royal Canadian Air Force Survival Training School, *Down but Not Out* (Queen's Printer, Ottawa, 1970).

[510] John Wiseman, *SAS Survival Handbook: The Ultimate Guide to Surviving Anywhere* (Collins, London, 2009).

[511] Barry Davies, *The Complete SAS Survival Manual* (Skyhorse Publishing, New York, 2011); Colin Towell, *Survival Handbook in Association with the Royal Marines Commandos* (Dorling Kindersley Ltd, London, 2012); Christopher Nyerges, *How to Survive Anywhere: A Guide for Urban, Suburban, Rural and Wilderness Environments*, 2nd edition (Stackpole Books, Mechanicsburg, 2014).

[512] Chris McNab, *SAS and Elite Forces Guide: Wilderness Survival: Military Survival Skills from the World's Elite Military Units* (Amber Books, London, 2011), *SAS and Elite Forces Guide: Prisoner of War Escape and Evasion: How to Survive Behind Enemy Lines from the World's Elite Military Units* (Amber Books, London, 2012), and Chris McNab, *SAS and Elite Forces Guide: Preparing to Survive: Being Ready for When Disaster Strikes* (Amber Books, London, 2012).

[513] Richard Graves, *The 10 Bushcraft Books* (CreateSpace, 2015).

wealth and knowledge and wisdom can be purchased on DVD – to be done before "power down.[514] There are many informative books[515] and websites.[516]

For example, Bob Holtzman's *Adventure Survival Handbook: How to Stay Alive in the Wild with Just a Blade and Your Wits*,[517] gives a minimalist approach to wilderness survival showing the importance of a good knife for making shelter and in fire and food preparation. He discusses the advantages and disadvantages of fixed blades and folders, and plain vs serrated edges. (I prefer a fixed blade plain edge and a serrated edge folder to have the best of both worlds). Holtzman gives a guide to sharpening knives and axes, as well as basic axe use, such as how to fell a tree, climbing, sectioning, splitting and hewing.[518]

After close to 50 years chopping wood, preparing fire breaks and clearing feral trees on my folk's Texas ranch and then my own, I prefer a good handsaw to an axe, and even to a chainsaw, especially on slippery hillsides and in the wet. I don't agree with the machete school of wood chopping either, for anything beyond a basic campfire. If you need to cut up literally masses of timber by hand, don't use an axe, use a biomechanically superior saw.

A great wilderness survival book from the editors of Stockpiles books is *Survival Wisdom and Know-How: Everything to You to Know to Subsist in the Wilderness*.[519] This is a large format book with three columns of print per page and fully adequate line drawings giving 7,845 skills and instructions on topics including animals, insects

---

[514] See www.backwoodsmanmag.com.

[515] See Michael Pewtherer, *Wilderness Survival Handbook: Primitive Skills for Short-Term Survival and Long-Term Comfort* (McGraw-Hill, New York, 2010); Dave Canterbury, *Advanced Bushcraft: An Expert Field Guide to the Art of Wilderness Survival* (F + W, Avon, 2014).

[516] See in general: https://survivalpulse.com/top-50-survival-blogs/.

[517] Bob Holtzman, *Adventure Survival Handbook: How to Stay Alive in the Wild with Just a Blade and Your Wits* (New Burlington Books, London, 2012).

[518] On the merits of a relatively thin-bladed knife for camp work (e.g. food preparation) see T. M. Trier, "Choosing an Outdoor Knife," at http://www4.gvsu.edu/trier/cache/articles/t1/outdoorknife1.htm.

[519] Amy Rost (compiler), *Survival Wisdom and Know-How: Everything You Need to Know to Subsist in the Wilderness* (Black Dog and Leventhal Publishers, New York, 2007).

and plants for food; packing and cooking food; water; hunting and fishing; fire; shelter traveling on land and water; weather and climate; navigation and first-aid – principally for a North American and Canadian audience. This book is essentially a wilderness survival encyclopaedia and is a clear "must have," as is John and Geri McPherson's *Ultimate Guide to Wilderness Living*,[520] which deals with surviving with just your bare hands and what you can scab in the woods. Here you will learn about making primitives tools, working flint and stone, and making wooden bowls and plates and primitive pottery and cordage. The McPherson's deal with the construction of basic shelters such has learn-tos and wickiups and more complex shelters. I have given this book to my three youngest kids to make up shelters for themselves in the hills on the farm while I have been scrub-clearing. They did fine in making both summer and winter shelters for themselves, although they got all manner of crap on the book.

Tom Brown's Field Guide to Living with the Earth[521] and Tony Nesters' *The Modern Hunter-Gatherer*,[522] also cover wilderness survival fundamentals, such as traps and snares, fire making, shelter construction, bow and arrow making, weaving stone and bone tools, hides and tanning (making buckskin), clay pot making and living simply without the trappings of civilization. These are classic books, well worth obtaining and studying.

Tony Nester in *The Modern Hunter-Gatherer* has given a very useful dot point list of the bushcraft skills which a complete survivalist will need to know. They are:

- How to make a fire in any weather (wind, snow, rain,) using modern fire making devices.

---

[520] John McPherson and Geri McPherson, *Ultimate Guide to Wilderness Living: Surviving with Nothing but Your Bare Hands and What You Find in the Woods* (Ulysses Press, Berkeley, CA, 2008).

[521] Tom Brown with Brandt Morgan, *Tom Brown's Field Guide to Living with the Earth* (Berkley Books, New York, 1984).

[522] Tony Nester, *The Modern Hunter-Gatherer: A Practical Guide to Living Off the Land* (Diamond Greek Press and Ancient Pathways, LLC, Flagstaff, AZ, 2009).

- Be proficient with a knife, axe and saw.
- How to dress properly and understand the insulative values of different garments and footwear.
- How to handle common backcountry injuries and deal with trauma.
- How to construct natural and improvised survival shelters as well as hogans and cabins for long-term living.
- How to ID, harvest, and know, how to use a dozen of the common edible plants of their region.
- How to use medical plants for healing injures and have made an herbal first-aid kit.
- Able to cook delicious (or at least, edible) meals over the campfire using variety of modern and primitive cooking methods.
- ID common animal tracks and have ability to follow the trail of a wounded animal.
- Be skilled in hunting small game with a pistol and rifle.
- Able to make primitive deadfalls and snares and successfully procure wild game with them.
- How to skin, clean and process wild game and fish.
- How to preserve meat and fish through smoking and air-drying into jerky.
- Be proficient at primitive methods of fire making such as the bow-drill and hand-drill.
- How to use at least 10 bush knots for lashing.
- Be skilled at navigating with map and compass, GPS, and barehanded/celestial methods.
- How to read the clouds and forecast inclement weather up to 72 hours away.
- Make improvised containers for cooking and know how to coal-burn utensils.
- Skilled at basic tailoring for mending gear and clothing.
- How to make improvised hunting weapons such as bows, atlatls, and throwing sticks.
- How to make quickie stone-tools and improvised cutting edges from natural materials.

- Be proficient at living in the deep snow and extreme cold weather.
- How to sleep well in the wild.[523]

It is a good, sensible list, especially the last point about the value of being able to sleep soundly outdoors. But, as a bushman who has living in the driest state on the driest continent on Earth, and the driest parts of West Texas, I would like to add to this list: be proficient at living in the extreme heat and how to find and purify water. Short-term survival methods of finding and obtaining water are well covered in the wilderness survival literature and include dew and rainwater collection, condensation methods using plants, water from plants especially plant roots, the solar still and improvised distillation. For both short-term and long-term survival, purification of water is needed to protect human drinkers from waterborne disease caused by parasites, protozoa, bacteria and viruses. Prior filtering of the water will remove large particles of dirt and mud and material that may protect bugs from disinfecting agents. Bleach and tincture of iodine can be used, along with stabilised oxygen products. Boiling for about one minute at low altitudes, and for several minutes at higher altitudes is a time-proven method of killing waterborne pathogens. Distillation—boiling water and collecting the steam—is also a way of dealing with salts, chemicals and heavy metals. Solar water disinfection, exposing water in plastic PET bottles to the sun's UV rays, can be used to kill the organisms causing diarrhoea, including viruses, bacteria and parasites.

Disaster Preparedness, Philosophy

The disaster preparedness literature, primarily manuals and information handouts from government organizations such as FEMA and emergency services organizations, is of course useful for general emergency preparation. In the disaster preparedness genre, Dr

---

[523] Nester, as above, p. 63.

Arthur T. Bradley's *Handbook to Practical Disaster Preparedness for the Family*[524] is outstanding for its stated purpose of meeting "likely" threats rather than TEOTWAWKI or the zombie apocalypse. Where I disagree is that one of our likely future threats is in fact TEOTWAWKI and the zombie apocalypse. Dr Bradley had more recently published *Disaster Preparedness for EMP Attacks and Solar Storms,*[525] a truly superb, much-needed book alerting us to this threat and showing how vulnerable modern technological society actually is to TEOTWAWKI and what I call the zombie apocalypse. Consequently, his *Handbook to Practical Disaster Preparedness for the Family* should not be your only reading in this field, but it is an excellent place to start, because the book is written as if you were with him out in the shed having a few cold beers.

Mathew Stein has published two books, *When Technology Fails*[526] and *When Disaster Strikes.*[527] The later book is more in the conventional disaster preparedness genre, definitely an "A" like Bradley's book and you would do well educating yourself with either. *When Technology Fails* through should be given an "A+" because this 439-page book in double columns essentially gives a synthesis of the disaster preparedness and self-reliance, self-sufficiency traditions, the later traditions originating from the "back-to-the-land" movements of the early 20th century and particularly in the 1960s. Stein has an engineering background and has hands-on experience with most of the technologies discussed in his book. The basics are covered including fire-starting, food, shelter, water, first-aid, what to do when high tech medicine fails (holistic health, herbs etc., the holistic health section is objected to, predictably enough, by some

---

[524]   Dr Arthur T. Bradley, *Handbook to Practical Disaster Preparedness for the Family*, 2nd edition (The Author, http://disasterpreparer.com/2011).

[525]   Dr Arthur T. Bradley, *Disaster Preparedness for EMP Attacks and Solar Storms*, (The Author, http://disasterpreparer.com/).

[526]   Matthew Stein, *When Technology Fails: A Manual for Self-Reliance, Sustainability, and Surviving the Long Emergency*, (Revised Edition), (Chelsea Green, White River Junction, 2008).

[527]   Matthew Stein, *When Disaster Strikes: A Comprehensive Guide for Emergency Planning and Crisis Survival*, (Chelsea Green, White River Junction, 2011).

on the net), clothing and textiles, heat and energy, metal working, black smithing, utensils and storing, not-so-modern chemistry and engineering, machines and materials. Each chapter concludes with a set of references with a synopsis and a brief discussion of a wide number of topics, such as the selection of sleeping bags which gets one column (but the information is correct as he favors fiber-filled synthetic bags). Obviously, other books mentioned earlier can offer further information. Nevertheless, *When Technology Fails* is highly recommended because it puts much information between two covers and it does so with the explicit recognition that our present society is unsustainable, and that we are facing a "long emergency."

I have already mentioned the work of leading US survivalist James Wesley, Rawles on retreats, and his novel *Patriots*. *Patriots* may not be great literature, but would be more helpful to a novice survivalist than a work of great literature. The novel is concerned with a group of patriots, who ultimately organise themselves as a militia, who face the socio-economic collapse of America because of crippling US debt and deficit problems. I won't spoil the plot. The most interesting read for me were long sections on survival preparations including: a discussion of survival knives and fighting knives, firearms selection, fuel storage, and how to fortify a house. There is a mention of the need for farming, but most of the book deals with the action part of retreatism rather than more monotonous manual labour. The preparation of explosives, Molotov cocktails and thermite use occurs. I just ignored all the annoying Christian bits, that were like mossies buzzing in my brain, and read for information purposes only!

Rawles' *How to Survive the End of World as We Know It*,[528] is essentially the distillation of the wisdom of his survivalblog.com between covers and one of the outstanding books on this field. If budget constraints for a reader were great that only, say, 10 books could be purchased, I would definitely put this book in the top 10 list, along with Stein's *When Technology Fails*, which jointly cover most of the bases including firearms and self-protection. Rawles adopts the

---

[528]   James Wesley, Rawles, *How to Survive the End of the World as We Know It: Tactics, Techniques and Technologies for Uncertain Times*, (Plume Books, Penguin, New York, 2009).

original approach to developing survival lists, giving a master "list of lists" from which people work on making up their own survival lists. Thus, the list of lists would cover the basic areas of water, food storage, food preparation, personal items, first-aid/minor surgery, chemical/nuclear/biological/pandemic defenses, gardening, hygiene/ sanitation, hunting/fishing/trapping, power, lighting, batteries, fuels, firefighting, tactical living, general security, security/firearms, communications and monitoring, tools, survival books, barter and charity. Rawles then goes into dot point details under each of these sub-categories.

Religion aside, Rawlesian survivalism embraces sound principles which I see as worthy of acceptance: lower populated areas are preferable to higher populated areas, exercise restraint, but be prepared to use lethal force if necessary. There is strength in numbers – retreat groups should ideally make use of a number of families for 24/7 security, the need for skills over technology, wealth in tangible goods rather than fiat currencies, seek good soil, clean water and adequate rainfall for agriculture, store adequate and surplus supplies, food storage is needed as crops may fail, undertake proper training with all tools including guns, use of "appropriate technologies"[529] such as a blacksmith's forge in collapse situations; the better prepared one is, the more can one help others - some technologies offer advantages in the short term (e.g. night vision gear and communication equipment), and some in the longer term (e.g. barbed wire and razor wire). Seek out skilled, reliable friends with practical knowledge, fortify your retreat, which ideally you should at live at all year round, and live simply and frugally.

Before moving on to consider worthy self-reliance and self-sufficiency books, nuclear war survival skills should be briefly mentioned. Dr Bruce Clayton's *Life after Doomsday*[530] is a still-relevant classic, and his more recent *Life after Terrorism*[531] updates

---

[529]   E. F. Schumacher, *Small is Beautiful* (Harper and Row, New York, 1973).

[530]   Bruce D. Clayton, *Life After Doomsday* (Paladin Press, Boulder, Colorado, 1992).

[531]   Bruce D. Clayton, *Life after Terrorism: What You Need to Know to Survive in Today's World* (Paladin Press, Boulder, Colorado, 2002).

things with a consideration of more recent horrors including biological and chemical warfare and much more. Available online is the respected book by Cresson Kearney, *Nuclear War Survival Skills* (1986).[532] The US Armed Forces, *Nuclear, Biological and Chemical Survival Manual* (2003)[533] is also worth consulting, as mentioned earlier in this chapter. I have not gone into detail about nuclear, biological, chemical and equally important, nanotechnology threats and survival strategy, as I plan to devote a future work to this if there is still time before doomsday.

Medicine and surgery, beyond basic first-aid, is an area requiring specialist knowledge, skill and training, and to preserve some of this knowledge, especially in the areas of public health and preventive medicine, is essential. There is no need for the world to go back to "bad air" and "evil spirit" theories of disease and books on pathologies can be acquired from university bookshops or second-hand book sales that are usually held by students at the beginning of the university year. Textbooks on anatomy, physiology, dentistry and surgical procedures, would be useful for general preservation of knowledge purposes and to better inform amateur medical and surgical practices in the desperate times ahead. Basic obstetrics and the delivery of babies should be learnt. I assisted my then-wife in the delivery of my first daughter, and if I can do it, you can too. Along with this, it is worthwhile having a basic surgical outfit of stainless-steel instruments – maybe someone qualified will wonder into your orbit, or you may be lucky and have someone come aboard before the collapse (but whose instruments are inconveniently back at the burnt-out hospital).

I have in mind here instruments such as a bone saw (amputations), Mayo and Metzenbaum scissors, lift-out forceps, dissecting forceps, an obstetrics kit, small curved clamps, large curved clamps, and an ample supply of disposable scalpels. Most survivalist books cite David Werner (with Carol Thuman and Jane Maxwell), *Where*

---

[532] Cresson Kearney, *Nuclear War Survival Skills* (1986), at http://www.oism.org/nwss/.

[533] US Armed Forces, *Nuclear, Biological and Chemical Survival Manual* (Basic Books, New York, 2003).

There is No Doctor: A Village Health Care Handbook[534] along with Murray Dickson, *Where There is No Dentist*,[535] as must-have books. I agree that these are very good texts, but they are not true collapse or survival medicine books for collapse situations. Here Dr Joseph Alton and Amy Alton's *The Doom and Bloom Survival Medicine Handbook*[536] offers instruction where the system has collapsed and there is no hospital to go to, true collapse medicine. Other books in the preventive and emergency paradigm, which consider grid down situations, are Ralph La Guardia, *The Doomsday Book of Medicine*[537] and Gerard S. Doyle, *When There is No Doctor.*[538] Useful books include William W. Forgey, *Wilderness Medicine: Beyond First Aid*,[539] Paul S. Auerbach, *Wilderness Medicine*[540] and Hugh L. Coffee, *Ditch Medicine: Advance Field Procedures for Emergencies.*[541] Obviously enough, in a collapse situation prevention is much better than cure – all the more reason to get a good diet and exercise in order to avoid the diseases of modern moron civilization such as heart disease and diabetes. There is room for herbal medicines and micronutrient therapy, perhaps even to tackle disease such as cancer.[542]

After the media image of survivalists as crazies tramping through the scrub with guns, comes the image of survivalists as stockpilers of supplies and food. So, let us not disappoint them. There are a

---

[534] David Werner (with Carol Thuman and Jane Maxwell), *Where There Is No Doctor: A Village Health Care Handbook* (Hesperian Foundation, Berkeley, Ca, 1992 and June 2003).

[535] Murray Dickson, *Where There is No Dentist* (Hesperian Foundation, Berkeley, CA, 2010).

[536] Joseph Alton and Amy Alton, *The Survival Medicine Handbook: A Guide for When Help is Not on the Way,* 2nd edition (Doom and Bloom, 2013).

[537] Ralph La Guardia, *The Doomsday Book of Medicine*, (Mindstir Media, 2015).

[538] Gerald S. Doyle, *When There Is No Doctor: Preventive and Emergency Home Healthcare in Challenging Times* (Process Media, Port Townsend, 2010).

[539] William W. Forgery, *Wilderness Medicine: Beyond First Aid* (The Globe Pequot Press, Guilford, Connecticut, 2000). See also www.wildernessmedicine.com.

[540] Paul S. Auerbach, *Wilderness Medicine*, 5th edition (Mosby Elsevier, Philadelphia, 2007).

[541] Hugh L. Coffee, *Ditch Medicine: Advanced Field Procedures for Emergencies* (Paladin Press, Boulder, Colorado, 2002)

[542] See Raymond Francis, *Never Fear Cancer Again* (Health Communications, Deerfield Beach, 2011).

number of excellent books available to help you get started on food stockpiling and preserving grown food. Kathy Harrison's *Just in Case*[543] and Peggy Layton's *Emergency Food Storage and Survival Handbook*[544] have already been mentioned, and both books provide a wealth of information on food storage and preparation. Harrison introduces the OAR system: organise, acquire and rotate, where you actively manage your food stockpile, keeping track of "use by dates" and using food then replacing it. The food stored will be foods that one's family actually eats. One of my friends, for example, stockpiled numerous tins of cheap meat without first trying it. When he did feast on the contents of a tin he and his family found the meat too fatty and salty to eat. Even the dog wouldn't eat it. Another take-home message is that while you can't live on bread alone, bread and soup is a possibility: soups and casseroles are excellent foods. Tin soup, mixed with rice or soup mix, can make a quick meal.

Jack Spigarelli's *Crisis Preparedness Handbook*[545] gives a comprehensive guide to emergency and survival preparations, including survival tools to store and stockpile: clothing, heat, cooking and light, sanitation, medical and dental, home preparation and management, communications, preparations for terrorist attack (biological, chemical and nuclear), but focuses largely on food and water stockpiling, food production and food preservation in chapters 5-19 of the book. Spigarelli, also says that one should store the types of foods that a family will normally eat, because children faced with an absolutely boring diet may starve. Adults too may lose interest in food if it is "oh no, not fuckin' baked beans again!" even if the mistake of my friend with the fatty, salty meat mentioned in the paragraph above is avoided.

There is merit in putting aside a large stockpile of the Mormon "basic four" of wheat, sugar (honey), powdered milk and salt. It is

---

[543] Harrison, as above, p. 804.

[544] Layton, as above.

[545] Jack A. Spigarelli, *Crisis Preparedness Handbook: A Comprehensive Guide to Home Storage and Physical Survival*, 2nd updated edition (Cross-Current Publishing, Alpine, Utah, 2002).

possible, if you know what you are doing, to add variety to these staples by making from gluten, the protein part of flour, a meat substitute which can be made into various dishes. But, as said, you will need to know how to prepare this and be a good cook. Further, the narrower the base of foods you have, the greater the risk of starvation if you or family develop allergies to a particular item, such as wheat and wheat products (gluten) and cow's milk (lactose). As well, this diet is lacking in fats and vitamins, although vitamins could come from fresh fruit and vegetables to be added to it. But, even then, the diet is lacking in essential fats such as omega 3 fatty acids. At a minimum, the Mormon basic four should be expanded to include as well as the four – oils (especially olive oil), a variety of grains and legumes, multi-vitamins and micronutrients such as selenium supplements, protein powder, herbs, seasonings and leavening agents. Olive oil trees can be grown both for oil and use can be made of olive leaf extracts, an excellent herbal treatment for a range of heart and respiratory conditions.

Stored food will deteriorate at various speeds, depending on storage conditions, losing nutrients, palatability and in the case of foods like yeast, thickeners and gelatines, their functional properties.[546] There is, surprisingly enough, little scientifically based knowledge on the shelf life of various foods and most of the figures cited in various books are estimates.[547] There is general agreement that salt and maybe sugar under ideal (moisture-free) storage conditions lasts indefinably, but beyond that there is little agreement. Some figures for illustration are: canned goods (two years, although under ideal conditions), canned fish (three to five years), dried dairy products (five years), dried fruits and vegetables (seven years), dried beans and legumes (seven years), grains (other than wheat, e.g. oats, 10 years), wheat (10-20 years), Meals Ready to Eat (MRE, 3 + years), dehydrated food (10-15 years), and freeze dried (7-25 years). As an example, decades ago I used to crash in a friend's office in Austin so I could get to college, readily while doing my science degree, then PhD in applied mathematics, part time. I generally ate "power muesli" for

---

[546]   Holly Drennan Deyo, *Dare to Prepare!* (Deyo Enterprises, Pueblo West, 2006).

[547]   Spigarelli, as above, p. 52.

lunch – oats, dried fruit, protein powder and powdered milk. One day I didn't/couldn't eat lunch and the guy renting the office said that he would store the contents in a jar and when we left the office, he would eat the power muesli. The food sat there for years, in an office under a tin roof (level four directly under that tin roof) and no air conditioning, exposed to light and often 40 C + temperatures in the summer. When we left the office years later I reminded him of his boast about eating the feast. He tipped out a handful and tossed it down. It was, "ok, I've eaten better." Talk about tough guys. But, did the oats have any worthwhile nutritional content?

Spigarelli cites a study that found that 40-year-old canned cream corn, fruit cocktail and green peas were about nutritionally equivalent to some freshly canned foods.[548] He says that canned goods retain, even after a number of years, 50-90 percent of their vitamin content, and all of their proteins, fats and carbohydrates.[549] Spigarelli puts the shelf life of canned food at 2 ½ - 7 years. However, I have tried to store tin food under "ideal conditions" (cool, dry etc.) and have never kept a tin of canned food "alive" more than about four years, especially with tomatoes in it (i.e. baked beans = acid) My bad luck! Thus, Lundin's advice is good advice: "take all prophetic advice about how long your vittles' will be vital with a grain of salt. The sure way out of this dilemma is to *rotate your food by storing what you eat and eating what you store.*"[550]

Dehydrated, air-dried, freeze-dried and canned foods, all have their advantages and disadvantages, especially with respect to cost, with freeze-dried and air-dried foods generally costing substantially more than canned food. On the principle of not putting all of one's eggs in the one basket, it is ideal to build up one's food reserves using a variety of these types of foods such as freeze-dried meats, dehydrated foods like powered milk, potatoes, cheese, eggs and soups and

---

548   As above.

549   Survival Diva, "The Mother of All Food Storage Myths," September 13, 2012, at http://survivethecomingcollapse.com/1970/the-mother-of-all-food-storage-myths.

550   Lundin, as above, p. 239; "What You Need to Know about Eating Expired Food," November 18, 2015, at http://www.backdoorsurvival.com/what-you-need-to-know-about-eating-expired-food/;

canned foods like fruit, vegetables and ready-to-go soups. There is no "one size fits all perfect food storage plan"; rather each individual survival unit, typically a family, will need to devise a plan to best suit their ends and tastes. In a collapse situation food will be one of the few remaining pleasures in life and for the purposes of morale, needs to be something to look forward to and keep one, keeping on.

It is important to properly store food in food grade storage containers that protect the food from insects and pests such as rats and mice. A friend prepared for the Y2K non-event, by buying various grain products and storing them in the plastic and paper bags they came in, in a storage area under the roof of his house. This was not wise in the first place because of heat, let alone mice. When I told him that he needed to deal with mice he arrogantly dismissed my concerns and put down rat poison and left the food. Not so! The entire stockpile was destroyed as the result of being an arrogant know-it-all. What self-respecting rat or mouse would go for rat poison over tasty grain? He would have got no food from me if a collapse had occurred because I would not want to pretend to be wiser than the forces of natural selection and aid in the survival of the dumbest.

In a nutshell, what food items should be put away by people on a tight budget, who just cannot think through all of these issues for themselves because they are so time-strapped from working long hours for minimal pay, just to keep body and soul together? "Health ranger" Mike Adams has put together a shopping list of 50 items.[551] Adams makes the point that salt will be hard to come by in a collapse situation, so sea salt (which has iodine) should be put away in large quantities. It lasts indefinitely under ideal conditions, and it is possible to store enough, in suitable *glass* containers, to last generations. There is almost nothing written on the ultra-long-term storage chemistry of food grade plastics because these things haven't existed long enough to judge their stability over a few hundred years. Will chemicals leak into the salt after 50 or more years? What about

---

[551]   Mike Adams, "Fifty Food Items to Stockpile Now: Health Ranger Releases Preparedness Foods Shopping Lists," August 22, 2012 at http://www.naturalnews.com/036907_emergency_foods_shopping_list_discounts.html.

100 years? Ideally, for ultra-long-term storage, use glass containers. In the distant future salt can be obtained from journeys to the oceans.

Self-Reliance and Self-Sufficiency Philosophy

The self-reliance/self-sufficiency and ecology movement has produced a range of useful works for the survivalist. Zachary Nowak in *Crash Course: Preparing for Peak Oil*,[552] gives a useful review of books and lists many useful websites, as does Ted Trainer's "Simpler Way" website aimed for small scale self-sufficient local economies, the abandonment of consumerism and adoption of simple living.[553] Some key books to consult are Carla Emery, *The Encyclopaedia of Country Living*,[554] John and Martha Storey, *Storey's Basic Country Skills*[555] and A. R. Gehring (ed.), *Back to Basics*.[556] Today the living simply/organic/permaculture/minimalism traditions are "mainstream" and newsagents often hold an array of magazines such as *Mother Earth News and Permaculture* (www.permaculutre.co.uk), *Grass Roots*, *Earth Garden* (www.earthgarden.com.au) and *Warm Earth* (www.warmearth.com.au). Of course, many more US produced magazines will be available. There are also many excellent "off-grid" living books, worthy to consider, because long-term survival in the future will definitely be off-grid, or rather, no grid.[557]

The late John Seymour, the father of self-sufficient living wrote some books of lasting value including *The Fat of the Land*,[558] *The Self-*

---

[552]   Zachery Nowak, *Crash Course: Preparing for Peak Oil*, (Green Door via Bonazzi, Italy, 2008), http://www.greendoorpublishing.com/.

[553]   See Ted Trainer, *The Transition to a Sustainable and Just World*, (Envirobook, Canterbury, New South Wales, 2010) and the "Simplicity Institute" website at http://simplicityinstitute.org/ted-trainer.

[554]   Carla Emery, *The Encyclopedia of Country Living* (Sasquatch Books, Seattle, 2012).

[555] John Storey and Martha Storey, *Storey's Basic Country Skills: A Practical Guide to Self-Reliance* (Story Publishing, North Adams, MA, 1999).

[556]   A. R. Gehring (ed.), *Back to Basics: A Complete Guide to Traditional Skills*, 3rd Edition (Sky Horse Publishing, New York, 2008).

[557]   J. Cobb, *Pepper's Long-Term Survival Guide: Food, Shelter, Security, Off-The-Grid Power and More Life-Saving Strategies for Self-Sufficient Living* (Ulysses Press, Berkeley, 2014).

[558]   John Seymour, *The Fat of the Land* (Faber and Faber, London, 1961).

Sufficient Life and How to Live It[559] and *The Forgotten Arts.*[560] This latter book gives an outline, albeit a brief one, of a variety of traditional crafts, including some surprising ones such as wooden fork and rake making. Covered as well is the production of various tempered blades by blacksmithing, including the slasher which I mentioned earlier (and wherever else I can fit it in), which could serve the dual purpose of a land clearing tool, far superior to any machete, as well as a pole axe weapon for pruning the zombie herd.[561]

Seymour's masterwork is *The New Complete Book of Self-Sufficiency*,[562] which in its 2009 publication by Darling Kindersley, compiles material from two of his older books, *The New Complete Book of Self-Sufficiency* (1976) and *The New Self-Sufficient Gardener* (1978). "Why should we all labour to enrich the banks?" he asks. Yes, screw the banks and the global financial conspiracy and all that. Instead, self-sufficient living, through moving from the cities to the countryside is a way of regaining our lost humanity: "[s]elf-sufficiency does not mean "going back" to an acceptance of a lower standard of living. On the contrary, it is the striving for a higher standard of living, for food which is fresh and organically grown and good, for the good life in pleasant surroundings, for the health of body and peace of mind which comes with hard, varied work in the open air, and for the satisfaction that comes from doing difficult and intricate jobs well and successfully."

Seymour advocated the method of "high farming" used in Europe centuries ago, which involved a balance of plants and animals e.g. plants feed the animals, animal wastes fertilize the soil. Crops are rotated and there are no monocultures, to control pests. Animals are free ranged. He felt that a five-acre holding could easily supply all the

---

[559]   John Seymour, *The Self-Sufficient Life and How to Live It: The Complete Back-to-Basic Guide* (Dorling Kindersley, New York, 2003).

[560]   John Seymour, *The Forgotten Arts* (Angus and Robertson Publishers, North Ryde, New South Wales, 1984).

[561]   The slasher is pictured on p. 53 and p. 74, as above. See also pp. 134-135 on blade making in John Seymour, *The New Complete Book of Self-Sufficiency: The Classic Guide for Realists and Dreamers* (Dorling Kindersley, London, 2009).

[562]   As above, p. 13.

food necessary for a large family, and has already been mentioned, it can be achieved with less than that. The color illustrations alone, are almost works of art in themselves and far more productive to view than much of the toxic sludge filling our modern art galleries. There is useful information about how to butcher a pig, chicken and rabbit breeds, clearing, draining and irrigating land, hedging and fencing, using working horses, preparing land and sowing, harvesting, how to make butter and cream, cheese, bread, bottling, pickles and chutney, jams and syrups, brewing and wine-making, compost, dry composting toilets and a wide range of crafts and skills.

Small scale, largely organic farming, without electricity, and using horse power, has been practiced by the Amish in America. Life there has involved lighting and cooking with a wood stove, water without an electric pump, washing clothes without a washing machine, entertainment without TV or video games, communication without a phone or texting, transport without a car, farming without a tractor and running a farm and woodworking shops without electricity. As Scott and Pellman put it: "Unlike many North Americans, the Amish value simplicity and self-denial over comfort, convenience and leisure. So they try to discern the long-range effects of an innovation before deciding whether to adopt it."[563] Electricity was seen to lead to a lifestyle contrary to church and family life (although some battery-powered devices are used). The Amish see "folly in a lifestyle that avoids physical labor, then creates exercise in the form of jogging or aerobics." For the Amish, the adoption of a self-sufficient lifestyle was done for the purposes of preserving their culture; but for us non-Amish, it will be needed to preserve our lives. The fact that a group of people has lived and striven to live this way indicates that it is possible, in the midst of our insane techno-industrial societies' death throes, to live an alternative life.[564]

---

[563] Stephen Scott and Kenneth Pellman, *Living without Electricity* (Good Books, Intercourse, Pennsylvania, 1990), p. 8.

[564] For a positive evaluation of Amish agriculture practices and lifestyle see Wendell Berry, *The Unsettling of America: Culture and Agriculture* (Sierra Club Books, San Francisco, 1977), *Amish Economy* (Adela Press, Versailles, KY, 1996).

Tools and the Craftsman

One topic sometimes mentioned in survival books is the need to have a supply of hand tools for a grid-down situation. Today, whether it be those who work with wood, stone, metal, or the garden, most work is done with power tools. Land clearing of feral trees and vegetation is done with a chainsaw, whipper-snipper/brush cutter instead of an axe/handsaw and machete, slasher and scythe. It is said that these tools are faster and more efficient that their hand equivalents. I have cleared many acres of territory of blackberry, olive and other weeds using a hand saw, slasher, machete and even a "don't care" katana. Here are my conclusions from a lifetime of hard sweat.

Petrol driven chainsaws, if they are a quality brand and regularly serviced, usually work well. They are about three to five times faster than a good saw or axe man. However, on steep land they can be extremely dangerous and I have seen one chainsaw accident (a co-worker) and don't want to see another. The axe and handsaw are much quieter and safer and do not require fuel beyond muscle power. Also, you don't breathe fumes. One government site on weed control says that chain saws and mechanical slashers "create high levels of soil and vegetation disturbance."[565] Chopping and sawing wood is one of the best forms of exercise, having immediate spin-off benefits for melee weapon combat. If one can use a wood chopping axe well, using a fighting axe (say a Viking short axe) or a tomahawk, is not too difficult. Hand-sawing is an excellent triceps developer. Hence, the art of the axe and saw needs revival. Further, one could bug out on foot with an axe or a good quality (sharpenable) handsaw, but it is impractical to lug around, while bugging out, a chainsaw, brushcutter and fuel. Consequently, the art and science of the axe and saw needs revival among survivalists.[566]

---

[565] "Physical Weed Control Methods," at https://www.business.qld.gov.au/industry/agriculture/land-management/health-pests-weeds-diseases/weeds-and-diseases/controlling-weeds-property/physical-weed-control-methods.

[566] See D. Cook, *The Ax Book: The Lore and Science of the Woodcutter* (Alan C. Hood and Company, Chambersburg, 1999).

In terms of clearing weeds such as blackberry on relatively flat land, the modern hand held brushcutter is not used and a tractor with a slasher attachment rules. There is no contest against it – assuming that you own a tractor and can maintain it. But, the wheeled tractor becomes dangerous on very steep slopes (tractors with tracks are better, but have their limits as well) and both cannot be used on extremely swampy land. The hand-held brush cutter though is inferior to the manual tool equivalents of a slasher/machete/sword/parang for tough scrub and a scythe for grass. I have worked with many guys who have used a brushcutter or a string trimmer and have always beaten them in terms of amount of scrub cleared per unit of time, using hand tools.[567] Much time is wasted clearing crap stuck in the whirly bits; not so for a scrub katana/machete.

The survivalist/prepper/doomsteader needs to stockpile various types of hand tools, general tools and supplies. For the shorter term, tools needed for automotive and electrical repair and maintenance are needed. e.g. oil filler, wrench, a range of sockets, spanners, compression tester, battery charger, fuse wire, etc. However, the concern in this book is for long-term survival in a coming dark age and our thoughts are for tools that are man-powered only. In general, one will need: gardening tools, metal working tools, wood working tools, masonry tools and a range of basic supplies, including such items as duct tape (the more the better), PVC electrical tape, safety goggles, dust masks, sun glasses, hearing protection, parachute cord (can't have too much), rope (can't have too much), plastic sheets, water containers, buckets, tarps, barbed/razor wire, fencing materials (e.g. star droppers, wire mesh), hacksaw blades, fire starting mechanisms (matches, flint and steel etc.), bleach, flashlights, work gloves, hoses, water pipe, chain, scales, paint, paint brushes, plumber's tape, wood and general purpose glues, massive quantities of nails and screws of various sizes, silicone sealant, washers, tire wire (the more the better), cement, WD-40, oils and lubricants and sand paper, to name but a few items.

---

[567]   On the hand-held slasher see Edward Mundie, *Go Country: A Troubleshooter's Guide to Successful Country Living* (Hyland House, South Melbourne, 1994), p. 53.

Woodworking tools include hand saws, rubber and wooden mallets, hammers, nuts & bolts, screwdrivers, chisels, adze, files, Stanley knives, drawing knifes, squares, tape measures, planes, dividers, and axes. Metal work and blacksmithing tools include a work bench, wrecking bar, nails, vice clamps, spanners, ball-peen hammers, files, (various types), hand-crank forge, bellows, grinding wheel, sledge hammer, forging tongs, a heavy-duty vice, punches, pliers, tin snips, leather apron, wire brushes, welder's gloves, work gloves, pliers, hack saws, safety goggles and so on. Masonry tools include shovels/spades, trowels, bolsters, manual mortar mixer, builder's square/tape measures, float, bricklayer's hammer, spirit level and cement edger and joiner. Garden tools include a slasher, machetes, spades and shovels, rakes (including a fork rake), forks (including a pitch fork), saws, axes, hatchets, block splitters, wheel barrows, crowbars/fencing bars, sledge hammers, post-hole diggers, mattocks (with both pick-end types and axe-like end types), pruning shears, pruning saws, sharpening stones, wedges and picks, among many other items.

Many, but not all commercially made tools are somewhat fragile, especially cheap Chinese made garden tools. I have purchased chipper hoes whose blade ends bend after hitting a few rocks, a problem due to either inferior slag-ridden steel incorrectly heat-treated, low carbon steel and/or thin hoe blades. Spades and shovels tend to be better so to make up hoes I have often cut up a spade and welded on a section to put a handle. Fork rakes can also be made up from garden forks. Anvils can be made from sections of heavy I-beams, railway iron or engine blocks. Knives can be made from old files, although they will be somewhat brittle as an impact tool or weapon, and thus need reforging and re-heat treating. Car (older models) and truck leaf spring steel is much better.

One could of course purchase hand-forged tools made by local blacksmiths, but this may be costly, and the extra life needs to be balanced against the cost. For the longer-term, a survival workshop centered on blacksmithing needs to be constructed now for the use of present and future generations.[568] There is likely to be enough scrap metal in the decaying cities of the future to supply all the metal that remnant blacksmiths will need, perhaps for centuries. However, most of the steel in such cities is soft, low-carbon mild steel that can be case hardened (on its surface), but not hardened by heat treatment. To make tools and edged weapons, a supply of high carbon steel needs to be secured before the collapse as it may be hard to find in Post Apocalyptica under the masses of decaying humanity and their garbage.

Tools, along with weapons are items which can, and should be stockpiled now at one's "Sustainable Autonomous Base," if one has one, or at least acquired now for early bird bugging out via a vehicle such as a light truck.

The use of hand tools was once an important part of manhood, replaced by industrialism and consumer culture. The idea of craftsmanship was abandoned, to be replaced by mass production.[569] But, in Post Apocalyptica this ancient ideal, once a philosophical aid in living one's life, will once more return.

Zombie Apocalypse Preparation and Survival Philosophy

Max Brooks' *The Zombie Survival Guide*[570] discusses a Class 4 or doomsday outbreak of zombieism driving humanity to the brink of destruction.[571] Such a scenario can be taken as a thought experiment

---

[568] James Ballou, *Long-Term Survival in the Coming Dark Age* (Paladin Press, Boulder, Colorado, 2007), pp. 29-63. On beginning blacksmithing see Alex Bealer, *The Art of Blacksmithing* (Castle Books, Edison, 2009).

[569] Brett McKay and Kate McKay, "Measure Twice Cut Once: Applying the Ethos of the Craftsman to Our Everyday Lives," July 3, 2013, at http://www.artofmanliness. com/2013/07/03/measure-twice-cut-once-applying-the-ethos-of-the-craftsman-to-our-everyday-lives.

[570] Max Brooks, *The Zombie Survival Guide: Complete Protection from the Living Dead* (Three Rivers Press, New York, 2003).

[571] As above, p. 155.

for the real zombie apocalypse, the coming collapse of civilization. Brooks sees any attempt at urban survival as futile, because if the "zombies" do not get you, human barbarians and savages living a parasitic existence will. To survive, a retreat to remote regions is needed, certainly to escape these bandits. This means a retreat from all civilization, or what remains of it. This remote retreat should have fresh water, good soils and the capacity to produce food. Ideally, it should have ample natural resources such as timber from trees for building and the terrain offer natural defenses. Brooks concludes that a permanent refuge requires at a minimum, food, water and extreme distance, otherwise "you seriously compromise your long-term survival." He considers deserts as offering protection from human raiders, but not necessarily Hollywood zombies, especially if the desert is between two population centers. There are, of course food and water issues for deserts, and perhaps a shortage of building materials.

Jungle regions have water, food and building materials. The vegetation will provide cover allowing both ghouls and Hollywood zombies to be neutralized, but they will be able to sneak up on you. There are specific challenges posed by jungle environments, such as disease and insects. However, jungles are preferable to temperate forests, which because of being a comfortable environment, are likely to be full of refugees and human predators, preying on them. Mountain regions, even in these zones, will offer good defense against human and zombie predators, especially if the terrain is rough and lacks roads and access paths. However, security issues will arise if it is necessary for obtaining water, food and building materials to go down the mountain to ground level.

Tundra and polar regions have the advantage of being improbable places for human and zombie predators to visit, at least in any concerning numbers. The main survival threat will be the harsh environment, the bitter cold, and unless one can live ultimately as the Inuits live, the threat of starvation. Islands will not offer safety from refugees – as the asylum seeker issue in Australia in past years showed. Pirates sail the seas today and will rule the seas in a post-collapse world, which makes living at sea on a boat, an unrealistic long-term option, certainly for a multi-generational scenario.

In conclusion, Brooks' approach to a doomsday zombie apocalypse, is consistent with the approach adopted by survivalists such as Mel Tappan, although the Tappan position is that some degree of remoteness needs to be sacrificed so that one has the advantage of safety in numbers of a small town. If Hollywood zombies (or disease infected humans) were a threat, then one would need to abandon seeking a community and strive for a high degree of remoteness and isolation, and take one's security risks.

One's Sustainable Autonomous Base (SAB)/Retreat will need to be fortified and defended in any SHTF/TEOTWAWKI situation, beginning with operational security by restricting information about what you are doing (e.g. blocking out windows, no cooking outdoors near the SAB; not having tell-tale waste lying around). A passive defense may be to hide in plain sight, using a low profile and camouflage to make the SAB look abandoned. Alternatively, one may go the way of overt fortification, hardening your SAB in various ways, such as structural hardening to prevent entry into the retreat. It is also possible to combine elements of both approaches to some degree, with context and circumstances ultimately determining which approach or combination of approaches is adopted.[572]

Conclusion

… The stakes of the game, for true men, will soon be to *survive*. That's all – to survive… [f]or one day, when the machine has exhausted all the possibilities of its original *élan*, it will totter and fall. Then, for us, it will be enough to be numerous, to maintain solidarity, so as collectively to regain control of our earth after we have fiercely defended our few areas of retreat. It is in order to be there, at that decisive moment, that we must

---

[572] See in general: Jim Cobb, *Peppers Home Defence: Security Strategies to Protect Your Family by Any Means Necessary* (Ulysses Press, Berkeley, 2012).

survive now. So, do not be ashamed: let us build our refuges! Remember that a rebel wins if he can hold out one hour longer than his adversary. Let us organise ourselves to do so.
- Michel Drac[573]

This chapter has given a guide to survival preparations for the coming collapse of civilization, the zombie apocalypse. Rather than adopt a "how to" approach, to cover the field, I have reviewed the literature which beginning survivalists should consult to acquire information about all aspects of survival preparations. Most disaster preparedness books and wilderness survival books say that the mental aspect of survival is the most important, the sheer will to keep going and not to give up. Some speak of people having a "survivor's personality,"[574] remaining calm and clear-headed when facing a survival threat and avoiding impulsive behaviour, carefully analyzing the situation and assessing options, and then taking decisive and correct action.[575] Where does this mental edge come from? Is it something a person just has inside them or is it a skill that can be developed? There are many fine books examining people in extreme survival situations;[576] the take home lesson is that knowledge, conditioning, survival kit and even sheer luck are all very important, but without the will to survive—the sheer, stubborn refusal to surrender and give up, the persistence to slog on however much it hurts and however hopeless things looks—people perish.[577] This question of survival will arise in another form regarding combat and self-defense and it is a matter

---

[573]   Michael Drac, "Foreword" to Piero San Giorgio, *Survive the Economic Collapse: A Practical Guide* (Radix/Washington Summit Publishers, Whitefish, 2013), pp. xx-xxi.

[574]   Al Siebert, *The Survivor Personality: Why Some People are Stronger, Smarter and More Skilful at Handling Life's Difficulties... and How You Can be Too* (Berkley Publishing, New York, 1996).

[575]   Laurence Gonzales, *Deep Survival: Who Lives, Who Dies and Why: True Stories of Miraculous Endurance and Sudden Death* (W. W. Norton, New York, 2005), pp. 262-263 and pp. 270-274.

[576]   Les Stroud, *Will to Live: Dispatches from the Edge of Survival* (Harper, New York, 2011), p. 222; Richard Harper, *Extreme Survivors* (Collins, Glasgow, 2013).

[577]   Kenneth Kamler, *Extreme Survival: A Doctor Explores the Limits of Human Endurance* (Constable and Robinson, London, 2004), pp. 302-303.

that I will address in the next book. My own view is that the mental edge of survival and combat is both innate and environmental; some people lack the capacity to fight and struggle for existence. Others have raw "guts," "nuts" and "true grit," which can be intensified by knowledge, learning from the mistakes of others (experience), and training. Survival prospects will be increased by knowledge and learning – hence the importance of learning as much as possible before the final curtain falls.

CONCLUSION OF BOOK 1

THIS COMPLETES the argument of book one in this two-part series. Here it has been shown that the zombie apocalypse is something of an outpouring from the Jungian collective unconscious of the hard times to come – in particular, that our number is up and the phenomenal luck of the human race has come to an end. The coming collapse of civilization means that ecological scarcity and natural forces will return with a vengeance, destroying our comfortable consumer world, and all of the ideologies that we presently live under. This should not be a startling revelation since such a conclusion was always lying on the surface of much environmentalist/collapseology work. But, as true cowards, environmentalists always offered false hope, that humanity will wake up just in the nick of time. However, dumb suffering *Homo sap* will not, and the future is doom, doom, doom.

Hence, it is time to prepare for the end of the world as we know it, and the beginning of a savage Dark Age that could spell human extinction, or at best, a die off of the majority of people on the planet. Many would not wish to live and perish in such a world, so they will die quickly, as their spirits are weak. Others, like me, and I hope you, may wish to persist regardless of what punishment this vicious and metaphysically absurd multiverse hurls at us—out of sheer cussedness—to be able to raise a "one finger salute" to the Cosmic Fates.

The next book in this series, *The Barbarian Reborn: Weaponry and Survivalism in the Near-term Post-Apocalyptic Wastelands*, is for those existentially stubborn warriors. In that book you will learn how to cast off the ideologies of modernity and postmodernity and express your inner barbarian. Be prepared for blood and profanity, as no sacred cow remains free from decapitation and impalement.

www.ingramcontent.com/pod-product-compliance
Lightning Source LLC
Chambersburg PA
CBHW031508270326
41930CB00006B/303